Emotions of life
The function, dynamic and healing power of feeling

Emotions of life

The function, dynamic and healing power of feeling

Martin Tidén

Inquire

Emotions of life
– The function, dynamic and healing power of feeling
First edition, 2022
Publisher: Inquire
Copyright © 2022 by Martin Tidén
Translated from Swedish by Lewis Lebolt
Illustrations: LAJ Illustration
Cover layout: LAJ Illustration
Cover photo: Maria do Carmo M. Iannaccone
(Flower: Aechmea multiflora)
Graphic design: LAJ Illustration
Print: BoD - Books on Demand, Norderstedt, Germany

ISBN 978-91-519-5401-1

ACKNOWLEDGEMENTS

I feel deep gratitude to my teachers, who shared
their knowledge and love with me:
Vivian Persson, Stèphano Sabetti and Antonia Lüdke

The content of this book developed over a period of ten years and many people were involved in it in different ways. First I would like to express gratitude to my dear friend and colleague Dorte Christiansen for her continuous support as she worked through the text and gave feedback. I am grateful for the work done by Lewis Lebolt in translating the text into English. I feel joy when I read his translation because it captures the essence of what I want to express. A big thank you goes to Claire Englund, who helped with the English translation. Illustrations and graphic design of this book were done by my friend Lars Ahlberg and his colleagues Mats, Jimmy and Garip at LAJ Illustration. I am grateful for their input and ideas which helped me rethink, clarify and find new ways of expressing myself on several occasions.

Contents

Forewords

The message of *Emotions of Life* is both simple and deep. It has an interconnected perspective on the body, emotions and cognition and focuses on the self-organizing principle common to all living organisms.

Martin Tidén connects neuropsychology and research into emotions with developmental psychology. The result is a cohesive picture of our inner universe and the book's examples from daily life offer a practical path for development. The evolutionary approach to the architecture of the brain presented provides insights into the function and dynamics of emotions and feelings, as well as disturbances in them. Sadness, happiness, fear and anger are dealt with as well as the particular power of love. In this way the reader gains insight into the emotional system as well as the possibilities and challenges that emotions create in human life, including the consequences of emotional trauma.

The book describes how a therapeutic and healing integration process can unfold over time. We are shown how to support personal growth processes in ourselves and in others and we are introduced to Affective Inquiry, a method of communication that supports the process of integration.

This book provides a rarely seen body perspective on human psychology that stems from Tidén's long professional experience as a supervisior, educator and psychotherapeutic practicioner. In all these areas I have myself had the pleasure of learning and working with Martin Tidén for a number of years.

I warmly recommend this book to others. *Emotions of Life* will provide insights and inspiration to everyone who wants to understand their own emotions of life. Professionals in education, psychology and therapy will also find new knowledge and inspiration in the book's theoretical breadth and practical cases.

I hope you enjoy this book.

Helle Winther
Associate Professor, PhD in dance, movement psychology and dance therapy at The University of Copenhagen, licensed dance and movement psychotherapist, author and editor of several books on dance-and-movement psychology in Danish, including "Kroppens sprog i professionel praksis" and "Bevægelsespsykologi".

~~~~~~~~~~~~~~~~~~~~~

I enjoyed reading Martin Tidéns pragmatic approach to the function and healing power of emotions. *Emotions of Life* presents theories from the 1970's and forward, that include works by body psychotherapist Alexander Lowen, infant behavioral researcher Prof. Daniel Stern and neuroscientist Antonio Damasio, together with modern trauma researchers such as Peter A. Levine and child psychiatrist Prof. Daniel Siegel. Together with this established research, Martin Tidén presents pedagogical models and examples showing therapeutic work focused on emotions and the body.

This book presents a broad range of knowledge that should inspire experienced psychotherapists as well as individuals who believe that it is possible to mature throughout life by paying attention to old emotional wounds and healing them.

Emotions of Life shows a way to change behavior that is a complement to change by the power of thought. This way involves a "bottom-up" focus that explores the organism's inherent, self-organizing ability. This exploration of somatic and emotional processes can lead to increased self-understanding, acceptance and self-esteem. This causes an increase in individual motivation for behavioral change. The exploration of feelings and defensive responses that are normally hidden can lead to re-establishing contact with old pain, fears, shame and guilt that were imprinted into us by early relational traumas. By coming into contact with and expressing these emotions in a safe, understanding and empathic relationship, a way opens to integrate these emotions into our personality. Inner conflicts subside and emotions that were previously treated as enemies can become resources as we deal with life's relational flows.

The world stands on the brink of a new paradigm that will make great demands on humanity. We need to raise consciousness about how we, each one of us, create our existence together and how we influence and are influenced by everything we do. An important element in this new understanding is knowledge about how our personality is formed by early relationships and relational traumas. We need to experience that we can become reconciled with unfinished inner emotional conflicts. When our mind is at rest we feel better and can contribute to making the world a better place. Each one of us is responsible for under-standing ourselves and this is why *Emotions of Life* is highly recommended for study and personal exploration.

A warning is however necessary. This is not an easy "feel good" book with advice on how to live a better life. There is a simplicity here nevertheless, one that inspires the reader to dare to face inner feelings as they present themselves to us in the present. This simplicity lies in accepting and understanding that as biological beings our organism has an ability to self-organize, a process connected to emotional regulation. Accepting this has for my part involved letting go of the notion that I control my choices and behaviors while still owning them as mine. Although this does not always necessarily make life easier, it fills life with sometimes unexpected meaning, acceptance, love and openness to the emotions of life.

Lasse Övling
Licensed psychologist and Gestalt therapist, previously Radio Psychologist on Swedish Broadcasting Radio P1.

Introduction

Feelings create life's variation and dynamic. They appear in good times and bad, through all stages of life. Wealth, sexual identity and ethnicity make no difference to feelings. We all have feelings and they do not care what we think or want. Though feelings are always present, we do not understand them very well. It is as if they live a life of their own that influences us. At times, feelings seem to be an external force that we must adapt to and follow – or shut out if we can.

In common usage, feelings and emotions are viewed as the same thing. However, in neuroscience, feelings are the experience of emotions and homeostatic processes in the body. Feelings are the experience of our living body.

Despite the enormous influence feelings have on our life and the quality of life, and despite our present knowledge about them, their function is little understood. Why do they exist? What do they do? What are they for and what can we learn from them? In books as well as everyday life, feelings seem to be pleasant, unpleasant or neutral. If a feeling is neutral or pleasant, we can simply carry on with life but if a feeling is unpleasant, we want to change or remove it. We particularly consider unpleasant feelings to be disturbances without value and we view pleasant feelings as normal. This intuitive misconception about what feelings are and do misses an important dimension of life. Feelings play a central and vitally important role in human life. They are our direct contact with life as it moves through us. When we avoid or ignore feelings, we lose contact with ourselves and our life.

This book is an attempt to answer questions such as: What are feelings and where do they come from? What is their function and how do they influence us? We will explore the physiology of feelings and show how fundamental feelings are for human life. They reflect our life processes and provide feedback about them. Feelings are our experience of the human organism's affective and emotional response processes. What we feel tells us about our inner biological state and how we are doing, that is, how life is moving and expressing itself through us. In early life, feelings contribute to shaping the person we become, and contact with feelings automatically provides contact with the part of ourselves we call "I" or "me", the core self and our unique, individual life process.

This book is for those who seek to understand human life and the emotional processes that form the basis of our experience of self and the world around us as well as how we relate to them. It is for those who, either out of professional interest or personal curiosity, want to learn more about life and the mechanisms that govern our behavior.

Chapter overview

The chapters deal with many facets of what it is to be human in order to better understand feelings and the emotional and affective responses behind them. Research from a number of interdisciplinary sciences are presented, including neuroscience (particularly interpersonal neurobiology and neuroaffective science), research in emotions, evolutionary psychology and insights and experience from several psychotherapeutic schools of thought.

The book begins with a description of basic human biological life processes followed by a presentation of the dynamics and function of emotional processes and feelings. This is followed by a description of how our early personality development is influenced by emotional processes. Finally comes a description of what happens when emotional processes are disturbed and how these disturbances can be resolved through emotional integration.

In **the first section** of this book, "The human organism: a living system", we look at the basic process of life and its organizing dynamic.

Chapter 1 describes the self-organizing principle that applies for all living organisms. This autonomous process is the human organism's foundation and it is experienced through feelings. It is this principle that makes complex and coordinated human life possible. At the same time, disturbances in this process cause many of the problems we experience.

Chapter 2 deals with the organization and functions of the brain. An evolutionary perspective on brain structure lays the groundwork for understanding feelings and emotions. We take a closer look at three evolutionary developments in the brain that explain the development of human life as well as the stability and flexibility of the human organism's central process: survival. Following a description of brain anatomy, focus shifts to three interconnected evolutionary areas: the body, emotions and cognition.

The physiology, function and dynamics of these three areas are dealt with in **the second section** of this book.

Chapter 3 takes a closer look at the physical body and biological life's tendency to self-organize. From single-celled organisms to multicellular organisms all the way up to complex multicellular organisms such as the human body, life forms itself into general biological structures and functions. We examine how the underlying human life process manifests itself in the biological organism and how the life process manifests itself further in the body's homeostatic process. It autonomously protects and takes care of the body.

In **Chapter 4** we turn our attention to the relational aspect of the human homeostatic system: the emotional system. Emotions are basically physical responses expressed in and through the body. The emotional system and its expressions are extensions of the homeostatic system and its response mechanisms. Their basic purpose is to promote physical survival and assist in relational interaction.

Chapter 5 discusses in detail the function, dynamic and expression of our basic emotions: fear, anger, sadness, happiness and love.

Chapter 6 takes a closer look at affective responses and processes that resemble emotions. Sexual affect is a central survival response. We investigate the function and dynamic of sexuality as well as the consequences of a disturbance in this response. Pain is another important survival mechanism. Contrary to common belief, pain is created entirely in the brain. Understanding its function and dynamic erases the boundary between physical and emotional pain. We also look at other human expressions that resemble emotions such as shame and guilt. These processes are not emotions although they resemble basic emotions in several ways.

Chapter 7 deals with cognition: the conscious and unconscious process that registers, remembers and makes it possible for us to relate to ourselves and the world around us. By means of conscious cognition we are able to abstract from, observe, cancel and to a certain extent adjust the expression of physical processes, including emotional expression. Cognitive ability also makes it possible for us to deceive ourselves, for example by not being honest about feeling sad or angry. This chapter also shows that to a great extent, what we call free will is partially our observation of automatically activated responses. We do not always decide what to do but instead automatically do what we learned is safe and then tell ourselves that it is what we want to do. Research in this area questions the extent of free will and how much we actually decide over our life.

Chapter 8 is about our feelings, often mistaken for emotional responses. Feelings are our experience of the body's autonomous response system, vitality affects and emotions. The ability to feel makes it possible for us to follow our body's autonomous homeostatic response processes. It connects the body to our self-awareness. Feeling ties the human being together into a single, conscious unit.

The third section of this book, "Personality", focuses on the organized patterns of behavior that we usually refer to as "who I am".

Chapter 9 shows how personality is established at an early age and how it is dependent on an attentive caregiver who can help the infant relate to or regulate affective and emotional responses. Without this, resulting disturbances in the emotional system have a negative impact on personality development. As a consequence some natural responses will be treated as threatening and personality develops defenses against them.

In **Chapter 10** we look at the defenses against threatening response processes that become integrated into personality. This chapter presents the dynamics of the five different defense systems and how to deactivate them.

Chapter 11 takes a closer look at adult personality and the core self, the source of personality. This chapter concludes with a model of the human organism.

What happens when the emotional system's natural functions are disturbed is the subject of **the fourth section**: "Wholeness disturbed".

Chapter 12 discusses the dynamics and consequences of emotional trauma. The human organism can mobilize three autonomous defense strategies when faced with a dangerous situation. If a defense strategy is not completed after activation, it becomes integrated into the defense system of personality.

The fifth section of this book, "The Integration process", deals with the path from emotional trauma to integration and wholeness.

Chapter 13 focuses on emotional integration. This process makes it possible for previously unaccepted emotional expression to be integrated into personality. By reconnecting to a natural process of integration, we begin to automatically regulate and integrate emotional expression. Through understanding of the integrative dynamic of feeling and the affective cycle (the natural, dynamic form of emotion), we can follow and support this process.

In **Chapter 14** we see how the process of integration shifts to the development of life-affirming emotional processes such as happiness and love. Focus on this part of the integration process strengthens psychological resilience and improves our ability to deal with psychological hardship and crises.

Chapter 15 describes how to facilitate and promote emotional integration in ourselves and others. Beginning with the mind's three integrative qualities – curiosity, empathy, and presence – we create a fertile field for integration. Affective Inquiry, a communication method used to follow and support the process of integration, is presented in this chapter. Since integration is a physical process the reader will learn how the body can be involved in this process. The chapter also looks at physical and relational manifestations of anxiety and how to use this understanding to intervene and effectively dissolve it.

The sixth section of this book deals with the consequences of insufficient emotional integration.

Chapter 16 summarizes the dynamic of emotion and explains how insufficient emotional integration creates the experience of problems and conflicts in life. Personal crises and psychological problems are the result of inner conflicts arising from suppressed emotional expression. A problem is a symptom of an inner conflict. By expressing and integrating suppressed emotions, the discomfort associated with a problem disappears.

The message of this book is that human biological life processes in the form of affects and emotions always seek autonomous expression. If this is repressed, psychological struggle and crises are experienced on our journey through life. By becoming conscious of this process however we can support it and experience more flow in life.

PART I

A HUMAN BEING
IS
A LIVING SYSTEM

Chapter 1

The self-organizing principle

A human being is a living system or, as some theoreticians call it, a complex self-organizing system. This means that every human is an independent life process that autonomously finds its way in life. Our interactions with our environment consist of automatic, inherited and learned response processes. The living system that we are registers what we need and automatically activates an appropriate response, for example an action suited to the situation.

This explanatory model does not correspond with our conviction that we always decide for ourselves and do as we wish. However it creates an exciting possibility that opens new perspectives and understanding of why we humans behave the way we do.

This book presents research that suggests that we do not have much say in our fundamental behavior. A large part of our personality's behavior is run by inherited and learned autonomous mechanisms that are predetermined to a great extent.

The definition of complex self-organizing systems is rooted in a classic systemic perspective. According to this perspective, the behavior of a system is determined by the way its parts are organized and the relation between those parts, rather than by the quality of the parts themselves and their individual behavior (Bertalanffy, 1969; Laszo, 1996). A synergy develops in which the system as a whole is greater than the sum of its parts. A concrete example of this synergy is when chemical elements combine in different ways to produce molecules with specific properties. For example, two atoms of hydrogen (H) and one atom of oxygen (O) become water (H_2O). A complex, self-organizing system such as a human being is a unity organized in a similar way but with a far greater number of parts. We are more than the sum of our parts.

A fundamental quality of a complex self-organizing system is that it always moves towards greater systemic efficiency. This is a hardwired, continuous pursuit of increasing complexity. The more complex a system is, the more stable and flexible it is in relation to changes in its inner and outer environments. The evolutionary development of humans and other life forms is a result of this natural systemic process. The system's pursuit of greater complexity involves increased integration of the system's parts relative to its environment in order to become more efficient. For a system such as a human being, development towards ever greater systemic complexity means being almost constantly in a continuous process of adjustment and change. We either develop or die. Status quo and stasis at a single level of development does not exist. In continuous development, the system learns by adjusting its expressions to ever changing influences. There is continuous interaction and development both within the system and in its contacts with its surroundings.

A system's life-long process of development may be viewed as a learning process in which system resources are given the opportunity to develop. The process is like an infant's development in its interactions with the environment before it is capable of abstract thinking, a process of trial and error where stimuli from the environment activate a response from the infant. The infant receives an influence which activates a response, it gets feedback to the response, learns from the feedback, adjusts its expression, gets feedback to this, etcetera. In this interaction infants find their path of development through a mutual and interactive dance of expressions, feedback and adjustments. It is a development without struggle, a continuous movement back and forth in which life finds its way in relation to a greater whole.

To conclude: from a systemic perspective, every system has a life of its own but its function is in relation to the larger whole that it is part of. A system is an essential part of a greater whole. The oxygen in H_2O is an essential part of water. Water is important because of its function in ecological systems etcetera. A human being also functions as part of a greater system such as a family and a social group. This systemic principle is interesting because as we will see later in this book, personality develops in interpersonal interactions. We emerge as a person and find meaning in life through relationships that make us part of a greater whole.

From this point on we will call the systemic unity that is a human being *the human organism*. This unity encompasses all of a human being's underlying, interconnected life processes.

Chapter 2

The brain
– a perspective on our development

Knowledge of the brain's evolutionary development and functional levels provides a basic understanding of human internal dynamics and external behavior. It is due to disturbances in the interaction between these functional levels that we experience problems and psychological difficulties. By understanding this dynamic we can find our way back to balance. Through our understanding of the brain's functions we can also see that there are no clear boundaries between the body, emotions and cognition. They are parts of a living, intertwined whole and influence each other's functions and processes.

In the human organism, the brain acts as an information processing system of extreme complexity. It consists of billions of neurons (brain cells), up to trillions of connections between these neurons and more than one hundred thousand kilometers of biological connections. The brain is an electrochemical network that transports information from neuron to neuron over a synaptic gap (the small space between neurons). Information transmission occurs through nerve impulses inside the neuron, and is aided by signal molecules (neurotransmitters) between neurons (Presti, 2016). Neurons are interconnected and form neural networks from which all activity in the organism proceeds. Small neural networks combine to form larger networks called *functional modules*. One example of a functional module is the facial recognition module, which remembers and recognizes faces. Functional modules combine to become elements in even greater systems, for example the visual system which in turn is part of the perceptual system (Hill, 2015). In this way the brain's functions build on different network levels that combine to form our brain capacity. It is truly a complex self-organizing system.

Generally speaking the brain developed from the bottom up over millions of years, from processing basic functions to more complicated tasks. It consists of a hierarchy of functional levels in which higher abilities determined by the will can inhibit certain lower automatic functions (Jackson, 1958). In the 1980's neuroscientist Paul MacClean developed his theory of *the triune brain* (MacLean, 1990). This theory describes the brain as organized into three complexes or layers: the reptilian brain, the paleomammalian complex and the neomammalian complex. Each of these constitute a level in human evolutionary development. We can picture how complex brain functions developed on top of more basic functional layers. This structure mirrors man's evolutionary connection with reptiles and lower mammals.

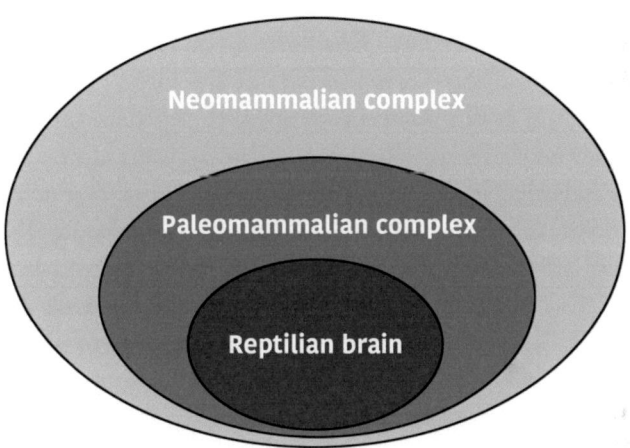

Figure 1: The triune brain according to Paul MacLean.

MacLean's theory has been criticized for its simplification of the brain's structure and function. His theory for example suggests that specific functions belong to specific levels of the brain. Research has shown, however, that the brain does not function in clearly divided and separate levels. The brain functions in a much more complex way. Its processes often involve several parts and levels that integrate both vertically and horizontally. Vertical integration means there is cooperation among so-called evolutionary levels and horizontal integration means cooperation between right and left hemispheres of the brain

(Cozolino, 2014). Social and emotional functions are for example primarily found in the right hemisphere and cognitive functions are in the left hemisphere. Despite criticism of MacClean's theory, dividing the brain into three evolutionary levels provides us with a simple conceptual model. It sheds light on processes involved in disturbances in human consciousness and behavior.

The three evolutionary levels in the physical brain

The three evolutionary levels correspond to the following areas of the physical brain: the brain stem (the reptilian brain), the limbic system (the paleomammalian complex) and the cerebral neocortex (the neomammalian complex).

The reptilian brain centered in the brain stem is the most primitive part of the brain and developed earliest. This part of the brain is fully developed at birth. As its name implies, this is the part of the brain that we functionally share with reptiles. It is not however identical to reptilian brains because our brains developed in different directions. The hypothalamus and thalamus are sometimes included in this part. The thalamus is among other things the body's switchboard for sensory signals to the rest of the brain. The autonomic nervous system, which branches out through the body and helps direct it, also belongs to the reptilian brain. The reptilian brain controls the most basic survival functions: homeostasis, drives and basic impulses of movement (Hart, 2006). These functions are genetically hardwired and autonomous, which makes them functionally reliable and at the same time difficult to consciously influence and change.

Structurally and functionally we share the paleomammalian brain complex with other mammals. Its center is in the brain's limbic system, which evaluates and activates a response to social and emotional information. Among other things the limbic system controls emotions, learning, memory and social behavior (Hart, 2006). The most important parts of the limbic system are:

- The amygdala, which coordinates and directs behavior. The amygdala warns us of danger and activates the autonomic nervous system and the endocrine system when an emotional response is required. It also records previous experiences of threats and danger to guarantee survival.

- The hippocampus, which organizes memories of events in time and space and emotional memory. This memory makes it possible for example to inhibit an emotional response.
- The hypothalamus, which is involved in translating conscious experience into somatic processes by activating the hormonal system.
- The orbitofrontal cortex, sometimes called the thinking part of the limbic system. It is part of both the limbic system and the cerebral cortex and executes the limbic system's most complex integration of information (Fuster, 1997). By means of the orbitofrontal cortex we can influence otherwise autonomous emotional and affective processes. This ability can be developed and improved throughout life.

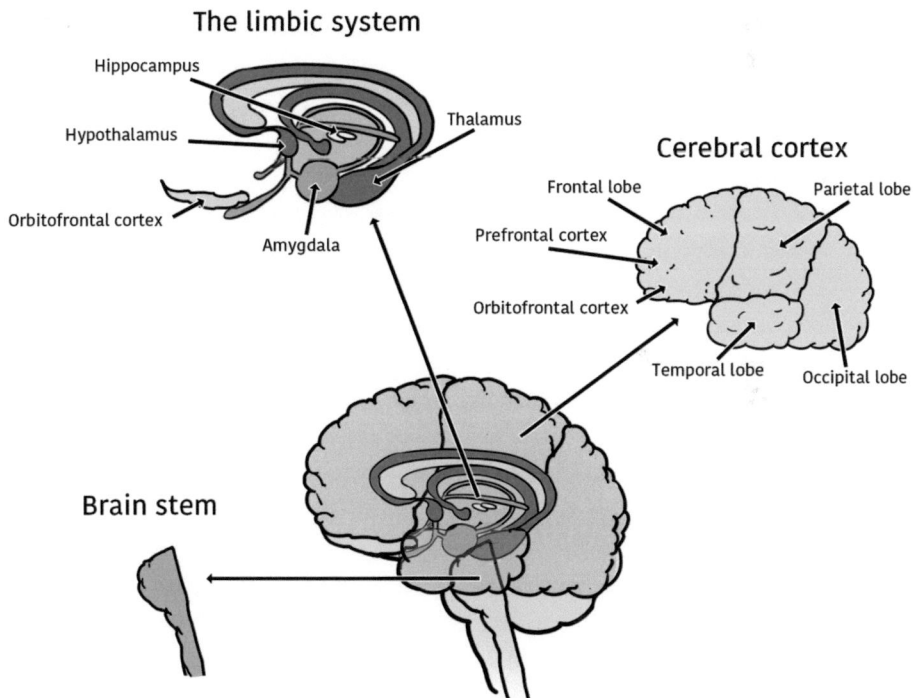

Figure 2: The anatomy of the brain.
Overview of the anatomy of the brain based on MacLean's three evolutionary levels: the brain stem, the limbic system and the cortex or cerebral cortex.

The limbic system is not fully developed at birth. It develops hierarchically from more primitive to more complex functions. As an infant's emotional system unfolds, its ability to experience, express and ultimately control its emotional expression gradually increases. The limbic system's most critical period of development is from birth to about eighteen months and it is strongly influenced by the infant's environment (Hill, 2015). During this period basic personality develops and the quality of caretaking has a significant effect on a child's future life.

The most recent part of the brain to develop is the neomammalian complex or cerebral cortex. Its development ends in early adulthood and it is the center of higher mental processes such as perception, attention, language and logical thinking (Hart, 2006). The central part of the cerebral cortex is the prefrontal cortex, which generates descriptive knowledge and understanding of ourselves and the world around us. This is the part we use for all cognitive thought processes. It makes self-awareness possible. Broadly speaking the cerebral cortex also consists of:

- The frontal lobe, which contains the prefrontal cortex. It is the center of our ability to execute conscious body movements.
- The parietal lobe, which is the center for integrating sensory impressions.
- The temporal lobe, which among other things is involved in understanding what we see and hear. It also contains the brain's language center.
- The occipital lobe, which is the brain's visual center. It contains most of the visual cortex.

Survival and the brain

From an evolutionary perspective the brain's primary function is to ensure the organism's survival. Without life there is no organism. Protection of life is therefore the highest priority. From this perspective every development of the brain's functional system is a natural expansion of this system and a more extensive "insurance policy" for survival. Beginning with the reptilian brain, each developmental level provides increased flexibility to the survival function (Hart, 2012). Increased flexibility here means improved ability to respond to the environment.

The reptilian brain's focus is on biological survival. The paleomammalian complex is a further development that makes it possible to protect the organism from its environment and with the neomammalian complex this protection is expanded. One might say that in a life-threating emergency, the function of the reptilian brain is to make the organism play dead to survive. The paleomammalian complex makes it possible to fight or run away (fight-or-flight respons). The neomammalian complex gives us the ability to plan so that a life-threatening situation does not arise and if faced with such an event, it provides us with the social ability to talk our way out of the situation. Each level uses increased complexity and flexibility to survive or resolve the situation at hand.

This architecture of higher and lower functional levels and survival capability also reveals itself in the ease or difficulty involved in changing or consciously controlling processes at various levels. The reptilian brain consists of unchangeable processes and action patterns. Its focus is on basic biological survival. Conscious adjustment and control would risk fatal mistakes and is therefore not possible for the most part. Luckily we are unable to decide to stop breathing or stop our heart from beating when life becomes a bit difficult.

We find a mix of unchangeable and flexible action patterns in the paleomammalian complex and the limbic system. The emotional memory of what is a threat to us activates an emotional response. We can to a certain extent learn and unlearn which situations that represent a threat; this shows a certain flexibility of response.

Compared to the other levels, the process of the neomammalian complex – the cerebral cortex and prefrontal cortex – is the level most capable of change. Its flexibility of response is great, which makes it possible for us to easily change our way of thinking and deal with shifting circumstances. One can however question the extent of free will and to what extent we can actually affect our thought patterns and behavior. As we shall see in the section about cognition, it seems that the way we think is directed by underlying processes in the limbic system and brain stem.

The brain's three evolutionary levels provide us with a stable and flexible ability to survive. If a survival process from a later developmental level cannot remove a threat, then processes from an earlier developmental level are activated. For example if we are unable to use our neomammalian complex (cerebral cortex) to reason our way out of a threatening situation, the fight-or-flight response of the paleomammalian complex (limbic system) will automatically take over. This is a built-in default setting that guarantees the highest probability of safety and security, something we will look at more closely later.

To gain a greater understanding of these three evolutionary developmental levels with their individual dynamics and interactions, let us look at the systems that they functionally correspond to in the organism. These are: the body, the emotional system and cognition.

PART II

THE BODY, EMOTIONS, COGNITION & FEELING

Chapter 3

The body

The body is a schoolbook example of a living, self-organizing system. Its primary function is to maintain, develop and transmit the life it is an expression of, a task we take for granted and which is performed without conscious thought. In this chapter we will see how the body's numerous and intricately connected systems and subsystems direct much of our behavior. The body is a direct manifestation of a complex and independent life process which defies the thinking being we are by not always doing what we would like it to do.

The human body is a product of billions of years of evolutionary development. Its basic structure consists of the same elements as all organic life: carbon, oxygen and hydrogen. The primary and fundamental principle of life from the tiniest one-celled life form all the way up to multicellular organisms, including animals and humans, is to protect and maintain life. One could say that life first and foremost takes care of itself. This process takes precedence over all of the organism's other processes.

A human cell has evolved from a clearly delimited and functionally independent unit: a eukaryotic cell. This was the first genuine cell in the evolution of life and it has the same general functional structure as a human body (Damasio, 2010). The body of a eukaryote has a border of skin (the cell membrane), a skeleton (cytoskeleton), organs with different functions (for example organelles) and a brain (the nucleus with its DNA). Its focus is on survival and it achieves this through information stored in its genes. Eukaryotes live and survive by responding to their environment. The life of a eukaryotic cell consists of finding nourishment, transforming nourishment into energy, removing waste products and using its energy to find new nourishment. The purpose of life for this primitive cell is to maintain and protect itself without self-aware regulation of its behavior. Through autonomic responses, eukaryotes live and survive in interaction with their environment.

The development of multicellular organisms was the next stage of development. Primitive, independent protocells formed communities with other cells. Becoming part of a larger organism, each cell received a special role or specialization. The cells became part of a larger body that protected them but at the same time made them dependent. If the body died, the individual cells also died.

The basic functions and behaviors of multicellular organisms are the same as those found in primitive eukaryotic cells. The organism's structural and functional complexity increased as it developed from independent, primitive cells to multicellular organisms such as algae, mites, mammals and humans. Increased complexity led to a more diverse behavior and improved the ability to survive. This process is similar to the basic relational and social conditions of humans. When we belong to a group like family or friends our security and chance of survival increase. At the same time however, belonging to a group makes us vulnerable in our relations with other members of the group.

Homeostasis

The body's autonomic process of life and survival is called *homeostasis*. Its primary function is to secure optimal conditions for the organism's inner environment in order to maintain and develop life. Homeostasis consists of several connected bodily processes, for example regulation of body temperature, blood pH, blood sugar levels and the elimination of waste products and toxins. Together they preserve our inner chemical environment within the limited range necessary for life to thrive and develop.

Homeostasis is an extremely complex and sensitive process. A fundamental of this process is to register the organism's inner environment. If a deviation from optimal levels is discovered, homeostasis activates a corrective response to restore optimal levels. This involves for example either supporting a positive process or stopping a negative process. It is for example homeostasis that makes us begin to sweat in order to restore an acceptable inner temperature when body temperature becomes too high. Another example is when we breathe more deeply and our heart beats faster if blood oxygen levels drop and carbon dioxide levels rise. The body's ability to quickly and with exquisite precision deal with and regulate a disturbance in its inner environment is both wondrous and thought-provoking. The organization of this process is a well-tuned autonomic masterpiece. If a human being were to deal with and regulate this process with our limited conscious resources, we would not survive for long.

Affects

Corrective actions activated in the homeostatic process are called *affective responses* or affects. For the human organism this is life's basic expression. Roughly speaking we see two types of affective response in homeostatic regulation: vitality affects and categorical affects. Vitality affects are a part of the body's homeostatic regulation of inner processes as previously described. Categorical affects are usually called *emotions* and will be dealt with in the next chapter. Both are part of the autonomous homeostatic system of evaluation and response. Homeostasis informs the organism about the meaning of different stimuli and activates an appropriate response to deviations from optimal conditions for life (Hill, 2015).

Vitality affects create the symphony of life and life movements that we encounter when we focus on and feel our body. They are the body's corrective responses in a self-maintaining feedback system which we can become aware of (Damasio, 1998). The experience of vitality affects is most often transient and can best be described using dynamic concepts such as rolling, exploding, streaming, warm, oppressive, cool or pulsating.

In addition to regulating the body's inner equilibrium, vitality affects also help us to actively seek whatever the body needs. An example of this homeostatic survival mechanism is when we react to hunger or thirst by actively looking for something to eat or drink (Panskepp, 2012). In this way inner regulation of body equilibrium influences human behavior and social interactions. Vitality affects also directly influence how we express ourselves and relate to our environment. They support human relational interaction in order to achieve and strengthen contact with others. This is for example done via the quality of eye contact, intonation and physical contact (Stern, 1985; 2004).

In conclusion: our body is an autonomous, complex and sensitive system. Its primary task is to maintain and perpetuate life, a task carried out without conscious control. The task of maintaining life has highest priority and is the basis for the development of the next two levels: the emotional and cognitive levels.

Chapter 4

Emotions

Categorical affects – usually called *emotions* – are a further development of the body's internal homeostatic regulation and are part of the basic autonomic life process of human beings. Their function is to maintain life and provide behavioral flexibility in our interactions with other people and our environment. We usually refer to emotions as *feelings*. There is however an important difference between emotions and feelings that is crucial to correct understanding:

An emotion is an autonomic physical response process.
An emotional feeling is our experience of it.

In other words, feeling is awareness of an emotional response (Ledoux, 1996). We will return to this later in the book.

Emotions are hardwired biological responses to stimuli from our environment. They have evolved into preprogrammed sequences of action to maintain homeostatic balance and ensure the organism's survival. The emotional response is in itself neutral, neither positive nor negative. The function of the response is to ensure survival and provide greater behavioral flexibility in interactions with our environment. To maintain natural flow in the homeostatic system, it is important that activated emotions are allowed to reach completion. If this does not happen, a disturbance in the emotional system develops that negatively impacts on our experience of life. An interrupted emotional response affects the body's homeostatic balance. This can cause symptoms in the form of muscle tension and can adversely affect our cognition, perception and thought processes among other things. A simple example of this is when someone crosses our boundaries and we do not express the anger that automatically activates. The withheld emotional response causes muscles of the neck to tense. Tense neck muscles can be painful and make us tired and irritable, which affects our ability to think clearly and behave in a balanced way towards others.

In this way the emotional system plays a decisive role in how we experience and assess our interactions and quality of life. A number of leading neuroscientists and researchers (Joseph Ledoux, Jaak Panksepp and Antonio Damasio among others) have also found that the cause of most psychological and relational problems and conflicts may be found in a disturbance in the emotional system. When we understand the disturbance we also find the remedy for the problem or conflict. This includes minor, everyday difficulties and conflicts all the way up to major psychic imbalances such as stress, burn-out and complex personality disorders.

This chapter will explore the function of emotions and the ways they are connected to and influence other parts of the human organism.

The emotional system

Processes in the emotional system interact with and involve several levels of the brain. The focus of the emotional system is in the limbic system but it also involves the cerebral cortex and brain stem in its processes. These processes are intertwined with many other human processes of motivation and need. Much physiological research into the emotional system particularly when it comes to fear has been conducted on animals, as our neurological anatomy is largely the same and mammals display similar emotional response processes (Panksepp & Bivens, 2012). This does not mean that we experience emotions in the same way, only that there is a resemblance between human emotional behavior and emotional behavior in other mammals.

Charles Darwin described emotions in his book "On the Expression of the Emotions in Man and Animals" in which he defined what he called *universal emotions* as early as 1872. In his travels Darwin had discovered several facial expressions of emotion common to different peoples regardless of location or cultural background. These emotional facial expressions expressed the same inner experiences and messages. He concluded that emotions are innate and common to all human beings and that emotional facial expressions function as nonverbal communication of inner experience and intention. Current research into emotions has followed in Darwin's footsteps and usually refers to six universal or basic emotions: anger, fear, sadness, happiness, surprise and disgust (Damasio, 2000). All other emotional expressions are seen as originating in these six basic emotions, either as variations of greater or lesser intensity or as a mix of several emotions.

Early in the 20th century physiologist Walter Cannon became one of the first to investigate the automatic fight-or-flight response that places the human organism on "red alert" when its life or safety is threatened. Cannon's research was the starting point for our understanding of the autonomic nervous system's function during emotional activation. He studied the digestive system of animals and discovered that digestion is disturbed when an animal is stressed. In particular peristalsis (the intestinal movement that transports digested food) stops. Cannon considered stress to be an autonomic emergency response. This led him to investigate the role of the nervous system in the fight-or-flight response (Cannon, 1927). He discovered that the sympathetic nervous system conveys the response and that the primary purpose of the fight-or-flight response is to redistribute the body's energy. Energy is withdrawn from physical processes that are not absolutely necessary and redistributed to areas, muscles and organs active in the emergency situation. Cannon showed that emotional responses are a way for humans and other mammals to adapt to an emergency or to prepare for one (LeDoux, 1998).

The function of emotion

The emotional system is a preprogrammed response system that autonomically ensures survival of the organism in a threatening environment. The emotional system has two related functions: to secure physical survival and to regulate and support social relations. Being a member of a group increases safety and the odds of survival and functions as a kind of extended life insurance.

As described in Chapter 3, automatic survival systems and mechanisms are basic prerequisites for all living beings. The purpose of the emotional system is to maintain life and emotional activations and their physiological responses protect the organism from and facilitate interaction with the environment. The speed required to perform this function is guaranteed by the system's autonomy. Preprogrammed behavior keeps us from stopping in the middle of a threatening situation to figure out if the situation actually is dangerous and losing valuable time that could make the difference between life and death. Instead we respond in a flash without thought. The fight-or-flight response is a prime example of this preprogramming. We will return to this later in this chapter.

Another purpose of the emotional system is to facilitate adjustment to social and relational behavior, which in turn promotes survival. Darwin described the emotional system as an interpersonal communication system. Emotional expression conveys how we are feeling in order to activate a specific response and behavior from others, as when we set boundaries for another's behavior by displaying anger or when we reinforce social cohesion by showing love.

Social community is extremely important for humans and other mammals. From an evolutionary perspective, belonging to a family or other social group increases physical safety. The relational function of emotion causes us to not only defend ourselves from others but also to seek relational connections with others. Emotions encourage us to enter into close relations with other people in order to create the best conditions for continued life, the establishment of a family and child rearing. Emotions also stops us from leaving groups we belong to. They discourage separation from close established relations, as can be seen in the pain and sorrow experienced when we are separated from those who are near and dear to us.

The physiology of emotion

The purpose of emotion is to activate muscles and generate physical movement in relation to an outer context. To understand this process let us look more closely at the physiology of emotion.

The brain's limbic system is the center of emotional activation. This is where the need for response activation is registered and where activation begins. Emotional activation is communicated from the limbic system to the rest of the body mainly through two systems: the nervous system and the endocrine (hormonal) system. These two systems, each with their own specific dynamics and functions, work together and complement each other in the emotional process. Together they make sure the emotional process is as vigorous, effective and persistent as the situation demands. An emotional response process is a so-called *global activation* (LeDoux, 2015). This means that it activates, focuses and gives direction to the whole human organism. The emotional response captures the organism's complete attention and claims all its resources. This is why we cannot ignore a powerful emotional response. It tends to hijack our awareness which is also appropriate, since survival is the organism's highest priority. Since the emotional response is so comprehensive, it influences other body systems. The immune system in particular can be negatively affected if it is exposed to an emotional response over a longer period. Research has also shown how fundamental the emotional system is to our physical health and general well-being (Cozolino, 2014).

The nervous system

The central nervous system, brain and spinal cord are connected to the body through the peripheral nervous system, which consists of the somatic and autonomic nervous systems. The somatic nervous system is controlled by our will and directs muscles and body movement. The autonomic nervous system directs body functions without the participation of the will. It regulates among other things the activity of inner organs and smooth muscles in blood vessels, activation of striated muscles in emotional expression, heart muscles and glandular secretion. It is the autonomic nervous system that transmits the emotional response.

The autonomic nervous system consists of two parts: a *sympathetic nervous system* and a *parasympathetic nervous system*. The sympathetic nervous system activates when a person is exposed to physical or psychological stress, which triggers the fight-or-flight response. Information in the sympathetic nervous system moves in two directions: from the brain out to the body in the form of responses (through efferent nerve fibers) and from the body to the brain in the form of sensory stimuli (through afferent nerve fibers). The purpose of efferent signals is to activate simultaneous changes in several different physical processes, for example increased heartrate, bronchial dilation, reduced peristalsis and so forth. They also transmit information quickly from the brain to striated muscles to perform an emotion's fixed sequence of movements, that is its *fixed action pattern*.

41

Emotional activation is predetermined and cannot be altered by the will. Depending on which emotion is activated, sympathetic activation takes place in different ways. The situation or degree of danger triggers a specific response with a specific force. For example when emotions like anger and fear are triggered, heart and respiratory activity increase in preparation for physical movement. In anger, blood supply to the arms and hands increases to prepare for striking. In fear by contrast, hands become cold while blood supply to the legs increases to prepare for flight (Ekman, 2004).

The physiological changes caused by emotional activation are substantial and multifaceted. For instance in the fight-or-flight response we see:

- Increased respiration, pulse and blood pressure in preparation for physical movement
- Increased blood supply to muscles and the brain in order to act quickly and forcefully
- Decreased blood supply to other areas of the body such as inner organs in order to mobilize all available energy against an external threat
- Trembling caused by increased muscle tension
- Decreased activity in the digestive system, to mobilize available energy against an external threat
- Pupil dilation and tunnel vision to sharpen focus on the threat
- Increased metabolism and blood sugar levels to provide energy for muscle activity
- Increased blood coagulation factor to prevent loss of blood in the event of injury
- A heightened pain threshold to prevent injury from stopping survival behavior
- Increased levels of adrenalin and cortisol in the blood for extra energy.

All of these physical changes are part of the body's red alert system. To increase the chances of survival and to prevent injury, bodily functions unimportant to immediate survival shut down and functions that address the immediate external danger are prioritized. The sympathetic nervous system is activated not only by fear, anger and sadness but also by positive experiences such as sexual arousal, infatuation and excitement.

Unlike the sympathetic nervous system's focus on survival in the short term, the parasympathetic nervous system is responsible for the organism's long-term survival. It regulates non-urgent homeostatic life processes such as energy conservation through lowered heart rate, repair and maintenance of the biological body, digestion, production of tears, sexual arousal and so forth. To avoid deterioration and ensure long term-survival, these are physical processes that must function properly. Among other things activity of the parasympathetic nervous system affects the body by:

- Lowering respiratory rate, pulse and blood pressure
- Increasing blood supply to the body's inner organs
- Stimulating digestion
- Contracting pupils
- Stimulating production of saliva and tears
- Inhibiting the release of glucose to the blood
- Reducing the secretion of adrenalin and cortisol
- Stopping activation of the sympathetic nervous system in general, which among other things inhibits the immune system.

The parasympathetic nervous system can also be activated in threatening situations. Through a process called *immobilization* it transmits a response to situations that the sympathetic nervous system is unable to resolve and the organism "plays dead". Immobilization is the last resort of the organism when faced with life-threatening danger.

Aside from these two subsystems of the autonomic nervous system, there is a third part of the nervous system which plays an important role in emotional responses. This is the tenth cranial nerve or vagus nerve. The vagus nerve is not just a single nerve but a complex communication system between the brain and body (Porges, 2011). Its anatomy extends from the brain stem down through the body, where it spreads out into many different body parts and organs. This is why it is called vagus, which means "wandering" in Latin. It reaches the throat, heart, lungs, digestive system and some of the striated skeletal muscles, among other things. With its fast feedback system of sensory and motor nerve fibers, it supports homeostatic regulation in the body. The vagus nerve supports parasympathetic regulation of long-term life processes such as digestion, physical growth and social communication. When the sympathetic nervous system is activated, the vagus nerve helps us remain in social contact with our environment. It prevents emotional activation from taking over awareness and behavior, making it possible for us to consciously adjust emotional expression and relate to others (Porges, 2011). Among other things the vagus nerve enables us to fine-tune our facial expressions in social relationships when we are emotionally agitated so we can continue to speak calmly and reasonably to a person we are angry with or afraid of. In this way the vagus nerve plays a decisive role in our ability to contain, deal with and regulate emotional responses.

The endocrine system

Parallel to the nervous system, the endocrine system is the primary partner of the emotional process. The endocrine system is our hormonal system, the body's powerful system of chemical communication. A hormone is a chemical substance secreted from a gland into the blood, where it is transported to organs and affect their behavior. There are more than sixty known hormones in the human body and each one is a messenger carrying specific information. This information supports natural processes in the body, for example metabolism, and every process requires specific hormones to function optimally. Hormones also carry information within the brain in the form of neurotransmitters that transmit information over the synaptic gap between brain cells in neural networks. The most important hormone-producing glands in the endocrine system are the pineal gland, the pituitary gland, the adrenal glands, the thyroid, thymus, pancreas, ovaries and testicles.

Basically, an endocrine gland receives a message from the brain to secrete a specific dose of a hormone into the bloodstream. The hormone is transported through the circulatory system to organs and attaches itself to receptors on the organ's cell membranes. Each hormone corresponds to a specific receptor on the cell membrane like a key in a lock which opens to receive the hormone's information into the cell. Some hormones transfer their information indirectly to the cell through the receptor, which forwards the information to the cell nucleus. Other hormones use the receptor to gain entrance to the cell where they transfer their information directly to the nucleus. In both cases the hormone transmits information to the cell about what behavior the organ should express. This results in a change in the behavior of the organ or body part that the cell belongs to (Kalat, 2001). In this way hormonal secretion affects cells and organs throughout the body.

The pituitary gland is the queen of glands. It produces and secretes its own hormones and also regulates much of the hormonal production of other glands. The hypothalamus is connected to the pituitary gland. As part of the limbic system, its function is to translate brain processes into hormonal processes. For instance the hypothalamus will take information about an emotional activation from the amygdala and translate it into a corresponding hormonal activation. This is communicated to the nearby pituitary gland, which either secretes the desired hormone directly into the bloodstream or secretes a hormonal message to another gland to secrete the desired hormone. In this way the endocrine system translates the entire spectrum of affective and emotional activation into chemical effects on body cells, which supports the emotional response transmitted through the nervous system. One example of this is vasopressin, a hormone secreted in the fight-or-flight response that stimulates heart cells to increased heart rate in preparation for immediate physical activity.

Fixed action patterns

The goal of the powerful activation of emotions is to stimulate the body to move or form facial and physical expressions that communicate a message. The task of the nervous system is to activate the striated skeletal muscles necessary for movement, for example in order to run away or defend ourselves in the face of danger or to signal our intent and experience through physical expression, thereby influencing the behavior of others. The aim of all physical processes triggered by emotional activation is physical movement in relation to our environment. This is the fundamental objective of every emotional response.

We are familiar with emotional movement in everyday life, for instance when we automatically raise our hands to ward off someone coming too close or involuntarily duck our head when we notice a fast object moving toward us. These are coordinated sequences of movement called *fixed action patterns* that require involvement from the entire body to be effective. Emotional movement does not always have to be large and dynamic. Small autonomic movements also send a message, for instance when facial expressions of pain and a somewhat collapsed upper body signal a need for care.

Physical coordination

Humans are equipped with a fascinating system of physical movement that to a great extent functions completely outside of our conscious control. As an example of the complexity the system works with, consider the process of taking down a shoebox from a shelf. The task may appear to be trivial but a closer look reveals it to be a masterpiece of automatically coordinated muscle activation.

> To begin with, perception of the shoebox must be coordinated with our body's position. Distance to the shoebox and the speed of approach must be registered. Lifting our hands toward the shoebox without thought, we simultaneously open our hands to grasp it. We stretch slightly to reach the shoebox. Just as our hands come into precise, gentle contact with the shoebox, forward motion stops. As we slide the shoebox from the shelf, our body adjusts to its weight. Legs, pelvis, torso and head shift position to maintain balance. A single error in this automatic balancing act would cause us to tip over and fall. In a gliding movement we bring the box from the shelf to the table, adjusting the body millisecond by millisecond to the shifting weight. We gently place the shoebox on the table and release it, keeping perfect balance as we let go of its weight. Our body returns to an upright position beside the shoebox.

In this small sequence of motions, most of the striated skeletal muscles in the body are activated autonomously without thought or focus. It is a complex and very well-coordinated process that we would not be able to perform if we had to consciously think through each muscle activation. During evolution a process using *fixed action patterns* developed in order to make this autonomous coordination of movement possible (Llinás, 2002). Fixed action patterns are hardwired and learned sequences of coordinated, simultaneous movements performed without conscious participation. They are a sequence of simultaneous muscle movements activated in parallel involving nearly all of the body's striated muscles. Fixed action patterns are not clearly defined motions but rather crude, general motor solutions that can be adapted to different situations. To better understand this, consider the simple act of walking, a fixed action pattern that we perform without thought. Aside from the general sequence of physical movements automatically activated when we decide to walk, we adjust these movements based on feedback from our environment. Out of the corner of our eye we may register a stone in front of us and automatically adjust leg movement to raise one foot a bit higher, adjusting the basic action pattern. In this way coordinated and automatic adjustment of a fixed action pattern takes place based on sensory information. We are often unaware of this information although it is registered and movement adjusts without conscious participation. Fixed action patterns are in this way integrated, preprogrammed movement templates that adapt to achieve optimal motor efficiency in a given situation without thought (Llinás, 2002).

Many fixed action patterns are inherited and universal. We can also learn new fixed action patterns which then become autonomous over time. Multiple repetitions of a specific movement are incorporated into the organism and become automatic. We see this clearly in crafts and sports, for example a carpenter's sense of how much wood to saw and the sawing angle to make a perfect fit or the tricky spin a tennis player may put on a ball without conscious focus.

Fixed action patterns of emotions

Apart from fixed action patterns automatically activated in concrete interactions with our environment, there are fixed action patterns that protect and preserve us or bring us closer to others. These are the fixed action patterns of emotions which express emotional activation through muscle activation and physical movement. The purpose of every emotion's physiological process is to support efficient and persistent activation of muscles and physical movement. This applies to every emotion, even those that are not involved in the fight-or-flight response. For example the action pattern of sadness, hunched over with head dropped, is not very expressive but it still activates striated skeletal muscles to protect ourselves when we experience emotional pain. An emotion's fixed action pattern involves complete activation of the body's skeletal muscles. This is necessary to keep us from injuring ourselves during emotional expression for example by losing balance or bumping into things. When a fixed action pattern has been expressed and there is no longer any threat or the emotional message has been received, emotional response activation ceases along with its fixed action pattern.

When an emotional response is activated, action potential in striated skeletal muscles quickly builds up. The intensity and power of emotional charge in an activated fixed action pattern is suited to the situation at hand, as previously described for other fixed action patterns. A fixed action pattern automatically adjusts to the amount of expression required in a given situation. One example of this is how we automatically run from a wasp and then just as automatically stop when we feel safe again. A healthy organism always aims for the highest possible level of efficiency and will therefore quickly adjust expression to the level the situation requires. In these automatic and precise responses to its surroundings, the human organism once again displays fantastic sensitivity and intelligence.

The action pattern of an emotion includes activation of facial muscles. An emotion's facial expression is part of its general fixed action pattern and it was these coordinated facial muscle activities that Darwin studied in 1872 and later Ekman in 2004, leading to the discovery of universal emotions. The function of an emotion's facial expression is to inform and warn others about the activated emotion or the emotional response that is about to be activated. We display an emotion through facial expression and others can relate to that before we physically act. It is a social signal about what may be about to happen. For example consider how a lion bares its teeth at an opponent to communicate what will happen if it attacks. A similar behavior is seen in humans when we inflate the upper torso and stick out our jaw to display strength and warn of a possible display of physical aggression.

Cognition and the emotional process

Cognition, that is our perception of reality and our thoughts, changes significantly during the emotional process. The stronger the emotional response, the more our ability to think clearly and flexibly is limited. Basic physical survival always takes precedence over more complex and sophisticated physical systems like cognition and abstract thought processes. This is why an emotional process tends to hijack awareness and limits our conscious freedom of action. Cognition is affected in different ways, depending on which emotion is activated. For example when fear is activated, attention shifts from a balanced internal/external focus to a strong, external focus. All our external senses become sharper and we become highly sensitive to our environment. The body prepares itself for action and there are no unnecessary thoughts. During fear activation it is impossible to think about pleasant things like a beach holiday or our favorite food. Activation for survival takes precedence in the organism and we cannot tell ourselves to calm down or that there is no real danger. The message of emotional activation takes over our perception of reality; you might say we become one with the emotion we express, for example anger or sadness. We can however, as we will see later, control the force of expression to some extent depending on the situation. In this way the emotional response does not completely take over our perception of reality although it continues to influence it.

The emotional response

In summary and as an example of the emotional response process, we can describe the fight-or-flight response as follows:

1. A threatening situation activates a fear response which places the organism on red alert through a cascade of parallel processes.
2. The sympathetic nervous system activates and signals facial and skeletal muscles to contract and prepare for a possible fight or flight. Intestines and superficial blood vessels contract while heartrate and respiration increase. The adrenal glands are notified to secrete adrenalin, enhancing short-term physical capability.
3. The hypothalamus and the hypothalamus-pituitary-adrenal axis (or HPA axis, a central component of the body's stress response) are activated. The hypothalamus translates emotional activation into the language of hormones and signals the pituitary gland to secrete stress hormones such as vasopressin into the bloodstream. Vasopressin affects cardiac cells, increasing heartrate and blood pressure. If the threatening situation continues, the pituitary gland will secrete adrenocorticotropic hormones (ACTH) into the bloodstream, signaling to the adrenal glands that they should begin secreting cortisone and other hormones that support prolonged emotional activation.
4. Cognition changes in parallel with physical activation. Our focus of awareness shifts from our internal physical environment to our external environment and our senses sharpen.

5. Activation is expressed through striated skeletal muscles. We either flee or fight the threat. The response displayed depends on preprogrammed, automatic outcome calculations that take into consideration things like distance to the threat, whether the threat has found us, possible escape routes and previous experience of similar situations (LeDoux, 2015).

Sympathetic neural activation is the rapid response to a threatening situation. Subsequent hormonal activation through the bloodstream is slower. The aim of hormonal activation is to ensure a more protracted response effect. It makes sure an emotional response persists when a threat continues over time. The physical influence of hormones prevents the emotional response from suddenly stopping. Instead emotional activation slowly dissolves as hormones leave the bloodstream. According to neuroscientist Jill Bolte Taylor (2008) it takes about 90 seconds for hormonal activation to clear the bloodstream after a threat has ceased and emotional activation stops. Continued emotional activation long after its cause has disappeared indicates a disturbance in the natural emotional response process and the emotional system.

To deal with intense, short-term emergencies, the human organism mobilizes its resources through extensive emotional activation. However if an emotional response continues for a long time as in chronic stress, the survival response disturbs natural physical functions and starts to break down the body. Incomplete sympathetic responses drain energy and resources from other essential long-term processes such as repair and maintenance of the organism. As long as a sympathetic response remains incomplete, the sympathetic nervous system continues to act as if it is in a threatening situation and the endocrine system continues to secrete stress hormones. The body does not get a chance to resume processes that ensure long-term survival. This strains homeostatic balance and over time results in physical symptoms such as irregular heartrate, physical tension, digestive problems and cognitive symptoms such as confusion and attention difficulties. Chronic emotional activation also impacts the immune system negatively, for example by inhibiting the production of proteins that are its building blocks. This results in a weakened ability to withstand diseases, from the common cold to more serious diseases (Cozolino, 2014).

Neuroception

How does the human organism know that an emotional response is needed? The amygdala, a part of the limbic system, is the brain's center for emotional response activation. The amygdala is a central part of our emotional memory and its main purpose is to create memories of positive and negative events. Emotional response is activated against this background of memories. The amygdala registers what is dangerous and should be avoided and what is safe and attractive so we can approach it. It continuously scans both our external and internal environment for threats in a process the psychiatrist Stephen W. Porges (2007) called *neuroception*. The amygdala also stores and recognizes positive stimuli, an ability that supports coupling as well as other social ties. This can be seen in the happiness activated when we meet a good friend and automatically open ourselves to contact or the love activated in interaction with our children, which makes it possible for us to prioritize their needs over our own. Although we do not notice it, neuroception is always switched on. If it notices a threat or positive stimulus, it automatically activates a fitting emotional response before we are even aware of it. Neuroception is in other words independent of conscious cognition. Its autonomy and swiftness minimize the risk of overlooking a threat to our safety.

Neuroception is quick because of the way external sensory information moves through the brain. Sensory information can take two different routes, a "high road" and a "low road" (LeDoux, 1996). The high road is a conscious route. It is exact and handles information slowly so we can recognize and understand sensory input and consciously act on our understanding. Neuroception uses the low road. It is swifter and its information is more general. This sensory information travels directly to the amygdala, which autonomously triggers a suitable response before we are aware of it.

The slow and conscious route for sensory information goes from a sense organ (for example the eye) to the thalamus in the brain. The thalamus functions as a relay that sends perceived stimuli to the part of the brain where information processing takes place. Visual information is sent to the visual cortex, where it is processed, patterns are recognized and we understand what we see. We can then act on what we see. At the same time as the thalamus sends information to the visual cortex, it also sends information directly to the amygdala. The amygdala continuously scans sensory information like a radar searching for emotional meaning. If the amygdala discovers something that matches an archived emotional memory, it automatically activates the appropriate emotion. This information route is more than twice as fast as the path from the thalamus to the cerebral cortex, which means that sensory information can lead to emotional response activation before we are aware of it. If the amygdala perceives something threatening in our environment, it activates an appropriate emotional response before the threat reaches our awareness. In other words, an emotional response is activated before we become aware of the activation and the stimulus that activated it.

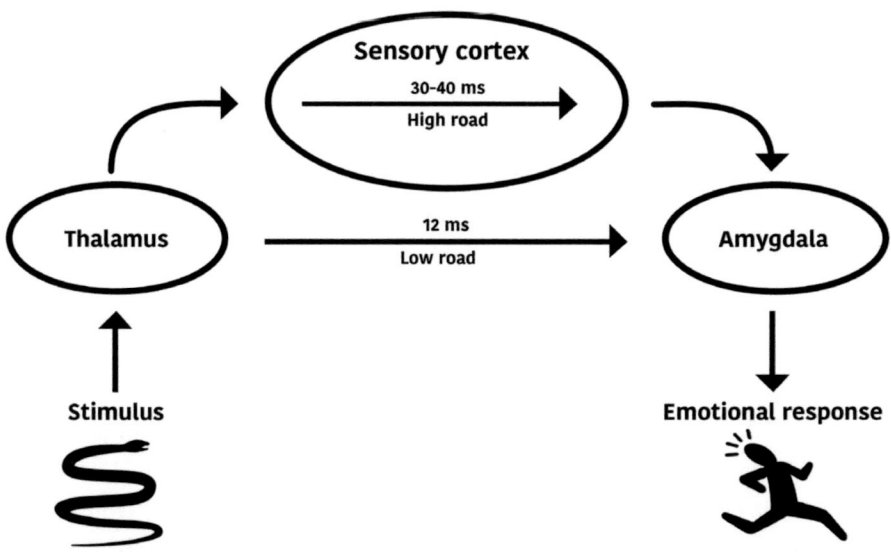

Figure 3: Two paths of sensory information to the brain: one slow and exact, the other swift and general. (LeDoux, 1996)
The organism uses two paths for sensory information. One path is slow and exact. Information travels through the thalamus to the sensory cortex where it is translated into conscious understanding. We can then act on this understanding. The other path is swift and general. Information travels through the thalamus to the amygdala where neuroception autonomously activates a quick response, if necessary before we are aware of what we are responding to.

Neuroception is to a certain extent active even while we sleep, which may be seen when we become completely awake in the middle of the night at an unfamiliar sound.

Neuroception in the amygdala scans all incoming sensory information. A sight, sound, smell or touch may for example trigger an emotional response. Neuroception can also trigger an emotional response to thoughts or feelings we have. If we are afraid of something, the mere thought of it can frighten us. In this way neuroception protects us and is an independent watchdog in the service of life.

The experience of emotion

An emotional response is primarily an autonomous physical response. Our experience of the emotional response is feedback from the response. The psychologist William James described this as early as 1884 in the following way:

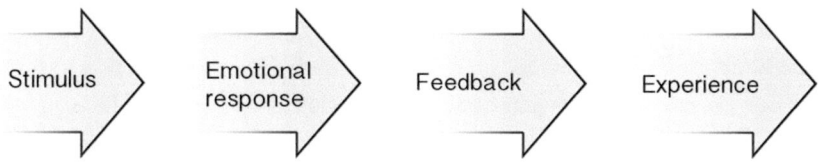

Figure 4: The experience of emotional response
In William James' model, sensory stimuli first activate an emotional response. Feedback from the response and our awareness of the response are our experience of the emotion.

James showed how different emotions cause different physical activations and that each emotion has its own specific feedback. The brain interprets feedback from an emotion in a complex process involving several memory layers before the emotional experience reaches our awareness. Neuroscientist Joseph LeDoux goes deeper and distinguishes between our emotional survival process and the experience of emotion. He describes the experience of emotion as a secondary process: a learned, cognitive feedback from an emotional response (LeDoux, 2015).

The scientist Nina Bull followed in James' footprints in her book from 1951. Bull discovered that most so-called negative emotions such as anger cause bodily movement in two directions. In one direction, the emotion is activated and moves through the body towards natural expression. In the other direction, an opposing force tenses muscles and inhibits natural expression. Particularly in the case of anger, Bull noted increased muscle tension in the jaw, lower arms and hands. Bull's research subjects described this as a way of inhibiting and controlling the emotional process. In her later work Bull discovered a causal relationship between the feeling of an emotion and the extent to which it is inhibited. If an emotion is expressed without any attempt to inhibit or control it, the intensity of the experience or feeling is low and quickly dissipates. On the other hand if emotional expression is controlled and physical expression is resisted, the experience is more intense and lasts longer. A logical conclusion from this discovery is that the emotions we experience are the ones we hold back. When a natural emotional response activation is held back, we feel it.

Imagine walking along a path and suddenly seeing a bear ten meters ahead. A natural fear response is activated which triggers a flight response that activates the body for flight. If we act on this activation's natural expression and run, we do not experience much fear but rather physical activation and its expression as we rush to safety. Once we reach safety, we feel elevated levels of activity in the body and the hormonal aftermath of emotional response activation. We may feel some fear if we begin to think about what could have happened. However if we hold back the activation's expression (for instance if we are paralyzed, cannot find an escape route or hesitate), we experience fear clearly, either in the situation or later. We experience the fear that was unable to convert into physical expression. The same applies in a relationship if we do not speak out when someone verbally violates our boundaries. The consequence of not expressing naturally activated anger is to feel fear or anger towards the person later. This feeling is the result of suppressed physical activation and can continue to affect us long after the situation is over.

Both of these examples show how a controlled and withheld emotional response leads to a subsequent experience of the emotion. We do not experience the emotion if its response is directly expressed upon activation. The emotion we do not express is the one we feel (Levin, 2010). This basically means that every emotion we experience has to some extent been inhibited or restrained in its expression, all the way from complete withholding of the emotional response to mild resistance. As a result the emotional response continues to affect the organism long after the cause of the emotional response activation is gone.

Affective and emotional responses as part of the brain's predictive process

It may seem obvious that affective and emotional response activations are triggered by external stimuli that result in a sudden start of neural and physical activity. Scientific studies have however found evidence that this is not the case and that the organism regularly initiates affects and emotions before an external trigger event. Research indicates that emotional responses are initiated by the brain to meet predictions of future events based on our knowledge of the environment. The organism is not simply a passive receiver of stimuli but actively relates to its environment (Barrett, 2017). As part of its basic process of life and survival, the brain is constantly trying to understand its environment and predict future needs. Instead of waiting for the environment to present a trigger for the organism to respond to, the brain proactively initiates emotional responses in the organism based on its predictions of outcomes and future needs. We initiate a response before something happens. This is a much more efficient dynamic for the organism from the perspective of survival, as compared to waiting and then reacting after something has happened.

The brain may be viewed as a prediction machine that constantly generates simulations and makes best guesses about what is happening and what will happen in the world around us (Seth, 2021). The brain assists in keeping the organism alive by comparing incoming sensory input to past experiences and generating predictions about outcomes and future needs as it constructs our world. The present moment we are experiencing is a prediction made by the brain a moment earlier.

For example: Every waking moment, the brain receives vast amounts of unsorted visual input through the eyes and optic nerves, information that in itself is without meaning. Drawing on previous experiences and its understanding of the world, the brain makes predictions and constructs our world on the basis of these predictions. Instead of experiencing the world around us we experience the world as seen in our mind's eye, projected back onto the world. It is only then that all the chaotic visual input gains meaning for us. The same applies to all of our sensory experiences: hearing, taste, smell, touch and everything we feel.

This process of prediction is a dynamic process. The brain continually issues a multitude of predictions about future events in prediction loops that are constantly tested against new information delivered by our senses. In this way predictions undergo continual updates. Predictions are adjusted on the basis of new information received as sensory input and new predictions are continually issued.

Physical action is closely connected to the process of prediction and is inseparable from information gathering. The brain guides our actions in its search for new information on which it can build further predictions and this new information changes perceptions and guides our actions. Every time the brain constructs our experience based on predictions, it prepares for automatic physical changes and may prescribe specific actions and physical movements before we are aware of any intention to move (Barrett, 2017).

Viewed from this perspective, emotional responses are proactive constructs initiated to meet our predictions of what will happen rather than responses to what has happened. Emotional responses affect the environment and reveal new information that makes it possible for the brain to adjust and refine its predictions and make corresponding adjustments to emotional response activity. Affective and emotional responses are thus parts of the organism's continual predictive process to achieve homeostasis through preventive physical resource allocation and autonomous responses. It is this process of prediction that guides the fixed action patterns described earlier in this chapter. Through a comprehensive predictive process we continually respond and physically move our body with greater or lesser intensity based on what could happen, without an external stimulus to trigger the response and movement.

5

The basic emotions

In this description of our basic emotions we have proceeded from a classic definition of the emotional system and basic emotional processes, making a few adjustments in the light of more recent research and clinical experience. Fear, anger, sadness, happiness and love are regarded as our basic human emotions. Disgust and surprise are often included in the classic definition but as we shall see, they are not distinct emotions but rather subcategories of anger and fear. Early research in emotions did not consider love to be an emotion. More recent research has however shown that love is one of the most important human social response processes (Fredrickson, 2013). It produces a positive life experience and plays a primary role in positive personality development.

Fear

The emotional activation of fear occurs mainly in two situations that cause the same physiological activation. One situation is when faced with a real, physically dangerous situation. The other is when fear is activated by another of our own affective and emotional response activations. Fear is the most well-researched emotion, particularly as part of the fight-or-flight response, and we can use this knowledge to gain a general understanding of fear. This section about fear begins by examining the biological process and function of fear triggered by a real, physically threatening situation. Based on this knowledge we turn to the fear experienced when we are not in a physically threatening situation. In this case fear is caused by our own emotional activation. The intention is to present a down-to-earth and clear picture of this relatively transient emotion so that it can be appropriately dealt with.

Fear in a physically threatening situation

Fear is a survival process that is activated when physical safety and well-being are threatened. It is a hardwired warning system that prepares the organism for a possibly life-threatening situation (Panksepp, 2012). Fear is the initial stage of the fight-or-flight response. It makes the organism hypersensitive, awake, and focused on a detected danger (LeDoux, 2015). Fear puts the physical organism on red alert in order to avoid or defend against a possible danger. Once activated, fear either leads to another emotional response expression or it dissipates. If we discover that the danger has passed or that there never was any threat, fear subsides on its own. However if it becomes necessary to either flee or fight the danger, fear turns into a suitable response.

As with all emotional response processes, fear is expressed through the nervous and endocrine systems. The activation of the endocrine system means it will take a while for the physical effect to stop if we discover there is no danger or that the danger has passed. Most of us recognize this delayed effect when frightened; fear continues to affect the body and cognition long after the danger is over. The body remains on red alert with tensed muscles and elevated heart rate and we feel the need to "come down". After focusing on discovering and locating danger in its environment, it takes a while for the human organism to regain its balance between the experience of inner and outer reality and reestablish contact with itself. This is supported by activation of the parasympathetic nervous system.

The memory of fear

Neuroception, which activates the fear response, is located in the amygdala. The amygdala contains both hardwired and learned knowledge about what is dangerous for us. A number of animals and circumstances were for example a real danger for early humans. This knowledge is imprinted in us from birth and can still activate fear. It would seem for example that we have a hardwired fear of spiders, snakes, heights and darkness. Aside from inherited knowledge we also learn what is a danger to us from experience.

Learning about danger is quick and efficient. A dangerous situation needs to occur only once to be registered and stored in the memory of fear. Afterwards neuroception will automatically activate fear when it perceives a similar situation

in interactions with our environment. For example if we have once experienced a dangerous situation involving drunk people, the amygdala labels drunk
people as potentially dangerous. When neuroception later receives information
that one or more drunken persons are ahead of us on the sidewalk, it triggers
a fear response. The body is activated, we become alert and we automatically
begin to scan the area for a safe spot away from the potential danger. Fear may
be followed by an automatic flight response causing us to change direction or
to hurry without thought over to the other side of the street. Neuroception is
extremely sensitive. It can discover a potential threat and trigger fear based on
little information. Small details are enough such as a raised voice, someone
who staggers as they walk or the sight of people outside a bar.

The memory of fear is such a basic survival function that the human organism
continues to activate fear when faced with similar stimuli for the rest of its life
or until we learn that the situation is no longer dangerous. For optimal safety
we learn about dangerous situations quickly and unlearn them slowly. We can
learn that a situation is dangerous by experiencing it only once, but unlearning
it takes many situations in which we experience that it is no longer dangerous.
The principle for the organism's "safety protocol" is that it is better to activate a
fear response one hundred times when there is no real danger than to unlearn
the response after ninety-nine times, only to find that the danger is real the
hundredth time.

As a result of this dynamic we continue to activate fear in specific situations
even though we know from extensive experience that it no longer constitutes
a threat. Some research even indicates that when it comes to safety, we never
forget a threat (Cozolino, 2014). The fear response will always be activated but
after a number of positive experiences, its intensity decreases.

Fear in situations that are not a physical threat

The function of fear is basically to protect life. Its purpose is to prepare a
defense for physical survival. Fear activated when we are not in a physically
dangerous situation activates the endocrine and sympathetic nervous systems
in the same way but the focus is different. This fear is activated to defend the
stability and survival of personality. It is a defense against affects and emotions
that we learned at an early age are a threat to personality. For example, in our

childhood an emotional response, such as anger, was not accepted by a caregiver or someone close and the emotion is therefore associated with separation from the caregiver. This separation threatened our existence and as a consequence we learned to defend ourselves from expressing our emotional response. Once this is learned, a fear response automatically activates every time the threatening emotional response activates. In this way fear becomes a defense against other response processes in the organism.

We see this dynamic for example when we experience fear because a colleague is mistreated at work. We are not afraid of the situation itself but of the anger or sadness it activates in us, which we have learned leads to negative consequences if expressed. A result of this fear may be that we do not stand up for ourselves or our colleague. We do not speak out against those who mistreat the colleague. Fear's function in this example is to secure the stability of personality. It does this by shifting our awareness away from the unacceptable emotional response, thereby avoiding the risk that the emotional response might become expressed.

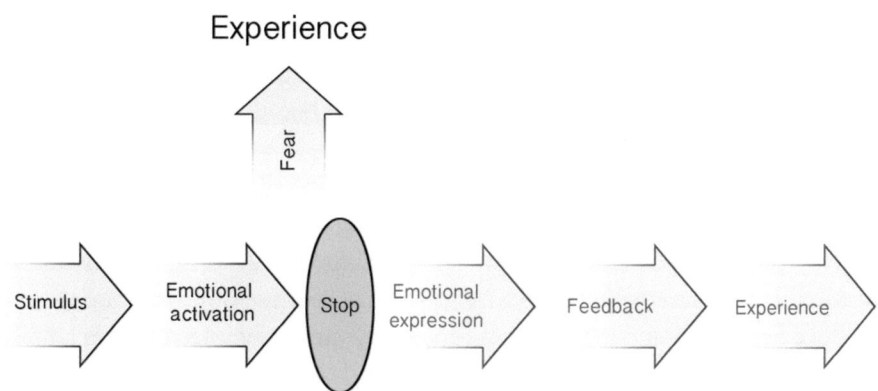

Figure 5: Fear as a defense against another response process
If we are not in a physically threatening situation, activation of fear is a defense against another emotional response in the organism. That emotional response threatens the stability of personality and its process is autonomously stopped. At the same time, fear eliminates our awareness of the emotional response. After this all the person experiences is fear.

Fear regulates relationships

An emotional response originally intended for physical survival is now used to "survive" human relationships, particularly to avoid loss of close relations (Frederickson, 2013). Experiences from earlier relationships are generalized and transferred to later relationships. Fear which was activated to protect against driving an early caregiver away is later employed to avoid driving others away. If we are afraid of someone or something that is not directly, physically dangerous, what we actually are afraid of is another emotional response that is activated in the situation and not the person or thing itself. It is this emotional response that we are afraid of.

Every time fear is activated it is because another emotional response was activated just before it. Fear of speaking in front of a large audience can for example be caused by a previous experience of not being good enough in a similar situation. The sadness activated at that time was not dealt with, which caused it to be stored in emotional memory. Later in life this sadness is automatically activated in similar situations and this activates a fear response. Fear is activated to avoid feeling the sadness that was activated. It is a defense against the expression of sadness.

Another example is when a person violates our boundaries, for instance when someone is loud. We are not afraid of the person but of the emotional response that the situation activates. It may be because we learned not to display anger when an important caregiver violated our boundaries, perhaps because it led to even greater violations. As a result our own anger is experienced as dangerous. Every time anger activates in similar situations later, it is perceived as a threat to personality and activates fear. We have become afraid of our own anger because we have learned that negative consequences follow when we express anger.

Fear in situations that do not directly involve other people is still connected to relationships, for example the fear of being alone. Earlier in life we may have experienced separation from a caregiver, which activated sadness. This sadness was not affirmed and accepted by the caregiver, which caused us to defend against it. Later, sadness activates in similar situations, for example when we are alone or think about being alone. Activation of sadness threatens the stability of personality, which activates fear. We are afraid of the sadness, not of being alone.

When we say:
"I am afraid he will leave me!" it may really mean, "I am afraid of the pain and sadness I feel when I think about him leaving me."
When we say:
"I am afraid he will say no" it may really mean, "I am afraid of the anger I feel at the thought of him saying no."
When we say:
"I am afraid to say yes to her" it may really mean, "I am afraid of my vulnerability and sadness if I open up to love."

When we feel fear and there is no real threat to physical survival, the fear is always activated by another emotion and not by the situation or person.

Emotion – fear – defense

As a matter of fact most of us are more fearful than we experience ourselves to be. To function practically in everyday life without being interrupted by attacks of fear (which many people actually experience), the human organism has developed a defense system that automatically cuts off contact with the activation of fear.

Fear is an uncomfortable experience. Basically fear is simply a physical activation of the sympathetic nervous system but since it is associated with threats to the organism, it is interpreted negatively (LeDoux, 2015). The negative value assigned to fear activation is called its negative hedonic tone, as opposed to a positive hedonic tone (from Greek hedone = pleasure, enjoyment). A negative hedonic tone is experienced as discomfort, indicating that the organism should keep away from something that is threatening. The closer we get to whatever threatens, the more discomfort we feel.

The discomfort experienced when fear activates is an important part of the defense against another emotional response that we have learned to see as a threat. This instantaneously indicates to the organism how it should deal with an otherwise neutral activation of the sympathetic nervous system. Personality then avoids the discomfort of fear by activating a cognitive defense that keeps us from feeling the fear. The primary aim of this cognitive defense is to avoid conscious contact with the activation of fear.

In a flash the sequence goes from an emotional response activation to fear activation to activation of a cognitive defense. Often we notice neither the activated emotion nor the fear. The defense takes over instead and fear is hidden from awareness. We do not have time to feel fear nor do we notice that a defense has been activated.

> In early life Claire learned that she was not allowed to be angry or sad because her mother could not deal with her when she expressed those emotions. Whenever Claire became angry or sad, her mother shut down contact with her. Claire learned that these emotional expressions resulted in an experience of separation from her mother, something Claire as a child could neither deal with nor relate to. Activation of these emotions became in themselves a threat to Claire's vitally important connection with her mother. Activation of sadness or anger from that point on activated fear in her.
>
> Claire's personality developed defense mechanisms and when these emotions became activated later in life, her defenses effectively eliminated her awareness of the discomfort of fear. As a defense Claire learned to direct her attention away from her own feelings and instead focus on and fulfill the demands and needs of others. As an adult Claire found it difficult to be in close personal relationships. Whenever she opened up in a relationship, fear was activated. This activation caused her to relate to the other person by trying to fulfill what she believed were the other's needs. This was the defensive behavior Claire had learned as a child in order to avoid feeling fear and another emotional response activation. As a result of this dynamic, she found intimacy difficult and did not stay long in relationships. She often felt lonely and isolated.

In therapy Claire was guided to focus on herself and her own feelings. This gave her the opportunity to feel fear without activating her defense. This brought her into contact with previously unaccepted emotions and she was given space to express them in her sessions. As Claire experienced that these emotional responses no longer resulted in negative consequences and were not dangerous, her fear of intimacy slowly began to fade. Fear effectively protects us from getting close to threatening emotions and our cognitive defense keeps our awareness away from the experience of fear. This is why we do not always experience fear even though fear is activated.

The physical dynamics of fear

Activation of fear initiates a physical shift from parasympathetic contact with inner processes to sympathetically activated muscle tension and a focus on external perception. Shoulders pull up and stay up, respiration becomes shallower and takes place high up in the body, eyes widen and we listen intensely. We are watchful and prepared for what happens around us. To discover possible threats in the environment, conscious focus moves up through the body to the head and its sense organs, away from contact with inner processes. Attention is directed outward and the body remains still, waiting, with all senses alert. This would be an appropriate process if it was about discovering and dealing with a real threat to physical safety. However fear activated by another emotional response that threatens the stability of personality is part of a defense. Instead of the open perception and alertness that comes before a fight-or-flight response, the dynamic of fear has become a defense against an internal experience and a flight from that experience.

The intensity of fear

Our experience of the power and intensity of fear is relative to how threatening the other emotional response is to the stability of personality. Personality can relatively easily deal with low intensity fear. Low intensity fear also makes it relatively easy to come into contact with the emotional response that activated the fear. The more dangerous the emotional activation, the more powerful fear activation will be and at some point our cognitive defense will be activated. In anxiety the cognitive defense can no longer contain fear; its intensity is too strong and personality is overwhelmed. This leads to various symptoms of anxiety such as panic, general anxiety and so forth. The cognitive defense and its mechanisms will be dealt with in more detail later and in Chapter 15 we will learn about the different levels of fear and how to deal with them.

Avoidance behavior

Avoidance behavior is the result of our fear memory, which makes a person physically or cognitively avoid situations that might activate specific emotions. Avoidance behavior often begins in childhood and later becomes a building block in adult personality. We avoid situations that activate fear both actively and passively. Active avoidance behavior is when we automatically avoid physical situations that could generate fear in us. Passive avoidance behavior occurs when we do not allow ourselves to explore new, unknown, uncontrolled situations. Avoidance behavior boxes us into a status quo that does not give us a chance to assess whether a situation is still so dangerous that we are unable to handle it. By avoiding a potentially threatening situation, we remove our chance of experiencing it and learning that it is not dangerous anymore. This makes it impossible to deprogram our memory of fear and experience the resulting behavioral flexibility and freedom. In this way avoidance behavior has massive consequences for our natural development and experience of life.

Anger

Anger activates to defend us. It is an emotional response that activates when our physical or psychological boundaries are violated. Physical boundaries are violated when someone injures or threatens to injure our body. Psychological boundaries are violated when someone pressures us, manipulates us or in some other way forces their will on us. In these situations the human organism activates an anger response to reestablish the boundaries that have been or are being violated. Anger can also be activated if we experience a potential threat of violation to our boundaries.

Figure 6: The anger response
Anger is a natural response that is activated when our physical or psychological boundaries are violated. The response wards off the threat, reestablishes boundaries and safeguards the organism.

The word "anger" is related to words that mean narrowing, strangling and distress. This is the experience that activates anger. External violation creates an experience of being painfully squeezed. This experience triggers an anger response to restore space for ourselves. Anger helps us repel the external threat that is pressing in on us and reestablish our external boundary. When the threat to our boundaries stops, the physical sensation of being squeezed stops and this causes the anger response to stop. Part of the fixed action pattern of an anger response includes movements of arms and hands to ward off or push away the person who is violating us. An outward movement of the arms with added power from the legs reestablishes or indicates our border. Striking with arms and hands are also manifestations of this expression. Anger is displayed through facial expressions and voice. Vocal expressions include unclear guttural sounds and words like "no!" "stop!" "go away!" and so forth.

Just as with every natural emotion, the intensity of an automatically activated, natural anger response is proportional to the degree of danger or violation. The intensity of our anger response is low when it comes to jostling in line at a store or if our partner tries to convince us to do something we do not want to do. It can be enough with a response expressed as a gesture, a raised voice or an angry look. When it comes to more serious violations as when somebody physically hits us or we discover that we have been manipulated for some time, the anger response will be more powerful and may be physical. We may counterattack physically and/or verbally.

As a physical survival response, the function of anger is to strike back at whatever threatens us. This is the fight response discussed earlier. James Avrill (2010) studied anger and wrote that the aim of anger (aggression) is to force another person to change or stop a behavior that can harm us. This means that anger is primarily about our own survival and safety, not the other person's well-being. A natural anger response does not take the other person into consideration, in fact quite the opposite. The most effective way an anger response can stop a threat is by pacifying it at its source, that is, the threatening person.

As mentioned earlier however, healthy anger is always expressed in proportion to the degree of threat to our boundaries. Anger expressed more forcefully than the situation calls for is due to a disturbance in the emotional system. This may be the result of long-suppressed anger or a reaction to other emotional processes. The same is true when the intensity of anger in response to a violation is too low to reestablish boundaries and end the violation or when an expression of anger is totally absent. These cases have to do with learned passivity and fear of the effects of others' or one's own anger.

Anger and boundaries

The relational function of the anger response is to regulate boundaries in interpersonal relationships and to reestablish and clarify distance between ourselves and others. Anger protects us when others violate our individual, intimate boundaries. It may for example be the extent to which we can tolerate and accept something without compromising our own needs and integrity. If this boundary is violated, the stability of personality is threatened and an anger response is activated to reestablish the boundary and defend the safety of personality.

The boundaries of personality are created early in the process of individuation when infants outgrow parental dependency and become independent individuals. In this developmental process, anger is naturally expressed as part of the separation process from the parent. For example we see this when a child says "No" to a parent simply to assert itself and its individuality. If a child learns that disagreement is not OK and that the child's anger is unacceptable to the caregiver, it may lead to suppression of anger later in life. The child learns that anger and setting boundaries make their situation worse and are dangerous in themselves. Later in life, instead of opposing the opinions of others that they disagree with, the person relates to others' opinion without opposition, with indirect opposition or simply avoids situations that they know would require opposition. We avoid expressing anger and setting boundaries for others later in life because it is connected to early rejection by a caregiver.

When we do not set natural boundaries and withhold expression of an anger response, others cannot sense our boundaries and relate to them. This can create a negative spiral that is difficult to break. If we do not set natural boundaries in a situation when someone violates our boundaries, anger is activated which is then suppressed. When our anger response is suppressed, the other person cannot sense our boundaries and may easily violate them. This activates anger again, which is also suppressed, and the spiral continues. The only way to break out of this spiral is by restoring trust in our own anger response and experiencing that it is OK and positive to set limits for others.

Anger and personal responsibility

Anger in relations is connected to a clear expression of who we are, what our needs are and what we stand for. When we respond in this way, we take responsibility for ourselves. Anger is often activated to reestablish the boundaries of personality when we have not expressed where we stand or have been unclear about what we want, mean or accept. If we express this clearly, our personal boundaries are obvious to others and most often we do not have to defend them.

If we experience that others do not respect us and our boundaries, it is probably because we have been unclear about where we stand. If we want clear boundaries that are not violated, we must stand up for ourselves in every situation, both great and small. When something we stand for is challenged, we must be clear about where we stand and speak our mind. By speaking out and disagreeing we actually say "yes" to ourselves and our needs. Conversely we say "no" to ourselves when we do not respect our natural boundaries and avoid expressing a standpoint.

Anger adrift

Expressing anger can be a sensitive issue if it is connected to early negative experiences. If anger was not accepted, we learned to suppress its natural expression. Suppressing the expression of anger means that the anger response is still activated as a physical process but we do not allow the process to reach completion through expression and then dissipate. This causes the action potential of the anger response to accumulate in the nervous system and muscles in a process similar to a pressure cooker.

However we cannot completely keep this action potential from expressing itself. Depending on how our personality is organized, the action potential of an anger response will seek other ways to express itself. This discharges the discomfort created by suppressed anger without clearly and plainly expressing it. One way of doing this is by letting anger seep out in the form of general irritability and grouchiness. Another way is by permitting more direct expressions of anger in situations where there is no relational risk. For instance instead of speaking out when our partner violates our boundaries, we yell at our children. It could also be that instead of speaking out and liberating ourselves from our parents, we are in constant conflict with everyone else and always looking for a fight.

It is also possible to relieve the discomfort of withheld anger by discharging its action potential and letting it express itself in the form of another more acceptable emotion or action. For instance instead of expressing anger, we cry, go for a run or channel the energy into work.

The case of Christopher shows how suppressed anger responses accumulate like a pressure cooker and are discharged in other, less dangerous situations.

> Christopher was in his final year at a teacher's college. He lived with a partner he loved together with their two small children. His final year at college involved writing a paper, something which according to him should not have been a problem. Once he began writing the paper however, he came into contact with performance anxiety and was unable to move forward. At the same time the manager at his workplacc was pressuring him. At home Christopher and his partner had discussed whether they should move to a bigger apartment now that they had two children. One evening while Christopher and his partner were eating dinner together, she raised the question of a move again and everything suddenly became too much for Christopher. He exploded, stood up from the table and screamed at his partner that she should stop pressuring him and then he left the room, slamming the door behind him. A half hour later Christopher returned and apologized for his behavior.

After this episode Christopher sought help to solve the chaos he was experiencing. Through the therapeutic process, Christopher came to realize that the inner pressure he had experienced for a long time and which had explosively expressed itself went back to his father's demands on him when he was a child, demands which Christopher still felt. He always felt that he must do better and that whatever he did was not good enough. This activated his anger, which he had learned only makes the situation worse if expressed. Christopher found it difficult to speak out when his boundaries were challenged. Instead he either withdrew or tried to fix the situation when his anger was activated. He saw that this also applied to his situation at work. To relieve the discomfort of accumulated anger responses, he tended to yell at his partner and their children when everything became too much. Afraid to express anger when it arose, Christopher discharged the resulting pressure by expressing anger in the one relationship where he felt safe.

For many of us anger and its expression are connected to physical and psycho-logical violence and violation, especially if we have experienced it in our own life. However, physical and psychological violence or violation are not natural expressions of anger. They are instead indications of an emotional disturbance, boundaries that were not set earlier in the person's life or the violation is a way of discharging the action potential of another emotion. The sole aim of natural anger is to reestablish a boundary that has been violated and its intensity is relative to the degree of violation. Violent anger is a flight from and defense against another emotional response. It is this reactive anger that causes an enormous amount of suffering in human relationships and is the cause of many of the conflicts we see in the world.

Not expressing or dealing with our natural anger has negative effects. Anger does not disappear when we ignore it; quite the contrary, it tends to grow. It can only be dissipated through expression in the context in which it belongs, aptly expressed in the poem "A Poison Tree" by William Blake (1794).

> *I was angry with my friend;*
> *I told my wrath; my wrath did end.*
> *I was angry with my foe;*
> *I told it not, my wrath did grow.*

Anger as disgust

The experience of disgust which Darwin identified as one of the six universal emotions is basically the same process as anger and has the same function (R.E. Jack et.al., 2014). Its function is to physically expel something ingested that is unhealthy for the organism, for example by vomiting tainted or poisonous food. When presented with tainted food or food we have had a bad experience with, we feel a loathing that prevents us from eating it. We react with disgust when we smell or see food that is bad for us.

The physical function of this response can be transferred to its psychological function. We may loathe and want to cough up others' opinions and values that have metaphorically been shoved down our throat, opinions and values that we may have been forced to adopt while growing up and could not refuse. They

71

poison our personality and degrade us. When we meet the same opinion later in life, it may activate a disgust response. The function of disgust and its physical process in this case is to maintain and reestablish a psychological boundary that was violated or is in danger of being violated. Instead of defending our boundary by pushing the person away, we vomit and expel the poison that had entered our system. We get rid of the poison swallowed or the opinion forced upon us and stay away from it.

Sadness

The function of sadness is to express and relieve pain caused by relational separation. We are social beings who live, develop and thrive in positive social connection with those close to us. When this connection breaks as in divorce, death or other separation, a natural emotional pain develops in the organism. This pain resembles physical pain and makes use of the same neurological circuits in the brain (Panskepp & Bivens, 2012). We see this dynamic clearly in children who spontaneously cry both from physical and psychological pain. In an evolutionary perspective, the purpose of pain caused by separation is to preserve social cohesion. It is an incentive to stay with others in a community for survival.

To understand what happens when a sadness response is activated, we can think of our closest social group as a relational body equivalent to our physical body. Our relational body consists of a close group of people who mean a lot to us, often family and others with whom we have a close relationship. Just as our physical body needs to heal after an injury, the same applies to our relational body. When separated from those we are close to, the relational body is injured or wounded and pain causes tears to flow naturally. The pain of separation encourages us to preserve and care for our close-knit social group, which from an evolutionary perspective provides greater physical safety. If we distance ourselves from those closest to us or if someone in the group removes themself, we automatically experience pain and sadness.

Tears

Tears are the natural expression of sadness. We see this clearly when a lonely child cries. The child experiences pain from relational separation and begins to cry.

When the child is comforted, relationship is confirmed and the pain goes away. Relational separation creates an imbalance in the relational body that threatens the stability of personality, which activates pain in the sympathetic nervous system. Crying dissolves this sympathetic activation, balance is restored and personality is stabilized. Research has shown that when tears are an emotional response of sadness, they cleanse the body from stress hormones secreted due to pain (Frey, 1985). By contrast, no biochemical cleansing takes place when we cry because we are sorry for ourselves. When we experience the pain of separation, the organism curls up in a short-term survival response to protect itself from further injury. Tears dissolve the survival response's sympathetic (stress-) activation and transform it into a parasympathetically activated condition in the organism. This is why we feel relaxed, cleansed and calm after crying.

Tears rolling down our cheeks and the injured, vulnerable aura we project when we cry are valuable evolutionary signals: they attract caring attention. A crying child evokes empathy in others, particularly the child's parents. Picking the crying child up and providing physical contact relieves the pain. Physical contact causes oxytocin to be released, a hormone that inhibits stress, promotes empathy and makes the child feel safe in contact with its parents. The child can relax again.

Many people experience discomfort when crying, especially in front of others. When we cry we show ourselves as vulnerable and defenseless with the same vulnerability which, coming from a child, attracts caring attention. Previous negative experiences can make it difficult for us to display this vulnerability. Instead we have learned to stop crying, to turn off the tears and stop whining. We once experienced the pain of sadness and cried, but the sadness was not acknowledged. The result was more pain. That is why we learn to conceal sadness: to avoid exposing ourselves to even more pain by being hurt again.

Sadness is often activated without expression. We are sad but hold the tears back and internally harden ourselves. Many years of withheld sadness and many situations in which we did not allow ourselves to cry can make it seem overwhelming to let go. It feels as if we would drown in tears if we opened up to them. This is why many of us feel sad for a long time. The sadness is real but its expression is forbidden. Instead of a naturally tearful expression and release from pain, we hold onto sadness and continue to be sadly depressed internally for weeks, months or years. Separation from someone close to us is a natural part of life and each separation needs its own time for mourning. If we do not allow ourselves the time it takes to mourn, each new separation reminds us of our unfinished mourning and is added to it. To release tears is to lose control and allow ourselves to be overwhelmed. When we allow sadness to unfold we feel better and our trust in the process grows.

It also happens that we cry when it is not a natural expression of sadness. We may cry because we feel sorry for ourselves and not as an expression of the pain of sadness. This type of sadness is a collapse. We flee from ourselves and defend ourselves against another emotional response, discharging its action potential by feeling sorry for ourselves. We may be angry but cry instead because we have learned that crying is safer than an expression of anger.

Sadness takes time

Sadness cannot be hurried. It is a slow, tear-filled, organic process. Just as with a physical wound, a relational wound needs time and care to heal. Wounds of separation become deeper the more a person means to us and they take more time to heal. It is common to think that mourning takes a long time, too much time before it is over. People in a long process of sadness often hear comments like, "It cannot be healthy for you to continue being so sad" or "Isn't it time to move on?". We may also think, "I do not understand why I am still so sad."

However the process of mourning and the pain of separation take time to heal. If we accept our sadness, allow ourselves to feel the pain we carry within us and let the tears flow, we will experience that our tears are not uncomfortable but liberating, not from the person but from the pain. Tears of mourning help us to let go of the past and give us the strength to move on. They are both closure and an opening in our further journey through life.

Happiness

Happiness makes us feel lively and satisfied. It is experienced as a positive emotion that allows us to relax and strengthens our bonds to those around us. Happiness and love are the so-called positive emotions. They are positive in the sense that their function is to initiate and strengthen relational contact and their activation leads us to seek out others. In contrast to the other emotions' focus on immediate survival and activation of the sympathetic nervous system, positive emotions activate the parasympathetic nervous system and are experienced as pleasurable.

Happiness and play are connected. When children play together, their happiness is evident in laughter, smiles and lively interaction. Unlike a great deal of adult daily life, play is a creative and pleasurable process involving relaxed and unrestrained interaction. Happiness is expressed naturally when we meet others in an informal give and take. Happiness is about being in effortless interaction with life. Adults have often refined this play and if it occurs at all, it is often less physical and more verbal and cognitive. This kind of play takes place in communication, social interaction and other creative expressions. In adult playful interaction we relax with an inner feeling of safety and ease. Happiness opens the organism in a process that effectively relieves physical and cognitive tension. It makes life less serious without becoming irresponsible. The biological usefulness of happiness lies in its activation of the parasympathetic nervous system, which relieves the stress of sympathetic activation.

Happiness functions as social glue. We are drawn to happy and smiling people and prefer to work with people who are fun to be with. Work is also easier when it makes us happy. Happiness is expressed in the smile, a fixed action pattern that displays openness and safety in relationship. A smile is a physical invitation. Together with an inviting body posture, it signals "I am no threat", "I would like to have contact with you". Most of us would also like to have contact with someone who expresses happiness in this way.

Since happiness has such a positive charge, we can feel great emotional resonance with someone who displays happiness. Happiness is infectious and mutual happiness generates a resonance that speaks of common interest and trust. It provides safety and a feeling of security. Happiness supports contact between people. It strengthens the ties that bind us together.

The dilemma of happiness

Why is it that happiness does not fill more of our life when it has so many positive qualities? Happiness is a natural expression of physical well-being, the exact opposite of one-sided cognitive focus or stressful work. It is a parasympathetic expression that promotes life by letting go of control over the life process.

This is the challenge of happiness: to happily let go of focus and control, qualities we have learned are important in defending personality from unacceptable emotional responses. When we let go and allow ourselves to experience natural happiness, we open up. We become vulnerable. As children many of us did not receive approval of our lively expressions of happiness. On the contrary, happiness may have been met with negative responses and we learned that displays of happiness had negative consequences. The lively happiness of a child can be challenging for a parent focused on structure and order. Children live and express themselves in their own organic time and their expressions of life can disturb a parent's perceived need for structure, such as the need to follow schedules and keep appointments. As a result, parents who are unable to deal with a child's natural, unbounded joy of life often brusquely cut it off. One example of this is when a parent stops their child's organic process in the morning and gets angry when the child is not ready to leave home. Another example is when a child is scolded for not ending an exciting game. In this way we learn to inhibit the natural process of happiness early in life and lose contact with natural happiness. A happy response which would be naturally expressed as part of open and playful contact with one's environment is gone. Instead we seek events and activities that put excitement and amusement into our life.

The natural happiness which many of us have learned is inappropriate and negative can be exchanged for forced, reactive and stressed happiness. While natural happiness is a balanced, physical expression of well-being in contact with life or other people, forced happiness is part of a physical stress response or a way to discharge the discomfort of stress.

Forced happiness is part of a chronic sympathetic stress activation when an experience similar to happiness is produced by endorphins released into the body, which wears down the organism. This is an unnatural expression of "happiness". The fixed action pattern of natural happiness activates facial muscles in a way that cannot be performed consciously without appearing forced or simulated. Guillaume Duchenne de Boulogne, a French neurologist, described the smile of natural happiness in the mid-19th century which is now called the Duchenne smile (Ekman, 2003). This smile involves contraction of both the muscles that lift the corners of the mouth (zygomaticus major) as well as small muscles around the eyes (especially orbicularis oculi). In a natural Duchenne smile we smile with both our mouth and our eyes. A forced or conscious smile activates the muscles around the corners of the mouth but lacks the natural activation of the small muscles around the eyes found in a Duchenne smile. In this way it is possible to tell the difference between natural and forced expressions of happiness.

Love

Darwin as well as many later scientists did not classify love as one of the universal emotions. This is strange considering its process and the enormous impact it has on our life. Love displays many of the functions and qualities typically found in universal emotions: it is activated in contact with others, it is an automatic biological response activation that may be felt and it motivates us to openly approach and help others. Love is also an important if not the most important ingredient of a positive experience of life. When we love another or are loved, life is experienced as meaningful and positive. By contrast, absence of love produces an experience of alienation and stress. The love response with its unifying quality resolves conflicts and promotes acceptance of ourselves and others. For many of us love is the most meaningful process in life, and it is one of the most essential human processes. Based on what we know about love, its quality and dynamic, we can call love the queen of emotions.

Love is a relational response that supports approach and attachment behavior. Its expression motivates us to approach and bond intimately with others, which increases our safety in an evolutionary perspective. Love is always expressed in relation to someone or something, it is autonomously activated and just like other emotions its expression can be withheld. The expression of love is multi-faceted and tends to get mixed up with other affective response processes. This causes its experienced quality to vary depending on the type of love involved. Research shows for example that romantic love is a combination of the love response together with sexual activation (Bartels & Zeki, 2001).

The physiology of love

Love, like happiness, is an emotion with positive physical effects not only in the sense that it is pleasant to experience but also because it strongly promotes positive, long-term development of the human organism. In contrast or opposition to the sympathetically activated flight-or-fight response, positive emotions and the love response play a major role in the lesser known calm-and-connected response coming from our so-called safeness system (Gilbert, 2009; Germer & Siegel, 2012). By bonding with others this response helps the organism shift from a sympathetically activated state to a parasympathetically activated state supported by hormones that make us feel calm and safe. We see this shift when a restless child is soothed by a caring parent. The same shift can also be seen when we as adults are comforted by others or when we express love and care for ourselves and others.

Activation of the love response involves several parallel physical processes in the organism. The brain's reward system is activated and it releases hormones and other chemical substances such as endorphins, dopamine and oxytocin that calm us and allow us to experience happiness and satisfaction. Endorphins are the body's own opioid pain-killers. They block pain signals in the brain and make it possible for us to use our body despite pain. Dopamine increases the urge for food, sex, social companionship and love, and in this way adds a drive to action. Together with endorphins and oxytocin, dopamine contributes to an inner experience of delight and happiness. Oxytocin is the "feel-good" hormone that takes a leading role in the love response and in social bonding. Oxytocin calms fears and supports social approach behavior. It heightens the organism's social and relational skills and improves our ability to understand and intimately interact with others. It motivates us to get closer to others. These chemical substances work together to make us happy and satisfied with life when experiencing love (Fredrickson, 2013). The love response also eases neuroception's rigorous scanning for threats in our surroundings and increases our ability to detect positive stimuli. In this way love makes us carefree and curious, and contributes to a positive, open-hearted approach to life.

Processes activated by the love response have a positive effect on our experience of life. However they do not simply make us feel satisfied with life but also have a directly positive effect on our health. They relieve stress and neutralize

78

its harmful effects. They promote the body's immune system and long-term life processes. In this way the love response has a substantially positive effect on the entire human organism in terms of how we experience and think about life, how we interact with others and our physical health.

An important and often-overlooked part of love is its physical expression. Just as with other emotional processes, an activated love response has a physical expression. Physical activation of love causes an expression of warmth, openness and accommodation. Due to the parasympathetic expansion that takes place in a love response, the expression is relaxed and alive with a genuine and warm smile that includes the eyes. It displays physical openness, often with open palms and a slight leaning in the direction of the person who is the object of the response, inviting and desiring contact (Frederickson, 2013). The head often nods slightly, indicating acceptance of the other. Eyes can tear up with overflowing love. The love response activates automatically. We cannot decide to love but we can stop the expression of love, which unfortunately happens all too often.

The many faces of love

Love is experienced in many areas of life. Love is seen between children and their parents, between couples, among siblings and friends. It occurs in romantic love, love of pets, spiritual love and self-love. Common to all these forms of love is its biological activation as well as the way love connects us and provides an experience of being part of a greater context. In love we no longer experience ourselves as alone and isolated but together and part of a larger whole. Love is inclusive. Our focus shifts from ourselves to others. Their well-being becomes important to us, not just for our own physical survival. This altruistic quality distinguishes positive emotions and particularly love from other emotional response activations which are self-centered and activate to secure our survival.

From an evolutionary perspective, love is a unifying force in relationships. It functions as a bond between people, the purpose of which is to protect and spread our genes and promote long-term survival. In this way love serves many purposes, as can be seen in its different qualities throughout life. The attractive force of infatuation is for example so strong that it shakes us loose from our natural boundaries of intimacy in relation to others. It can be experienced as a kind of magnetism, bringing us together with and opening us up to another person who just the day before may have been a stranger. Sexual activation and lust accompany infatuation in a deeply felt wish to physically unite with the other. This is a strong urge that biologically functions as a way to reproduce by having children, which from an evolutionary perspective increases our odds of survival. The more children we have, the more likely it is that we will be taken care of and survive when we are old and unable to take care of ourselves. The effect of the happiness of romantic love on the brain is similar to the effect of cocaine (Breitner et al., 1997; Schlæpfer et al., 1998) both when it comes to the natural intoxication we feel when close to the other as well as in the dependency that develops to the other. When apart, symptoms of abstinence and discomfort appear which makes us long for the next meeting and a new "kick".

After a time infatuation turns into mature love in a relationship. We feel calm and stable together with someone we trust. This form of love provides the perfect conditions for establishing a family with a safe and stable foundation for child development. The care we give to children and the love we feel for them seems to have evolved out of infatuation's focus on reproduction (Panskepp & Bivens, 2012). Love of our children makes us put their needs before our own. This love is the main ingredient in optimal child development. As we shall see later, children depend on love from caregivers and we are biologically hardwired to feel rewarded when we treat children lovingly. Loving interaction with children activates the reward system in adult brains. Oxytocin and endorphins are secreted, hormones that create a feeling of well-being and provide an incentive to continued positive contact and care. A caregiver's loving expressions and interactions demonstrate to the child that they are welcome, which makes them feel safe. This experience of fundamental safety makes optimal development possible for a child. On the other hand its absence can lead to serious consequences for the development and stability of the child's personality.

Love grows

Love and natural happiness display a dynamic that does not appear in sadness, anger or fear. Unlike emotions expressed when the organism is threatened, love is self-reinforcing. Every time we express a natural love response, our ability to express it grows stronger and activates more often in life. This creates a positive feedback loop for the love response.

Barbara L. Fredrickson describes in her research the biological causes of this positive dynamic which amplifies our natural ability to enter into loving relationships. According to Fredrickson (2013), the love response makes us open to and interested in other people. This makes it easier to have positive relationships, which creates a fertile ground for more loving relationships. Oxytocin levels in the body rise when we experience and express love, making us more receptive and motivated to enter into loving relationships. The more love we display, the higher the oxytocin level, which influences us to enter into even more loving relationships.

Love also restructures the neural networks that govern behavioral choices. Expressions of love make it more likely that we will enter into healthy and loving social relationships in the future. Through this neuroplasticity that is the brain's ability to change its neural networks, love creates more love. The expression of love itself improves our ability to express it. As with most emotional expressions, many of us are not used to expressing love due to our early upbringing, so every time we express love, our trust in its expression grows and this further improves our ability to express it. In this way love generates more love in a self-reinforcing dynamic that causes expressions of love to grow both in frequency and in strength.

Self-love

Self-love, that is love and acceptance of who we are, is another aspect of the love response. The difference between self-love and other forms of love is its focus on ourselves rather than on something or someone outside us. It is a love response to ourselves, not to be confused with narcissism or self-glorification. Self-love comes from acceptance of who we are with all our strengths and weaknesses. It is a loving self-acceptance which has a positive relational effect that makes us more accepting, open and receptive to our environment and the relationships we are part of. In natural self-love we give ourselves the acknowledgement that we seek from others, ending our dependency on others and allowing us to be who we are.

The basic dynamics of what we experience as life problems stems to a great extent from an absence of loving care early in life (see Chapter 11). An early experience of some degree of this absence seems to be a universal human experience regardless of how well-functioning and loving our childhood was. As a consequence we seek a substitute for this absent love outside ourselves later in life. It can express itself in a hunger for attention, the next best thing for a child when natural love is absent. However seeking attention and getting attention from others never stills the inner sense of love lost. Quite the contrary, seeking attention and love from others is actually a defense against feeling the effects of absent love. As adults our focus on getting attention and love is a way of shielding ourselves from the emotional discomfort and pain caused by earlier absence. It is only when we confront, relive and accept the emotional pain caused by an early lack of love that self-acceptance and self-love can grow.

If we later in life experience the love and safety that was absent earlier in life, it can have powerfully positive effects. The negative effects of insufficient loving care can partially be dissolved in a stable and loving relationship later in life. A partner, friend, teacher, therapist or other person we meet later in life who lovingly accepts us as we are can be a powerful force for healing. However the psychologist Louis Cozolino (2014) points out that this must be in a relationship where we are loved for who we are and not for what we do. Despite learning early in life that we cannot be loved for who we are and that we are unworthy of love, loving acceptance of who we are later in life proves the opposite to be true. We experience that we are loveable and this makes it possible for us to accept and love ourselves.

Strangely enough, though we long for love, many of us have a hard time taking it in when it is there. How can this be? When we open up to receive or accept love from another we also feel the unresolved earlier emotional pain of love's absence. To deeply accept that we are loved and loveable is painful. We experience a mix of expansion, happiness and pain. If we intend to activate self-love, we need to become aware of the pain of that early absence of love and accept it. Allowing the pain to be felt is the doorway to self-acceptance and self-love. By remaining in contact with our pain, the pain dissolves and self-love is activated. When we stop protecting ourselves from this inner discomfort, we let self-love unfold. Only self-love can fully resolve the inner experience of early absence and fill the void many of us feel.

An early experience of the absence of love is painful and makes us vulnerable later in life. There has to be a good reason to risk coming into contact with that experience again. As long as we are not aware of it, we defend against it automatically and unconsciously and it is almost impossible to come into contact with that painful memory. It often takes a personal crisis later in life to be able to reconnect to it and become motivated to allow its process. The painful intensity of a recent personal crisis or a relational separation from someone close to us, as in divorce or death, connects us to the pain of that earlier separation and the absence of love. We can then experience, accept and express this pain, allowing the process of self-love to spring into bloom if we let it.

The process of self-love

The psychologist Abraham Maslow wrote that emotional maturity is a non-judgmental, loving acceptance of ourselves (1968). Self-love may be described using words such as self-acceptance, self-empathy and the like. These words describe a positive and accepting attitude to ourselves. However self-love does not only consist of a positive attitude to ourselves. It is primarily an emotional response to ourselves. As an emotional activation, self-love seeks natural physical expression. Its biological process and results are the same as in the love response. It activates the parasympathetic nervous system, infusing life into the body. There is a biologically and cognitively relaxed and open quality to the process and expression of self-love. At the same time we experience an inner connection to people or things. Together with love's quality of expansive warmth, we feel the vulnerability that appears when defenses are lowered. This causes pain to come into focus. When that happens, the tension that the pain expresses begins to ease. We are touched and tears come naturally. Tension and pain dissolve when we allow their expression. Afterward we experience stable, expansive and warm openness and are filled with a feeling of wholeness. The case of Lois can serve as an example of this.

> Lois grew up with an emotionally inhibited mother. According to Lois, her mother always found it difficult to be in emotional contact for more than a short time. As a result Lois had a very ambivalent relationship with her mother. She could not stand her mother's behavior or manner while at the same time she deeply longed for the loving contact that was missing earlier in life. This powerful longing made

her repeatedly interact with her mother, unconsciously hoping to get the love she missed with no thought to the consequences. Contact always ended in conflict and disappointment.

During a therapy session, Lois came into contact with the pain that she had been avoiding by continuing to hope for something that she had never gotten. She realized that her recurring conflicts with her mother were a way of avoiding confrontation with her own reality: that she did not get the love she needed while growing up and that it still hurt. This realization brought her into direct contact with that old pain and sadness. Tears of sadness brought relief from pain and after a while there was a calm and inner acceptance of what was and is. This brought more tears but now instead of cramped tears of sorrow, her tears ran freely down her cheeks without struggle in loving acceptance of herself. Later she explained that staying with her pain released a self-love that could fill the void created by that early absence.

Expressions of self-love display a physically relaxed expansion. Muscles are relaxed and alive, particularly noticeable in the face. Facial features radiate warmth and eyes appear soft, open to contact and touched. The process of self-love has a melting quality, particularly expressed in the tears that are its main expression. We do not cry from sadness when in contact with self-love but as an expression of the process of giving in after holding back. Just as ice melts to water as it warms, tears express the melting of inner hardness. With growing trust in this process, tears can flow almost unabated and the more we allow them, the more we feel self-love.

Self-love and selfishness

There is a big difference between self-love and selfishness or narcissism. Self-love is actually the opposite of being self-centered. In the absence of self-love, we develop an exaggerated focus on ourselves and an urge to display our excellence. Exaggerated self-centeredness and narcissism are according to the psychoanalyst Heinz Kohut an emotional dysfunction stemming from an early absence of loving care and support for a natural, positive sense of self (Mitchell & Black, 1995). A person develops exaggerated self-glorification as a defense against the pain caused by the early absence of loving care. A narcissistic person does everything possible to show the opposite: that they are fantastic and loveable, thereby avoiding their painful inner reality.

As a result of self-love we can act freely in relationships. Self-love is a safe and secure inner base that reduces our dependency on others. We no longer need approval from others to feel good enough. We can be honest and stand up for ourselves. In this way self-love frees us to love others. Natural self-love changes our approach to our surroundings. From being isolated and only seeing the world from the limited perspective of our own personality, self-love opens us to others. You and I become we, our understanding of others increases and life opens up. We become one with the world we live in. In self-love the quality of love that transcends personality makes us genuinely interested in others' well-being. The happiness of others is our happiness and their sadness is our sadness. This motivates us to get involved and help others for their sake, not because we need to show that we are good enough to receive their love. Self-love gives us integrity and an honest interest in others.

This quality of love that transcends personality makes it a central process in many religious and spiritual traditions. According to many of these traditions, love is one of the most essential human processes and should be nurtured through contemplation and practice to develop and realize our true human potential. Concerning this fundamental quality of love in life and the possibility it opens up for humans, Jiddhu Krishnamurti (1975) wrote: "When you love there is neither one nor many: there is only love. It is only when there is love that all our problems can be solved and then we should know its bliss and its happiness."

Chapter 6

Other affective responses similar to emotions

Human homeostatic regulation motivates behavior and includes survival responses that are in a gray zone between vitality affects and emotions. Examples of these responses are sexuality, pain and curiosity. Each of these response processes has a specific function in promoting life and is a natural part of the organism's homeostatic process. In a similar way to interrupted emotional responses, if their expression is held back it leads to a disturbance in the organism's self-regulation.

So-called complex social emotions are a combination of basic emotions and the ability of our higher mental functions to influence emotional expression. We will look more closely at the most well-known examples of complex social emotions: shame and guilt. Chapter 6 ends with a discussion of reactive emotional processes. These are easily confused with primary emotions but are in fact a reaction to and defense against them.

Sexuality

Sexuality is a primary, multifaceted human function that may be experienced in many ways. For one person, sexuality may be one of the most intimate and beautiful forms of human contact. For another, it may be connected with negative experiences of violation, shame and guilt. Sexuality has many forms of expression and there are many theories about its function, dynamic and expression. It would take a separate book to give a full presentation of this complex subject. In this chapter we limit ourselves to describing sexuality from the perspectives of evolutionary psychology and neurobiology. We will review what research has to say about sexuality and consider the consequences this knowledge has for our understanding of healthy sexuality versus unhealthy, disturbed sexuality.

The biological function and goal of sexuality is reproduction. It is a further development of homeostatic survival in the sense that the organism lives on by transferring its genes (and in this way its life process) to a new organism. It is a process more highly developed and complex than cell division in which cells copy themselves and pass on their life. The aim of every biological and cognitive process activated by sexual affect is to support the continuation of human life.

Human sexuality originates in the homeostatic sexual affect and it shares some properties found in other homeostatic affects. It is similar to the physical urge to satisfy basic needs such as the affects of hunger or thirst in that its activation is connected to a powerful longing. Unlike those affects however, unfulfilled sexual need does not expose us to mortal danger. Sexual affect is also similar to emotional response processes in that it is relational, activates the entire body and has the same kind of dynamic structure of charge and expression. This is displayed in sexual lust, excitement, copulation, orgasm and physical relaxation (Panskepp & Biven, 2012).

Different perspectives on sexuality

Freud (and later the entire Western world) considered sexuality to be a drive with a regulatory function for the organism. The sex drive, which Freud called libido, is in this perspective an expression of basic human vitality and a central element in healthy human development and life. The build-up of sexual energy is seen as a natural inner pursuit for the organism that automatically seeks expression and gratification. If this build-up is not allowed it leads to imbalances in the organism and different degrees of personality disorder. Metaphorically speaking, sexuality is in this perspective like a bladder that automatically fills up and needs to be emptied when full. This perspective explains the urgent character of sexuality as frustration drives a person to sexual satisfaction and orgasm.

There is however not much scientific evidence to support this one-sided view of the sex drive and a good deal of research points in a different direction. For example not even the most extreme sexual deprivation can be shown to produce any biological trace or disturbance in the body. In other words sexuality does not seem to have a physical, regulatory function (Ågmo, 2007). Many people live without any apparent psychological disturbance despite a total lack of sexual activity. In contrast to hunger or thirst which quickly develop life-threatening consequences if their needs are not met, it is possible to live in perfect physical and psychological harmony without sexual expression.

The experience of sexual frustration is due to activation of the sympathetic nervous system and can have long-term negative consequences such as stress. When this is the case, sexual activity and orgasm followed by physical relaxation can temporarily restore balance to the organism. However it is the body, emotional system and cognitive system that cooperate to form our experience of sexuality. Our experience of sexual frustration occurs in the brain and is the result of disturbed emotional and cognitive processes. What we regard as a physical sexual drive is actually a physical mobilization toward something we associate with the satisfaction of desire. This way of looking at sexuality is called the incentive approach (Ågmo, 2007). According to this approach, scxual desire is activated by specific information or stimuli that we have learned can lead to gratification (orgasm and fertilization) in the same way that basic emotions are activated by specific inner and outer stimuli for a purpose.

The biology of sexuality

The sexual affect is aroused by stimuli and intensifies in direct relation to these stimuli. If the stimuli are removed, sexual activation stops and this is why sexual activation requires continuous stimulation to reach orgasm. In this way a real or imaginary person, object or situation arouses and intensifies sexual affect with a promise of satisfaction (Toates, 2014).

Sexual desire arises in the interaction between sensory stimuli and the meaning given to them. A simplified description of this process is as follows: the amygdala perceives sexual sensory stimuli and sends this information to the hypothalamus. The hypothalamus directs the pituitary gland to secrete hormones that in turn cause sexual hormones to be secreted, particularly estrogen and androgens such as testosterone. These hormones sensitize areas of the brain that encourage sexual desire (Regan & Berscheid, 1999). There are for instance neurons in the hypothalamus with specific receptors for testosterone that make it extra sensitive to sexual stimuli (Georgiadis & Korrekaas, 2010). Androgens also affect the supply of dopamine to the nucleus accumbens, the part of the brain that generates the experience of magnetic, irresistible attraction to a specific stimulus. Dopamine, a part of the brain's reward system, is a hormone that incites us to action. Dopamine secretion in the brain creates a strong sexual desire before and during expression of the sexual affect. It also causes the powerful longing experienced when we are separated from the object of desire. Dopamine incites us to sexual action.

Another person (or object) and their behavior activates the sexual affect. The strength of sexual desire stems from various hormonal activations and the type of stimulus. Testosterone in particular affects sexual interest in men. Men also tend to become more sexually aroused by explicit sexual stimuli than women, for instance by the sight of a woman or a man (in real life or in a picture), through direct physical contact or by inner images and thoughts about sexual activity. The hormones and processes that arouse women are not as obvious but there are many indications that estrogen is of great importance as well as testosterone to a certain extent. Sexual desire in women appears to be aroused by more psychological factors such as a partner's behavior, characteristics and status (Ågmo, 2007). These factors are important from an evolutionary perspective when it comes to defending and maintaining a family.

Individual sexuality is formed early in life in the interaction between autonomic, innate, inner processes and outer influences. The stimuli that activate sexual desire are both innate and learned. Facial symmetry for example is innately attractive from an evolutionary perspective because it signals healthy physical development and a greater chance of having wholesome and healthy children. Outer influences that shape sexuality come from family, culture and later on our circle of friends. Sexual behavior and interest are established in adults through sexual experience and interaction. As we grow up we learn what appeals to us sexually.

Sexual activation takes place over several separate stages. A sexual stimulus arouses a desire which can develop into sexual excitement if it remains in focus. Sexual excitement then activates a response in the sexual organs. Sexual excitement and its physical response can however arise without prior desire. In child development for example it seems that physical excitement develops first and the desire associated with it comes later (Spiering & Everaerd, 2006). Over time this process changes until the object of desire arouses the desire that develops into sexual excitement and a physical response. Sexual excitement

89

prepares the body for sexual action in the same way emotional activation prepares the body for emotional expression. Our physical movements in the sexual act are driven by escalating excitement toward orgasm and fertilization. The pleasure of orgasm also functions as an incentive to increased desire. We learn that sexual activity gives great pleasure, a reward that supports and encourages further sexual activity. All this takes place simply to guarantee that our genes are passed on and that we survive in a broader evolutionary perspective.

Sexual disturbances

Sexual affect - desire, excitement, sexual movement and orgasm - is a natural human expression and an expression of who we are. Just as with other affective responses, positive sexual development requires acceptance and understanding while growing up without violation of intimate boundaries. If this does not occur, it results in a disturbance of the natural process and expression of sexuality. Natural sexual affect becomes inhibited and to varying degrees suppressed, while personality can begin to use sexual expression to gain control over other feelings or to avoid them.

Since sexuality is formed by both early and later relational experiences, most sexual disturbances are entangled with disturbances in other emotional processes. Sexual disturbance is the result of negative experiences of sexual expression, either our own or others', that violate our intimate boundaries. We may have had a caregiver who did not understand and accept infant sexuality or we may have been a victim of sexual violation. A disturbance in natural sexuality has negative consequences for how we deal with sexual activation and its expression later in life. It leads to relational problems and can result in physical symptoms such as erectile dysfunction and coital pain. A violation of intimate sexual boundaries causes pain, anger and sorrow. It can later lead to discomfort in sexual activation or from the mere thought of entering into a sexual relationship. This discomfort stems from the fear of unaccepted, suppressed emotions connected to an earlier violation of intimate boundaries. In extreme cases a person may repress their sexuality and from then on avoid sexual relations.

Discomfort with sexuality can also be avoided by separating sexuality from the body's other emotional processes. When sexual affect is used to avoid other feelings and affective processes, we say that we have separated sexuality from love. In this case the defense against unaccepted emotional processes can use sexuality to retain control over either oneself or another, or it can exploit sexual satisfaction and its subsequent relaxation to avoid or numb other negative feelings. This is possible because sexual affect leads to one of the most pleasurable human experiences, one that we even can administer to ourselves. This is a highly potent cocktail. The ability to give ourselves both enjoyment and a kick can be difficult to resist, resulting in the numerous sexual preferences, behaviors and dependencies we see in the world.

Flirting, sexually inviting behavior or providing sex can give an experience of control over others and thereby over oneself. This control is achieved by making oneself the object of others' sexual desire. The "sexual hunt" and "bagging the prey" can also boost weak self-esteem. This form of sexual behavior is often the result of an early experience of loss of control or self-esteem (Meston & Buss, 2003). The ability to attract others and achieve physical closeness through sexuality can give a sense of being appreciated that can for a while drown out the feeling of absent contact and love.

Desire, excitement, the sexual act and orgasm can also be used to avoid other uncomfortable feelings. We see this in various forms of sexual dependency such as promiscuity, sexual perversions and addiction to pornography. Sexual dependency has quite a lot in common with other forms of dependency such as excessive gambling or drug addiction in that it can be used as a defense against life situations that create emotional discomfort. The sexual act shifts focus from what is experienced as difficult and helps a person relieve tension. Sexual dependency also has a physical component that makes the body crave the positive physical and chemical experience of the sexual act. A person can therefore experience symptoms of withdrawal such as emptiness, depression, discomfort and irritability if the body does not get what it is dependent on. At the same time dependency results in an experience of loss of control over one's behavior and life. An addict experiences being driven to whatever he or she craves and a large amount of mental focus is spent on this dependency. Parallel to the experience of being driven, an addict experiences inner conflicts with shame or guilt connected to their addictive behavior.

Dysfunctional sexual behavior is a defense against natural sexual affect, and the disturbance is maintained by repeating the behavior. Healthy sexuality can only develop by confronting the suppressed emotions connected with natural sexual expression.

Pain

The physical pain response can be viewed as a homeostatic affect comparable to hunger and thirst in that it autonomously motivates the organism to behavior that directly preserves life. Pain is a danger signal that makes us pay attention and avoid whatever is causing the pain. Similar to the physical pain of injury to the body, emotional pain stems from an injury to what we call the relational body, the internalized relations important to us that are part of our personality. Since these two different types of pain have the same basic dynamics, let us begin by looking at the function of physical pain to better understand emotional pain.

Physical pain

"Pain is made by the brain. 100% of the time. No exceptions. Ever." (Moseley, L. & Butler, D., 2015, p. 7) There are no particular pain sensors or pain signals that tell us that our body hurts. There is no pain center in the brain that registers that we are in pain. There are instead numerous nerve sensors in the body that inform the brain about the condition of the body and its environment and changes that occur. There are millions of these so-called interoceptors in the body. Each interoceptor has a specific role in registering changes to different parameters such as pressure, temperature, injury, stress and movement. Some of them register everything that happens, others only register if a safe, homeostatic level in the body is exceeded. Interoceptors send information to the brain. The brain reads this information to discover if parameters have exceeded safe limits, that is if there is danger and how serious the danger is. When there is a clear and present danger as is the case when we touch a hot stove, automatic physical activation pulls our hand away before we are aware of pain. Afterwards the brain provides the experience of pain to enable us to consciously deal with the situation. Pain is generated through a general assessment of many different types of information that indicate threats to our safety. The greater the threat, the greater the pain (Louw, 2013): a smart, automatic function that makes us take a situation seriously.

The function of pain is to preserve the human organism. It is part of our survival system. Nothing is as effective as pain when it comes to changing harmful behavior. When we hurt, we stop stressing the part of the body that the pain is coming from and do what we can to alleviate the pain. We go to a doctor, rest or take care of ourselves in some way.

Aside from information about physical danger and injury, many factors influence the experience of pain and how much it hurts. These factors include:

- Physical conditions of the body such as temperature and health
- The level of stress
- The level of perceived danger
- The level of safety and our familiarity with this and similar situations
- Personal beliefs regarding the situation
- Other emotions activated in the situation
- Knowledge and experience of the injury suffered.

We see a clear example of how the experience of pain is influenced by surrounding factors when a child falls and hurts itself. The child screams loudly from experienced pain, yet often if the child is embraced by an adult who blows a few times on the injury, the child will run around again without pain a few moments later. The pain disappeared when the child went from being in an unsafe, threatening situation to a safe one. Another example is when we sprain an ankle in the midst of an emergency situation. As long as the emergency continues, we probably feel only a little pain. As soon as the emergency has passed, we experience pain strongly. If there were pain sensors, we would immediately notice the sprain and feel intense pain. We can in other words be distracted to the point that the pain of injury temporarily disappears (LeDoux, 2015).

Many factors influence and determine the degree of experienced pain. The more we experience safety, acceptance of the situation and life in general, the less we experience pain. Pain activation is also an activation of the sympathetic nervous system similar to the dynamic seen in the fear response. As is the case with fear, pain is activated by the organism's general level of security or insecurity and it makes us awake, alert and attentive. In Figure 7, neuroscientist Adrian Louw (2013) describes how a pain signal is triggered after an accumulation of various danger signals taken together put the accumulated danger beyond our threshold of pain.

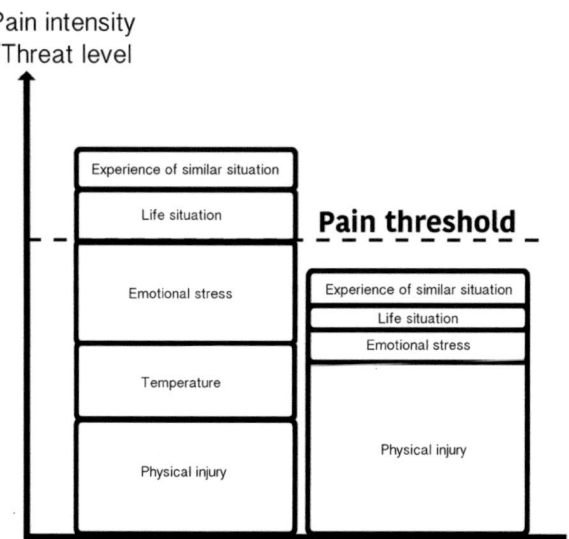

Pain intensity /Threat level

Figure 7: The pain threshold vs. the degree of danger
Pain is an expression of the organism's total assessment of threats to the organism. The severity of pain depends on several different factors: sensory information, emotional status and the person's experience of safety and pre-dictability in the situation. A small injury can produce a stronger sensation of pain than a larger one if a person experiences that the circumstances are unsafe or dangerous.

Chronic pain

While acute pain has a protective function, it seems that chronic pain is caused by hypersensitivity to pain. In chronic pain, pain's warning system activates more easily. Hypersensitivity makes it easier for the brain to perceive and magnify existing danger signals long after the actual danger and need for protection has passed (Louw, 2013). This means it is possible to relieve chronic pain by learning to de-program it and consciously stopping the organism from overreac-ting through training in Mindfulness or conscious, physical sensing (Haines, 2015). In this we see a parallel between relieving pain hypersensitivity and the treatment of hypersensitive fear activation. Hypersensitive fear activation can be treated with so-called exposure therapy (LeDoux, 2015) in which a person repeatedly confronts the object of fear and realizes that it is not dangerous. Fear is alleviated by approaching what we are afraid of and pain is alleviated by approaching what hurts.

Emotional pain

Physical pain is a construct created by the brain's overall threat assessment and here we clearly see a connection to emotional pain, which is also created by perceived danger to the organism. In emotional pain the same criteria are used to assess the danger level but the primary focus is on emotional and relational factors. Group affiliation and close relationships are fundamental to the stability and survival of personality and our relational context is an integral part of personality. Relational separation or the threat of separation from people important to us constitute a threat to the stability of personality. When the relational body is injured by separation from others important to us or by the threat of separation, emotional pain appears.

The physical reaction to separation and a break in relational connection is similar to physical pain. Inner tension is sympathetically activated in the body as the organism responds to protect itself from further injury. Emotional pain is triggered when a relational threat becomes too great and we experience a life crisis in the form of separation or the threat of separation from others important to us. The pain can stem from a situation in the present or from a prior experience of separation that has not been worked through and integrated.

Emotional pain indicates that there is something we need to deal with. Just as physical pain makes sure that we protect and treat whatever hurts, emotional pain shows us that we need to deal with the consequences of a relational break. We need to leave the automatic tendency to shift the focus of awareness away from what hurts and instead meet it directly, giving space to the pain. This is the same procedure used to dispel fear.

As we can see, physical and emotional pain have the same basic dynamics. Both are created by the organism's overall threat assessment. The severity of physical pain is determined by many non-physical factors and is more or less emotional and on the other hand emotional pain manifests itself physically.

A good deal of research has also shown that chronic physical pain does not depend on physical damage such as a problem with the body's joints or tissues but rather on other emotional factors (Butler & Moseley, 2003; Lederman, 2010; Ingraham, 2014). Research indicates that the experience of physical pain in the form of headache, back pain and muscle ache is actually caused by a disturbance in the emotional system to a great extent.

Complex social emotions

Some human processes and experiences are similar to affective or emotional responses but are actually learned manipulations of natural responses. These processes are the result of basic emotions that are not naturally expressed but instead controlled and transformed into expressions that are safer for personality. Neuroscientists Jaak Panksepp & Lucy Biven (2012) call these processes *complex social emotions.*

Complex social emotions are formed by a combination of basic emotions and our higher mental ability to suppress and distort emotional expression. Complex social emotions include shame, guilt, jealousy, hope, admiration and so forth. Common to all of them is that they stem from natural activation of an emotional response and make use of the emotional response system but they turn this into a defense against natural emotional expression. They are misleading distortions of basic emotions that relieve the discomfort of an affective charge. An example of this is when we continue to hope that a former lover will return in order to avoid the pain and sorrow activated by separation. Hope prevents sorrow from being expressed and is a defense against the emotional consequences of separation. Activation of complex social emotions are a learned, safe behavior that is autonomously activated without conscious participation. To gain a deeper understanding of complex social emotions, let us take a closer look at two of the most common experiences and processes that have massive negative consequences for many people: shame and guilt.

Shame

The experience of shame begins when a child is twelve to fourteen months of age. At that time the orbitofrontal cortex and dorsolateral prefrontal cortex have developed to the point that they can inhibit displays of impulses and responses in order to allow for others (Bentzen & Hart, 2012). Natural shame regulates self-esteem and behavior by signaling the need for self-correction. According to neuropsychologist Dr. Allan N. Schore (1994), this skill is decisive for the personal and social development of children. Natural shame helps children moderate omnipotent and self-aroused affective states to achieve more balanced expression and make it easier to enter into social contexts. It is a process that supports the development of social skills.

The experience of shame is however a very chaotic and painful state for children. Shame activation involves a quick shift from a positive and aroused state that the child wants to share with others to a state of frozen dread. Shame is a sudden and painful internal collapse caused by unexpected rejection (Schore, 1994). When correcting a child in shame, it is important that the caregiver help the child with empathic comfort so the child can come out of the parasympathetic immobility of shame (a state that will be described later in Chapter 12). When natural shame is allowed to develop, the child learns to stop pleasure-filled activity and calms down when necessary. It is a process in which a caregiver stops the child, makes the child feel shame and then quickly repairs the shame by showing that the child is still loved. In this process a child develops a tolerance to negative experiences and learns to shift from a negative state to a neutral state (Hill, 2015). However if a child is exposed to exaggerated shame from a caregiver without necessary repair to the relationship immediately afterward, a disturbance will occur in experienced self-esteem. This disturbance expresses itself later when an adult's life is limited by the experience of shame.

The central dynamic of life-limiting shame is the experience of being exposed, naked and vulnerable. It is the experience of being "caught with one's pants down" without protection. This is the same experience the person had when shamed by a caregiver. It is associated with being wrong, not good enough or unworthy of love. A caregiver's criticism in early life becomes internalized, leading to destructive self-criticism of who we are (Brown, 2012). Now we are the one doing the criticizing. This self-criticism can be so strong and uncomfortable that a person experiencing shame may consider it life-threatening to expose even the slightest bit of who they are or to express an honest opinion about what they are feeling. As a result, honest self-expression is suppressed. In early psychoanalytic literature, shame was often associated with exposed sexuality but today it is understood to include all forms of self-expression: ideas, feelings, opinions and so forth. Shame is a process that stops us and punishes us for showing ourselves and expressing who we are.

The central expression of shame is self-criticism, an anger response directed at ourselves. In children the sequence of shame begins with an honest expression. The child is corrected and experiences being exposed. The experience of being exposed comes from this violation of the child's intimate sphere, which naturally activates an anger response. Through experience the child learns that expressing anger toward the caregiver does not make the situation better and in fact makes the situation worse. To get away from the experience of being exposed and bad and to repair connection with the caregiver, the child learns to turn their anger against itself and say to itself that it is bad and unworthy of love. Through this self-aggression and a simultaneous submissive attitude, the child learns to restore connection with the caregiver and forces itself to do what the caregiver wants. This is what happens when adult shame activates. When an opinion or feeling is honestly expressed, the person experiences being exposed. This activates anger which turns inward and becomes self-criticism since it is dangerous to show anger. The function of the harsh self-criticism of shame is to avoid the feeling of being exposed, vulnerable and insecure and to avoid the expression of anger that is threatening to burst out.

The dynamics of shame create a negative spiral that can be difficult to break. Any attempt to get out of it is potentially even more dangerous for our personality and leads to more shame. This is why a powerful shame process often results in a person using a great deal of energy on the suppression of all honest personal expression.

Shame's self-criticism can come immediately after a person says or does something but it can also come hours or even days later. An example of this is when we come home after having made a successful public speech and experience the unpleasantness that comes with shame together with thoughts about what people might have thought about the speech. This self-criticism activates without actual feedback to indicate that what was said or done was wrong or incorrect in any way. Shame strengthens the conviction that we are wrong and a victim unable to do anything about the situation and this is often followed by an inner collapse and a feeling of hopelessness. This inner implosion explains why there is substantial correlation between shame, depression and suicide (Brown, 2012).

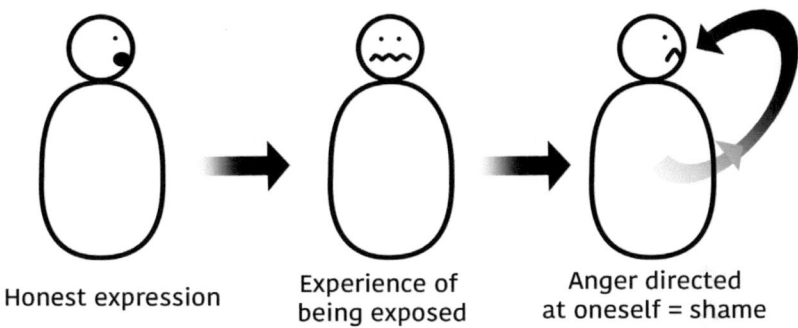

| Honest expression | Experience of being exposed | Anger directed at oneself = shame |

Figure 8: The dynamic of shame

To terminate the process of shame a person must first become aware of it and its dynamic. The next step is to become aware of the feeling of being exposed and uncertain after expressing something that activates shame without activating shame's self-criticism. In other words a person must dare to stay with this vulnerable and often painful experience at the root of shame's dynamic without self-criticism. In this way the natural, outward-moving anger that was buried in self-criticism can be accepted and expressed and the person can move out of the state of shock and parasympathetic immobility that appeared from feeling exposed. It is a process easy to describe but as anyone who feels shame knows, difficult to carry out in practice.

Guilt
Guilt develops later than shame since it requires that the child has acquired a language. The ability to distinguish between right and wrong which is necessary for guilt develops around the age of three (Bruner, 1990). Parents show their children what is right and wrong behavior by correcting them and in this way they learn how to relate to others. This is a process in which children are helped to enter into a social context and learn from their own mistakes. One might say that the process of correction draws an inner behavioral map of social norms

for children which they learn to navigate. The function of natural, balanced guilt from that point on is to serve as behavioral self-correction in order to join and get along with people in a social context.

If correction of a child's behavior is too severe or if the caregiver does not show care in helping the child get through the discomfort caused by taking on guilt, it can lead to problems with guilt later in life. Similar to shame, guilt feelings stem from the absence of loving support from a caregiver or other authority to help the child through the uncomfortable feeling of overwhelming guilt (Bentzen & Hart, 2012). As a result the experience of guilt will in various degrees control and limit a person's life.

When we experience guilt, our conscience punishes us for not living up to our own internalized standard handed down from early caregivers. To experience guilt does not just mean doing something wrong. It also means being bad and unloved. Natural guilt in children is an incentive to self-correction and adjustment of social behavior. When we experience guilt later in life, we punish ourselves for improper behavior and being unlovable. It is a sensitive dynamic automatically activated at the least sign of imperfect behavior or even for no real reason at all.

The dynamic behind the experience of guilt later in life is that while growing up, we learned that we must act in a particular way to be loved. Being loved or unloved depended on our performance. We learned that when we were not good enough, positive connection with our caregiver broke off and when we lived up to our caregiver's standards, we received acceptance and love. The caregiver's punishment for improper behavior may have been direct and verbal or it may have been indirect, for example by being ignored. When we experienced that the caregiver did not accept our behavior we became naturally angry. Expressions of anger were forbidden however because they made everything worse and the caregiver would become even more emotionally distant. To solve the situation, we struck a compromise and found a way to avoid being unloved. We learned to turn our anger inward against ourselves and our behavior. In this way we take over the role of punishing caregiver and by turning anger inward, force ourselves to be better and avoid the pain of not being accepted.

The experience of guilt is a dysfunctional expression of anger. We punish ourselves for not being perfect in the same way that we were punished when we were children. Guilt is a self-destructive behavior that restricts the process of life. At the same time it keeps us from standing up for our natural, outwardly turned anger. If we want to be free of guilt feelings, we must dare to turn our anger outward instead of inward. We need to confront our past, stand up for ourselves and dare to feel the uncertainty and vulnerability that initially arise when we accept that we are not perfect.

A central dynamic in both guilt and shame is outgoing anger turned inward. The difference between the two is that guilt is directed at a specific behavior while shame is directed at and undermines a person's entire self-understanding and self-esteem. With guilt there is hope that something can be corrected. With shame, the experience is of something irreparable and that there is no hope.

Reactive emotional processes

Many of our emotional expressions are actually not expressions of a natural emotional response but rather a reaction to it. Instead of expressing a naturally activated emotional response, we turn the activation into a more acceptable emotion-like expression. Psychoanalytic theory calls this dynamic *reaction formation*, a defense against emotional responses and impulses that incite fear (Laplance, 1973). In reactive emotional expression a basic emotional response is exchanged for a more acceptable one as a defense and to retain control. It is a manipulation of the natural response process and a defense against it. We trick ourselves and others into believing that it is a natural response in order to avoid the emotion that is actually activated.

When expression of an unacceptable emotional response is suppressed, an uncomfortable emotional charge builds and is held in the organism. To release this held charge and relieve discomfort, we lead the emotional charge into a more acceptable channel in the form of an emotion-like expression. The problem with reactive emotional expression is that it does not complete the activated emotional response. The emotional charge grows in intensity again and continues to seek natural expression. Reactive emotional expression is a learned behavior used to avoid contact with an activated emotional response

101

as opposed to a natural emotional response, which is the organism's natural answer to an outer influence.

As previously described, two reactive emotional processes in particular are employed as a defense against natural emotional responses: crying that is similar to sadness and reactive irritation which is similar to anger. One example of this is a woman who deals with her divorce with reactive irritation because she has learned that expressions of pain and sorrow are unacceptable. Every time she experiences pain and sorrow over the end of her relationship, she reacts with irritation. Another example is a man who gets angry at his partner but instead of displaying activated anger, he withdraws, becomes sad, cries and feels sorry for himself.

It also happens that we display irritation or sorrow when experiencing love or fear. Depending on upbringing, we have learned to use a specific, reactive, emotion-like expression that is similar to an emotional response in order to defend ourselves from another emotional response activation. This dynamic is clearly on display when for instance a person cries while saying they are angry. The person may not even be aware of the contradictory nature of this display or be able to explain it. It is a collapse into sorry self-pity brought on by the fear of anger and its consequences if the anger is expressed. Similar to anger, reactive irritation is a defense against inner pain and sorrow. Fearing to appear vulnerable, we have learned to fight back with displays of seeming anger.

Reactive irritation is the primary explicit expression in every conflictual process. We feel attacked and strike back to defend ourselves and conceal our vulnerability. This is why a conflict can only be resolved through honest expression of its underlying natural emotional responses. Many emotional expressions seen daily are reactive. We are so used to a reactive defense against natural emotional responses that they end up seeming natural to us. We often feel it is our right to express them. At the same time reactive emotional expressions are unhealthy for the organism. Since they do not complete the activation of a natural response, the response remains active and incomplete, stressing the organism. The function of a naturally activated emotional response in relational interaction remains incomplete as well, for example when we need to set a boundary but do not and the emotional response continues to be activated.

This is why all reactive emotional expression is unhealthy: it inhibits natural expression and flow in the organism.

Chapter 7

Cognition

In terms of evolution, the cognitive system is the human brain's most recently developed level. It is seated mainly in the neocortex. Instead of simply returning automatic responses to outer and inner stimuli, the cognitive system enables us to experience, reflect, think and consciously initiate behavior. By definition cognition cncompasses all mental activities. It includes the ability to notice, perceive, represent, remember, reflect and all forms of thought. Cognition is the conscious and unconscious process that registers and recalls. It makes it possible for us to handle ourselves and deal with the world around us. Our high degree of self-awareness and ability to think at several levels of abstraction constitute a developmental leap compared to other mammals.

According to neuroscientist Rudolfo R. Llinás (2002), cognition developed out of our ability to predict coming events, a necessary condition for the survival of a mobile organism like ourselves. Had we been immobile we would not need this complex cognitive ability. To survive we need to be able to predict what will most likely happen in our environment so we can move in relation to it.

Fixed action patterns are part of this predictive system of movement. They help us to move quickly and precisely without losing our balance. In order to avoid colliding with people and things we need to continuously respond and adjust movement to incoming data that indicate new developments in our environment. For instance if you are walking down a street and see a piano being drawn into a fifth-floor window ahead of you, you unconsciously predict the risk of it dropping and landing on your head. Without thought you make a small detour to avoid passing directly underneath it. We take in an enormous amount of information from our environment that must be connected and coordinated to predict what might happen every second, including the possibility of being hit by a falling piano. Based on what we know and perceive in the physical world we make unconscious calculations and predict future scenarios. Our prediction automatically activates a safe, fixed action pattern that moves our body. In the case of the piano, a detour around the point of impact is made without thought or conscious decision. The ability to predict possible developments in the world around us is a basic necessity and not just when it comes to danger. Without this ability we would be unable to move without bumping into people and things. It is a necessary condition for any moving organism.

Reality Maps

To make predictions we need to know how the world is structured and functions, how it looks and what it means for us and our ability to move about. A human organism's understanding of the world is built on inner images or reality maps. These sketches of physical reality are drawn in early life and are simplified versions of complex contexts that we can quickly relate to. Since survival is the most important theme of the human organism, our reality maps are created from the perspective of biological survival (Damasio, 2012). This means that every object, situation and person is mapped relative to its safety or potential danger for us.

It is the reality seen and experienced in early life that becomes our inner map and perspective on life. Later in life it constitutes the background of understanding that guides our behavior and physical movement in interactions with our environment. Reality is mapped using data from all the senses and these reality maps provide a comprehensive inner understanding of reality. Created in early life, they seem to receive only minor adjustments in adult life. Our understanding of reality remains basically the same throughout life.

What we perceive as we move through physical reality is compared to our reality map and our understanding. We experience, see, hear, smell, taste, perceive and comprehend reality based on previously created understanding and reality maps. The physical reality we consciously perceive and understand is therefore not external reality but an earlier construction of inner images and understanding. We apply what we have learned about reality like a template on information received by our senses and only see what we already know with little opportunity for adjustment.

Language

The implicit part of cognition described here is an automatic process based on our learned decryption of reality and the learned responses that go with it. We understand, predict and act. This underlying, unconscious, invisible process directs a large portion of our behavior, if not all of it (Harris, 2012). The explicit, conscious and self-reflecting part of cognition is connected to language development, which makes it possible to exchange complex information with others through words and symbols.

Body language is an early, more primitive form of communication compared to verbal language, which developed later. Its function is to express feeling and intent to others in our environment. Body language connects us to those close to us and sends a message. It is an autonomous expression that displays the human organism's natural, response-based relational interaction. Others nearby notice our body language, understand the message and act on what is communicated. Emotional facial expressions are part of this early body language. When for instance a person displays anger, those nearby notice it, understand what is being communicated and stop behavior that violates personal boundaries. Spoken language is a further development of our body language's physical communication of feeling and intent. By using voice and words to say what we want, efficiency of communication is enhanced.

The sound of language made with the voice can be understood as articulated body movements. Words are oral sound structures, articulated gestures and movements created in a process in which we attach symbolic form to things, situations and experience. From this perspective language development may be seen as a linguistic and symbolic refinement of early, primitive, physical and emotional communication. Over time this evolved into the precise and conceptual language of today, a development that increased the flexibility of communication and the odds of survival in our physical environment and in our relations (Cozolino, 2012). In a similar way children acquire language skills and move from expression of experience via body language to the rich vocabulary of modern language.

We can imagine how this linguistic evolutionary development enhanced flexibility and the odds of survival for a group. If one of our early ancestors came upon a poisonous snake and wanted to tell others about it, communication would take place using body language such as pointing in the direction of the snake, grunting and a display of the fear experienced. Others would understand that there was danger in that general direction and be extra careful. However body language may not be enough to precisely convey what to be afraid of. Communication becomes more precise when we develop the ability to symbolize and articulate. Communication deepens and information improves when we go from making a sound like a snake to saying the word "snake" and explaining which way it was moving. A person receiving this information would then have a better chance of avoiding a snakebite. Better language skills improve the chance of survival.

The words we use and the way we form and understand them remain connected to our experience and ability to move. Experience based on movement is the unconscious source of spoken language. According to neuroscientist Marco Iacoboni (2008), we see this connection in the fact that the brain's movement center activates when we speak. Actually it is often activated even before words are formulated. This indicates that speech stems from the experience of movement in the organism, which is a physical expression of emotional or affective response processes. We witness this connection daily when we use body language while communicating. The hand and arm movements displayed in intense and engaging discussions do not simply reinforce what we say. They begin before the words are formulated and speech follows this movement. This process is obvious when we cannot find the right words to express what we want to say. Hand and arm movements become more intense to support and reinforce verbal formulation of what we want to say. The words we use can from this perspective be seen as a more detailed form of the experience and intention we wish to express.

We make use of the same process when we receive and decode others' speech. Helped by so-called *mirror neurons*, words transform into movement and make it possible to experience the feeling communicated. We understand speech on the basis of its spoken context and how it is expressed. This is why it can be difficult to understand a sentence taken out of context or when context is unclear. This is also why personal contact when communicating is of such importance, since underlying intention and emotional information is decoded by reading all the hidden information contained in the contact itself. It also explains why word choice needs to be more precise when we communicate in writing (such as email or SMS) to avoid misunderstandings and why we turn to emojis (figures that convey feelings) to show our intention and avoid misinterpretation. When we are unable to read a sender's intention or feeling, we lose an important part of the information communicated. This leaves the field open to personal interpretation. To understand others we have to take them in with all our senses.

From this perspective language and vocabulary develop out of the fact that we are part of and express ourselves in a social context. We connect to others in daily life through words and the underlying experience they communicate. We achieve a shared experience of reality as language develops. Meaning and understanding is worked out in a familial and cultural context. We understand each other's intentions and feelings and feel we are in a safe zone. As part of this development, the meaning of words changes. Meaning goes from having exclusively personal significance to being a product of interpersonal interaction (Stern, 1985).

Self-aware linguistic cognition

Language development is closely connected to the development of self-awareness. Before children acquire language skills they can for example only respond unconsciously to stimuli. As children acquire linguistic symbols for events they begin to relate to their environment and their experience. Linguistic cognition and self-awareness make it possible to distance ourselves from events and think about them instead of just being a part of the process of life. This permits us to rise above, understand and also distort experienced reality (Stern, 1985). We can choose what reality to believe in and are able to lie to ourselves and others about our reality. Self-awareness makes it possible to say, "I am not angry" when we are and actually believe that we are not angry. We are able to shield ourselves from the living organism that we are and ignore its feedback. As a result words do not always have a direct connection to the organism's response processes. and without this, emotional connection to those spoken to is lost. When we shield ourselves from ourselves, we hide from others as well.

Linguistic self-awareness is also the reason why we hold onto inner and outer conflicts. It makes it possible to ignore the organism's discomfort when natural response processes are suppressed. By limiting self-awareness to just mental (verbal) processes and treating our body as separate from ourselves we are able to shut off physical experience. For instance if we registered the organism's feedback when stressed, we would immediately experience discomfort caused by the physical imbalance of stress. This feedback would motivate us to do something about the disturbance and restore flow in the organism. Instead however, we are able to neglect the organism's signals until we no longer can maintain control and the imbalance breaks through. This can express itself in the form of physical pain, conflicts with others or psychological difficulties such as extreme mood shifts, burnout, anxiety etcetera. Self-aware linguistic cognition gives us the ability to distance ourselves from the organism's self-regulating feedback process and lays the groundwork for our emotional and relational conflicts.

Free will: an afterthought

Conscious decisions and free will exist within a subjective understanding of reality and not in an objective, external reality. We act consciously on the basis of an interpretation of reality created early in life. Connected to this interpretation we have developed a safe and reliable pattern of behavior and action. In daily life we compare what we perceive with our understanding and autonomously activate appropriate, learned behaviors. In other words, conscious free choice is an afterthought (Wegner, 2002). We do what we usually do, which is what we have learned is safe and reliable. Self-awareness – the thinker we identify as "I myself" – does not rule our life. We are ruled by learned and automatic processes that we only later become aware of (Damasio, 2012). Our self-aware ego is in reality an observing awareness that imagines it is running the show.

To a great extent conscious cognition – what we perceive, how we perceive it, what we think about it and the evaluation process involved – occurs in retrospect after an autonomous process. The logic is: "Since I acted, I am the one who did it in precisely the way I wanted to." According to consciousness research, most behavior is automatic and outside of conscious control (Bargh, 1997; Zajonc,

1980; Wegner, 2002). It is difficult to act outside of this framework. We can at most make marginal adjustments to our behavior to fit a specific situation. This is why substantial behavioral change can only take place when our inner reality maps change. To make a real change in behavior, we must change the way we unconsciously interpret perceived reality.

From an evolutionary perspective of survival this explanatory model makes sense. It would be altogether too risky to rely on our relatively limited conscious cognitive capacity to determine safe and reliable behavior. In a crisis there is no time to think everything through and then activate appropriate behavior. Ben Libet, a neurophysiologist at the University of San Francisco, was the first to perform controlled experiments that demonstrated the connection between autonomous behavior and conscious decision-making. He was able to show how the conscious decision to move a body part, in his experiment a finger, is made 300 milliseconds after the area in the brain responsible for finger movement had begun preparing for movement (Libet, 1983). By measuring activity in various areas of the brain Libet observed the following process:

1. *First comes autonomic preparation for movement (-535 ms).*
2. *Then there is awareness of wanting to move the finger (-204 ms).*
3. *After that comes awareness of moving the finger (-86 ms).*
4. *Following this the finger actually moves (0 ms).*

Libet's experiment showed how the decision to do something is more a statement about what will happen than an actual decision. Awareness of moving the finger actually occurs before the finger moves. Conscious cognition and free will are in other words built on a foundation of unconscious, automatic fixed action patterns and behavioral responses that seem to share common characteristics with emotional responses (Bargh et al., 1996; Zajonc, 1980). In the same way that neuroception autonomously activates emotional responses, there seems to be an expanded neuroception that perceives and activates responses to every life situation before we are aware of it. This understanding corresponds to the theory of a predictive brain described in Chapter 4. According to this theory the brain constantly generates simulations and makes best guesses about what is happening by comparing incoming sensory data to past experience (Seth, 2021). From this it proactively initiates responses in the organism based on its predictions of what will happen and future needs. A description of how our understanding of reality and our response repertoire develop in early childhood can be found in Part III, Personality.

> You can perform a little experiment yourself to experience predetermined behavior. Go to a place where there are many people moving about, for instance a pedestrian shopping street. Focus on your breathing and your body, relax, and while you maintain body awareness, walk slowly forward. Look at the people you meet, maintaining good contact with your body and without focusing on thought processes. Notice that your impressions touch something inside you: a recognition. Do not spend much time on any one person, only two or three seconds. If something stands out - a person's facial expression, clothes, movement - notice how this influences you and your attention. By performing this action without reflection you will become aware that you identify aspects of what you see and in fact most of what you see is identified in awareness. Something in you knows what is seen. It is recognized from earlier experience and every bit of perception contains a host of information. If you linger a little longer in this recognition, knowledge of a predetermined basic image or understanding of a person's features may appear. You may have an idea about the person at least in a general way, such as positive-negative, dangerous-safe. We already possess a preconceived interpretation of reality. We access it. It becomes our reality. We even know what to expect if we happen to interact with someone. We meet a person with this knowledge or preconceived idea and have a number of predetermined response patterns ready to be deployed depending on how the person acts.

This experiment demonstrates how the world we see is the world we know. We see a preconceived, subjective interpretation of reality and not objective reality itself. We carry within us an automatic, preconceived interpretation and then automatically act on this interpretation.

Chapter 8

Feeling

Emotion is a response process that seeks expression; feeling is our experience of emotional and other affective response processes. Emotion is an autonomous response; feeling is the result of a higher cognitive ability. Thinking about the life process is an abstraction; feeling the process of life is direct contact with life. When we say that we are "in contact with a feeling," we experience the human life process, a process that expresses itself through our affective responses: vitality affects, categorical affects (emotions) and the affective responses in between.

Feeling fills an important function in linking the human organism's three parts: body, emotion and cognition. Just as emotional experience is feedback from an emotional response, we may experience every affect as part of a system of values and interpretations that help the organism to relate to and deal with itself and its environment. A feeling is an evaluation of an emotional or other affective process. When we are aware of feeling, we are able to consciously experience, follow and understand our body's life processes. Feeling connects us to the human organism and makes us aware of it. It is a central process for humans.

Feelings are at the same time the foundation on which we come into contact with what we call "ourselves" (Damasio, 1994). The relatively stable background of affective responses in the organism generates an inner structure. When we feel this structure of affective responses, we experience it as "who we are". We are anchored in ourselves when we consciously allow ourselves to be with our feeling and when stressed we may experience the need to return to ourselves. Feeling is in this perspective feedback from the self which our self-awareness can choose to pay attention to, or not.

The physiology of feeling

Interoception is our sixth sense. It is the ability to perceive physical states and processes using interoceptors spread throughout the body including our inner organs (Porges, 2011). As previously described, these are the same physical sensors that provide the brain with information about the degree of danger and create the experience of pain. Interoceptors are specialized nerve endings that register physical states: physical contact, pressure, heat, cold, chemical influence, strain, injury etc. They transmit this data to the brain where it is interpreted (Fields, 2008). When necessary this data and its unconscious interpretation activate affective responses that change the organism's inner or outer environment. Balance and spatial perception also make use of interoception and interoceptors as they map the relations between our body parts and the body's relation to its environment.

In homeostatic regulation, interoception is both perception and a functional evaluation of affects. Interoception has both a conscious and unconscious aspect, which is to say that it can be experienced as a feeling but this experience is not necessary for its function (Siegel, 2010). As a functional evaluation, interoception provides qualitative data that the organism can respond to and deal with by regulating physical states. This functional evaluation provides each feeling with a distinct quality that triggers appropriate behavior. A feeling of disgust will for example automatically make us distance ourselves from the source of our disgust.

In unconscious, physical, homeostatic regulation, all body activities are compared to an inner image or understanding of the body that is stored in the brain. This comparison can trigger an adjustment through autonomic responses. When we are aware of interoception, we are aware of information from the body through feeling. Awareness of our feeling provides us with distance to the body's processes, allowing us to deal with them more freely and making it possible for us to choose to express or suppress a response. For example when we go to the dentist we know there will be pain and we are able to keep our head from turning away when the pain appears. When the treatment is over we can relax the muscle tension caused by our suppression of this natural response to pain. When we ask ourselves what we are feeling, it is our awareness of feeling that we refer to.

Emotional awareness is the experience of affective responses: vitality affects, emotions as well as affects such as sexuality and pain that are between vitality affects and emotions. When we discuss a feeling it is either a *background feeling* or an *emotional feeling*. Background feelings are our experience of vitality affects including affects such as pain and hunger, and emotional feelings are our experience of emotional responses (Damasio, 2010).

We experience our physical, homeostatic process as background feeling. The homeostatic process is the continuous stream of information and feedback between the physical processes and vitality affects that are regulated by the brain to protect our body. In the background of awareness we can feel our heart beating, blood flowing in our veins, warmth, chill and so forth in a constant background murmur of life processes which can be brought into the foreground of awareness at any time. Data passes from the body to the brain and the brain makes adjustments based on this information by activating responses. Since the autonomic nervous system directs these processes, our ability to consciously influence them is quite limited. Normally we are not aware of background feeling (if we do not focus on it) but it enters awareness when the homeostatic system registers events outside the way our system normally functions, or its optimal range for life. This happens when a disturbance in physical processes becomes so great that we experience discomfort, pleasure or something else that we are not used to experiencing.

Emotional feeling is our experience of an emotional response activation but not all emotional responses cause emotional feelings. As discussed in Chapter 4, an emotional response that moves unhindered through the body and is freely and immediately expressed does not appear to result in an emotional feeling. Only withheld emotional responses seem to result in emotional feeling. If for example we speak out directly when someone crosses a personal boundary, we do not feel anger towards that person in the midst of the situation or afterward. It appears that the only thing we experience while the situation is ongoing and immediately afterward is physiological activation in the form of increased respiration, pulse and so forth. However if we do not give expression to this natural response activation and remain silent, we may feel anger later.

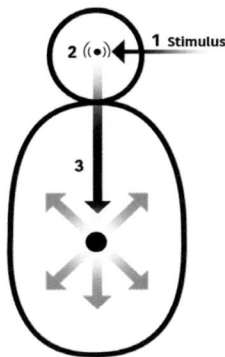 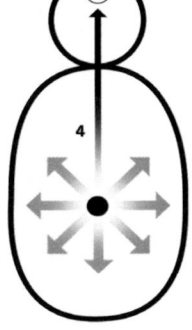

1. Emotional activation   **2.** Emotional feeling

Figure 9: The difference between emotional activation and emotional feeling
1: A stimulus (1) is discovered by neuroception (2) which autonomously activates an emotional response (3). **2**: Feedback from emotional activation (4) is evaluated and enters the foreground of awareness as an emotional feeling (5).

A feelings hedonic tone

The *hedonic tone* of a feeling is the value given to that feeling. It is a subjective value which autonomously influences behavior (Hart & Bentzen, 2012). A feeling's hedonic tone helps us navigate our environment. Hedonic tone may be plotted on a scale ranging from extreme pleasure to extreme displeasure. We approach something that generates pleasurable (hedonic) feelings and avoid and distance ourselves from something that generates unpleasurable (dyshedonic) feelings. When we experience an unpleasant feeling, that is when we register a negative hedonic tone, a response activates that enables us to quickly avoid whatever is causing our displeasure. We do not need much understanding of the experience. It is enough that it is unpleasant and the organism immediately activates an avoidant response.

A feeling's hedonic tone is either inherent as when we experience the discomfort of pain or learned as when we experience displeasure with certain emotions. When an emotion is connected to a negative experience it acquires a negative hedonic tone. For instance if we have learned that expressions of anger lead to negative consequences, we may come to experience displeasure at anger itself. The same logic can be used to unlearn an emotion's negative hedonic tone by associating the emotion with positive experiences and an absence of negative consequences. Displeasure with anger can disappear if a person has positive experiences or at least receives no negative feedback when expressing anger.

Emotional feeling

Emotional feeling occurs when an activated emotional response is held back in any way. We have at some point learned that an activated emotion is unacceptable and therefore we keep it partially or completely unexpressed. Most of the time an emotional feeling is not clearly and fully experienced but rather appears in a vague form that we do not directly associate with an emotional response. We hold back emotional expression and at the same time personality's cognitive defense strives to keep our focus of awareness away from the resulting emotional feeling.

As a result of this dynamic we experience only low-intensity feeling from an unaccepted, held back emotion assuming our cognitive defense lets us become aware of any feeling at all. An example of an emotional, low-intensity feeling is when we say, "I am not angry, I am just a little irritated." Irritation is a low-intensity feeling of anger. In its least intensive form, emotional feeling often appears as a physical sensation without direct connection to emotion, such as heaviness when we are sad or lightness when we are happy. From lowest to highest intensity, the wide range of emotional feelings that we experience are all caused by our defense when it holds back "unacceptable" emotional responses.

Emotional feelings appear on a scale of intensity ranging from low intensity, which resembles a neutral physical experience, to high intensity with a slightly paralyzing quality. Both low and high intensities express a defense against natural, emotional expression. The dynamic of the different intensities of feeling is as follows: when we focus awareness on what we are feeling, our experience of the feeling grows into a clearer emotional feeling. If we focus on a low intensity feeling it naturally grows in intensity until a clear emotion appears in the foreground of awareness which may be expressed if we allow it. If we focus on a high intensity feeling, for instance a feeling caused by emotions that have been excessively bottled up, a calm and stable focus of awareness on the feeling results in lower intensity and its paralyzing quality eases. This makes it

116

possible to naturally express the emotion. For example by bringing an experience of low-intensity restlessness into our focus of awareness, it may develop into irritation and later grow into clear anger if we let it. If this natural expression of clear anger is withheld, the feeling may grow into high-intensity rage. By maintaining a calm and stable focus of awareness on the intense feeling of rage, its intensity drops and we can express the natural anger behind it.

Low intensity				Basic emotion			High intensity
restless	⟷	irritation	⟷	**anger**	⟷		rage
heavy	⟷	sad	⟷	**sadness**	⟷		drowning in sorrow
relaxed	⟷	satisfied	⟷	**happiness**	⟷		overjoyed
nervous	⟷	anxious	⟷	**fear**	⟷		terrified
inner warmth	⟷	softly open	⟷	**love**			

Figure 10: Different intensities of emotional feeling
An overview of the intensity scale of emotional feelings. Emotions are shown at their experienced values from low to high intensity.

Due to early negative experiences many of us have made ourselves more or less insensitive to certain emotional feelings. This often leads to an experience of alienation and lack of deeper meaning in life. Awareness of emotional feeling is fundamental for humans. It is part of the organism's natural function and is connected to a satisfying experience of ourselves.

Every feeling is the experience of a homeostatic response

In summary we see that all our feelings are our experience of responses (affects) in the body's homeostatic system. Figure 11 on the next page is an overview of the three types of affects previously described, their function and the various feelings they give rise to. Sometimes however we find it difficult to define our feelings and emotional states. We may for example experience vague depressive moods, soft energizing well-being or confusing frustration. These kinds of feelings can arise from a low-intensity experience of an affect, a mix of several affects at the same time or as a consequence of our defense against a specific affect.

Homeostatic response	Function	Type of feeling	Experienced feeling
Vitality affects	Somatic regulation	Background feeling	Heat, cold, pressure, flow, pulsation etc.
Categorical affects (emotions)	Survival in one´s environment, social regulation	Emotional feeling	Fear, anger, sadness, happiness and love at various intensities
Affects between vitality affects and categorical affects	Motivates action in the environment	Other feelings	Thirst, hunger, pain, sexual excitement, curiosity, etc.

Figure 11: Feeling as the experience of homeostatic responses
The figure shows how all of our feelings are our experience of feedback from homeostatic response processes (affects). These response processes have specific functions for survival and we use our higher cognitive ability to interpret these responses as experienced feeling.

PART III

PERSONALITY

Chapter 9

Personality develops

Personality is the learned organization of the human organism's life processes that we use in our interactions with inner and outer reality. The primary function of personality is to secure stable, effective and most importantly safe behavior. We begin Part III by looking more closely at personality and later focus on the center of human life: the core self.

The word "personality" comes from Latin personare, which means "to sound through". Personality is symbolized by a mask that forms our sound or expression in the world. The mask of personality gives us our specific character and behavior, and it defines our role in life's interactions. Life moving through us passes through this mask of personality and creates our specific, individual expression. The word *identity* is related to the word personality and provides another insight into personality. Identity comes from Latin indentitamen, which means the same or something that is repeated. In this sense, our identity is our patterns of repeated behavior or actions.

Viewed from the outside a person's behavior, actions and thoughts tend to repeat a pattern. Our behavior is an extension of our autonomous responses which are activated against the background of our basic understanding of the world. This explains why there is a strong tendency to repeat behavioral patterns. We feel the same as usual when we get up in the morning and start the day. We eat the same kind of food and have a relatively fixed program when it comes to work, family and recreation. Our actions express our autonomous responses and our autonomous responses support our actions. We act and relate to life the way we usually do even when we know it is not good for us. Our behavioral patterns can be so hardwired that we do not even consider them; it is just the way we are. We can alter some superficial expressions of our behavioral pattern

123

in the same way we change perfume, clothes, jobs or even partners but the basic patterns remain the same. Personality's patterns provide us with safe behavior and we feel insecure if we try to change them and act differently.

Personality is the clear and characteristic pattern of thoughts, feelings and behavior which taken together make up a person's individual style of interaction with their inner and outer environment.

From the standpoint of developmental psychology, personality is the way we deal with inner and outer influences that we learned while growing up. Inner influences are experiences and thoughts. Outer influences occur in interaction with the environment in the form of people, places and situations. Our behavior is the actions we have learned to either get what we want or to avoid and protect ourselves from what we do not want. When we find a specific behavior that fits our purpose we repeat it in similar situations. In this way personality is an accumulation of safe and efficient methods to deal with inner and outer stimuli. Through repetition a behavior becomes automatic, which means we no longer think about what to do in similar situations. We learn a behavior that works and repeat it. Automation is an integral part of the organism's safety and survival protocol.

Personality's automatic activation of behavior is supported by a basic dynamic in the brain's organization and function. A specific behavior creates a specific neural network of linked brain cells. Through repetition, the neural network becomes the brain's most efficient and preferred network. In other words the more we repeat a behavior, the deeper its behavioral pattern imprints itself. The neural networks that the brain uses most often and their associated behaviors are the ones that offer the least resistance. If a person for instance repeatedly expresses reactive aggressive behavior, the neural networks created will be streamlined and made easier to use, becoming the brain's normal and most efficient way of functioning. The same holds true for any frequently repeated behavior.

A biological explanation of how neural networks become more efficient through repetition is found in a process involving the brain's glia cells (Fields, 2011). Activation of a specific neural network attracts glia cells which produce an insulating layer around the nerve fibers (axons) involved. This so-called myelin

124

sheath thickens through repeated use. Each time we perform a specific behavior, electric impulses move through a specific neural network and each time that happens, the impulse attracts glia cells which attach to the associated cells' axons and thicken their myelin insulation. Myelin insulation makes electric nerve impulses move more quickly and precisely through nerve fibers (Fields, 2011). Each time a neural network is used, more myelin is produced, insulation improves, nerve impulses move faster and the neural network becomes more efficient.

Because the human organism always strives for optimal efficiency in all its processes, the behavior chosen is that causing least friction and it becomes the brain's normal, automatic way of functioning. This automatic functioning also makes us less aware of what we are doing (Coyle, 2009). We no longer need to focus awareness on what we are doing. This process of brain network optimization makes it possible for us to develop skills, such as a craft or some other professional skill to perfection. Through practice and repetition, behavior becomes more efficient, automatic and part of our nature. We no longer need to think about what we are doing.

As described, personality is imprinted into the brain's biological structure as the brain's most efficient way to function. To change behavior, new neural networks must be created. New neural circuits need to be trained until a new behavior becomes the most frictionless and efficient. Until a new behavior becomes the most efficient, it will require more focus and energy than the old way. Due to this biological process, change takes time. Repetition of a new behavior streamlines the behavior's neural networks over time and suppressing an old behavior reduces its efficiency until its circuitry of networked brain cells ultimately dissolves.

Mirror neurons

Personality is created through a child's interactions with its caregivers, such as a mother or a father, as well as with other important people close to them. The ability to read other people and communicate with them without use of explicit cognition is necessary for this process to take place. This ability makes it possible for a child and caregiver to enter into the early, non-verbal interactions that lay the foundation for a child's personality (Hart, 2006). The ability also makes it possible for us to know how to deal with others and their behavior before they have expressed their behavior verbally. We can quickly deal with the intentions of others and automatically activate appropriate behavior before there is conscious awareness of what is happening.

Although previously known from experience, a possible scientific explanation for this fascinating ability came only in 1996 when neuroscientist Giacomo Rizolatti discovered a specific type of brain cells called *mirror neurons*. Mirror neurons are special because they activate both when we move our own body and when we observe someone else moving their body. When we observe someone's physical movement, mirror neurons imitate the movement as if we were performing the action ourselves. Mirror neurons make it possible for us to experience the specific feeling activated and expressed in the other's movement. For example, this function helps us to decide if a person waving at us is friendly or unfriendly. The other's movement expresses a specific emotion or other affect activation. Their pattern of muscular activation is mirrored within us and we experience a corresponding emotion or affect.

We see this dynamic when we are close to someone who is injured. Seeing pain expressed in another's face can cause us to feel pain ourselves. Mirror neurons translate observed muscular expressions of pain in the other's face and body, activate the same movement in us and we feel their pain. In this way, mirror neurons erase the difference between the observation of someone experiencing something and experiencing it ourselves. They dissolve the boundary between our environment and ourselves. Becoming one with our relational environment is also the basic process behind our ability to feel empathy.

As discussed earlier, every emotional activation has a fixed action pattern of movement as its natural physical expression. This holds true for all affect activation. Everything we feel has its own specific physical expression and every affective process is continuously and naturally expressed through muscle activation of the face and body. Just as we experience our expression of biological responses through interoception and feeling, mirror neurons allow others to experience them as well. Autonomous physical expressions wordlessly display our state of being. Every second, they communicate the organism's response expressions, vitality affects and emotional processes. Others read our response expressions both consciously and unconsciously: consciously when they understand what we experience and unconsciously when their neuroception activates an autonomous, unconscious response. In this way all human interaction involves a great deal of non-verbal and unconscious communication. We respond unconsciously to others' responses and they respond to ours. We relate to and interact with each other without thought.

Subjective interpretation of others

Our knowledge of how to interpret mirrored action patterns is both inherent and learned. We interpret others' response processes in the same way we interpret our own. Through experience we learn to interpret and understand different expressions. Since our subjective interpretation of a mirrored emotion is created in advance, the interpretation may however be incorrect. When specific experiences are connected to positive or negative circumstances, positive or negative hedonic tone is applied to similar experiences later on. For example if we have connected our own sadness to an experience of loneliness, we may interpret a crying child as lonely. We may think the child needs comfort when in fact it may be hungry and needs food. A loud, powerful voice together with expressive body language may also be interpreted as expressions of anger in Northern Europe while in Southern Europe the same sounds and gestures may be interpreted as personal and lively engagement. The way we experience, interpret and respond to others is always colored by our own history and background.

Contagious emotions

Mirror neurons are the reason why feelings, emotions and other affects are contagious (Cozolino, 2006). When another person smiles at us their smile is registered, mirrored and we smile back. Their happiness is mirrored and experienced as our own. The reason for the smile is unimportant; happiness is contagious in itself. This is why we are attracted to people who radiate emotions that we see as positive: being with them awakens the same emotions in us and we may be inspired and motivated to new perspectives and possibilities. On the other hand, this same dynamic can lead to dependency and manipulation if contact with the other is maintained to avoid facing challenges in our own life. If for example we avoid insecurity or loneliness by holding onto another person because we get a kick out of the mirroring that takes place when together, a dynamic is established that can easily be exploited by the other, as seen in groups that gather around charismatic persons.

Emotions are also contagious in large crowds, for example at big demonstrations or sports events. Anger and violent behavior can spread among groups of supporters to such an extent that otherwise peaceful people become brutally violent. People in a group can get carried away by powerful expressions that are mirrored and experienced internally. For a susceptible person, outside influences such as these can be difficult to resist. The mirroring of group emotions is also seen in positive social situations such as manifestations of aid in the midst of a disaster when empathic caring is awakened and supported by the group. The advertising industry also exploits this dynamic by associating a product with a particular feeling. They know that the product is purchased not only for its function but to a large extent for its associated experience. The product promises to provide the purchaser with the feeling associated with it.

Pattern recognition

The human organism continually communicates autonomic responses, needs and intentions through the body. We cannot escape response activation but we can to a certain extent hold back its expression with our striated muscles used for movement. When this happens, the body's affective expression consists in part of the response's natural expression and in part of muscular immobility caused by the fact that a natural expression is being held back. A lie is accompanied by physical signals that indicate inconsistency between what is said and an honest response. There may be a stiffness in the face, a nervous tic or lack of eye contact. When we communicate with others, we receive this information unconsciously and take in the entire expression. Without thinking we notice the withheld natural movements that interfere with complete, honest expression.

This ability to recognize patterns makes it possible for us to prepare for and deal with potentially dangerous situations. When a person lies or withholds information, some natural expression is held back and we perceive the resulting muscular immobility. We sense that things do not add up when physical information autonomously perceived and mirrored does not correspond to what is said. We can sense when things are not what they seem but this sense can early in life be influenced by "double messages" and we may stop trusting the information we sense. An example of double messages is when a caregiver says, "I love you" and shows something else, for instance irritation.

Relationships: the foundation of personality

Personality is the result of our early relationships. We become a person and define ourselves in relation to others. Personality is built through relational interactions with people around us and exists so that we can take part in relational interactions. You might say that personality exists outside ourselves in a relational space with others and not as we normally perceive it as being inside ourselves (Siegel, 2017). The central response system for relational interaction is the emotional system and when it comes to forming personality, the emotional system is the primary response system.

According to John Bowlby (1969), a leading theoretician in the school of psychoanalytic object relations, personality as an organization of the human psyche is established in the child's attachment to its caregivers. Attachment takes place during the first two years of life and its quality has great impact on our relationship with ourselves and others for the rest of our life. Bowlby describes attachment as the emotional bond between child and caregiver. The strength of this bond determines the infant's experience of being loved and therefore safe and secure. A strong, positive and secure attachment occurs when a caregiver provides for the child's needs and helps the child deal with inner tensions, affects and emotions that the child cannot deal with alone. Weak attachment, on the other hand, leads to various psychological disturbances later in life.

In the mid-1960's psychoanalyst Mary Ainsworth investigated the consequences of incomplete attachment in an experiment she termed "The strange situation procedure" (Ainsworth et al., 2015). In this experiment Ainsworth demonstrated that different degrees of attachment result in different relational behaviors and different degrees of personality disturbance when a child is exposed to a frightening situation. This behavior continues for the rest of the person's life. After Ainsworth's experiment, later studies confirmed that a child's environment and specifically its early caregivers are decisive in determining the way a child's inherent potential is realized (Ciccheti & Tucker, 1994).

The infant's dependency on its environment

Human infants cannot survive early life on their own. They are both physically and emotionally dependent on a caregiver. A number of studies have shown that children growing up in orphanages with good physical care will not develop normally if they do not also receive good emotional care (Spitz, 1946; Fisher et al., 1997). To bloom, children must have continual loving care as well as having their physical needs met.

Compared to other mammals, the human brain is poorly developed at birth. We would have to remain twelve months in the uterus to reach the same level of brain development as other mammals at birth (Gould, 1977). To emphasize this relative lack of maturity, the first three months after birth are sometimes referred to as the fourth trimester. Being born at such an early stage of brain and nervous system development is one of the reasons why human infants are extra sensitive and immensely dependent on care from others. A newborn baby leaves its enclosed, protected fetal environment prematurely and still needs a clear experience of being protected and part of someone else. Newborn infants are therefore extremely sensitive and need sensitive caregivers who can attune themselves with the infant's individual temperament and way of being.

An infant needs loving care and support in dealing with its own affective responses, also called *affect regulation* (Hart, 2008; Hill, 2015). An infant's affective responses are its earliest relational communication with its environment. These affective responses communicate the infant's needs and are their autonomous responses to outside stimuli. The infant requires help from caregivers to integrate these affects into its developing personality. At the beginning of life, communication consists mostly of responses to basic physical needs such as pain or hunger to achieve need satisfaction. Communication of responses develops from that point on to include the expression of other affective and emotional responses.

An infant's responses need to be met with acceptance, indicating that they are accepted and still one with the caregiver. The caregiver supports the infant in this process through sensitively attuning to them in order to help them regulate their responses. A caregiver's attuned interaction involves feeling what the infant is feeling and showing this through facial and vocal expression. When an infant's expressions are met with attunement from the caregiver, the infant experiences acceptance and love. Through sensitive attunement and response regulation, the infant learns to deal with its own responses as a natural and accepted part of itself. Supported by this interaction with its caregiver, the infant learns to integrate its responses into an organized structure or personality during this developmental process. If an infant's response is not met and regulated it will not be integrated into its personality and later activation will be experienced as a threat to the infant's personality. When this happens, expression of the response is held back, the affective system's natural functions are disturbed and there will be negative consequences for the future development of the infant's personality structure.

Affect regulation is the process of becoming attuned to and regulating the infant's affective and emotional responses.

Becoming one's self

An infant learns to regulate its own responses through shared regulation with an attuned caregiver. These interactions and processes take place through the communication of affective responses between the infant and its caregiver, mostly in the form of non-verbal communication with physical contact, body language and voice. Contact is synchronized through mutual small expressions, so-called *micro-interactions*, that create a resonant emotional field between infant and caregiver.

The infant develops in this harmonious symphony of mutual contact in which the caregiver constantly seeks interactive resonance by adjusting contact to continuously adapt to the infant's expressions. Along a wordless affective and emotional spectrum, the infant and caregiver adjust to each other for maximum contact, support and development. These micro interactions are both physical and verbal as well as through eye contact, particularly in the infant's contact with the subtle and sensitive gleam in a caregiver's eyes (Mahler et al., 1975; Kohut, 1971). This eye contact creates an open connection between the infant's and the caregiver's nervous systems. They move in a dance of affective resonance, shifting between challenge and oneness. In this challenging and unfolding dynamic, the infant is gradually allowed to express and integrate its responses. For the infant, it is a process which may be described as becoming friends with oneself.

The motivation and goal for this attuned interaction is the child's process of separation. It supports the child in becoming an independent individual. Developmental psychologist Daniel Stern (2004) called this a "development towards intersubjectivity". Intersubjectivity takes place when children become independent from others without experiencing separation from them. An inner understanding of this intersubjectivity arises out of the attuned micro-interactions between the child and its caregiver. It is important for a child to receive support and acceptance in this natural process of individualization.

To be able to separate from our original caregivers, we need to experience that we are still emotionally attached and that external separation from dependency does not mean inner separation. This is achieved when a child is accepted in the moment of separation by the person they are attached to. When separating from its caregiver, the child must experience that they are accepted and still part of a social context. With this support external security in the form of dependency on a caregiver is replaced by inner security.

The three stages of early development

The organization of personality in early child development goes through three distinct, overlapping stages during the first three years of life: *imitation, proto-conversation* and *affective attunement*. All three stages require *attuned emotional contact* with a caregiver. Attuned emotional contact is a developed form of early caring physical contact and provides the child with comfort and security through its experience of being part of the caregiver.

Imitation

From the age of two to three weeks, children are physically able to imitate and thereby understand others (Meltzoff & Moore, 1977). Children relate to their environment by physically imitating others and in so doing experience what others express. In this attuned imitative interaction children develop and expand their ability to respond. A child's imitation is globally oriented, which

132

means that the child is able to transform input received to other areas rather than imitating only through direct mirroring. A child can for example hear a voice and imitate it by moving its hand to the rhythm of the voice.

Children can also recognize imitation of their own expression in another form if the imitation is attuned and has the same quality, for example if the child's sounds are imitated in the form of a movement. If imitation does not have the same quality, the child will not be receptive to whatever is being communicated. This demonstrates the importance of flexible and attuned empathic openness in a caregiver.

The ability to give a child a qualitatively equivalent response reinforces attachment and provides the child with space for its needs and development. For example if a child displays physiological affects such as pain or agitation, a caregiver may provide comfort and security by attuned imitation of the child's expressions while connected to their own feeling of calm and loving care. In this way, pain or agitation is regulated. The caregiver meets the child's discomfort, shows that the child is accepted and shows a way back to calm. By contrast, if the caregiver's imitation is not attuned with the child's expression, the child will not associate the caregiver's imitation with its own expression, regulation will not occur and the child's discomfort will not disappear (Stern, 1985).

Protoconversation.
From the age of about two to three months, children start to engage in social communication that not only imitates others but also begins to relate to them. The child begins to respond to its environment with other abilities than movement and voice. At this time the child will smile, gesture and emotionally express itself in relation to its environment. This early form of social communication is called protoconversation (from Greek *proto-*, first or earliest form).

The caregiver vitalizes and supports the child's expressions. In this way the caregiver helps the child to regulate its responses and find its way in social interactions (Stern, 2004). A child at this age can read and match a caregiver's expression and this provides space for the child's own affects as it finds its way in social interaction. At this point it is no longer sufficient for the caregiver to respond in an attuned way to the child's expressions; it is also important for the caregiver to invite interaction and exchange by vitalizing contact and initiating and motivating interaction. In protoconversation, the intensity of affective response increases naturally in the dynamic between child and caregiver. This supports the child to regulate its own continually increasing intensity of response expression and gradually learn to integrate increased affective and emotional charge.

Affective attunement

The final form of communication in early child development is affective attunement, a more sophisticated level of imitation and protoconversation. Affective attunement occurs when the child begins social behavior together with protoconversation and it is the most common form of communication at nine months of age (Stern, 2004). At this stage children develop the ability to feel what others are feeling and to feel and experience that others understand their feelings (Hart, 2006). This ability enables children to share an emotional state with others through protoconversation, sound and movement.

With affective attunement, children share affective and emotional experiences with their caregiver. The caregiver responds with so-called affect mirroring in which the caregiver returns what the child is presumed to be feeling through gestures, facial expressions and sounds. The child can then continue to explore the affect by amplifying and changing it in a shared experience with the caregiver. For the child this interaction confirms that others feel what they feel and provides an experience of connection to others (Stern, 1985). This gives the child a sense of security and enables it to organize inner experiences and relate to their own affects instead of simply reacting to stimuli.

In this process a child experiences that it is connected to its environment and develops the capacity to emotionally relate to other personally important people later in life. The child develops the ability to maintain its own perspective or experience while dealing with someone else's. This process lays the groundwork for our empathic ability: the ability to feel what others feel without mistaking it as our own feeling. As a child develops, affective attunement continues to play an important role in forming the child's personality and future behavior.

134

A template for personality

The basic structure or template of personality forms in this early development of mutual contact between a child and its caregiver. The caregiver relates to the child's different expressions and selectively regulates them, saying "yes" to some and "no" to others and this shapes the child's personality in relation to the caregiver. A caregiver's hopes, desires, inhibitions, fears, etcetera are transferred to the child in this selective attunement and become a part of the child's evolving personality. Our personality is colored by our parent's personalities, which were colored by their parents' personalities. In this way character traits and behaviors are passed on in families over generations.

Interactions with primary caregivers that form personality expand after a while to include other important people in the child's life. Friends, teachers and the surrounding culture now become an important part of personality formation. The child mirrors itself in these social interactions and finds the best way to survive, live and develop in relation to its established capacity. To fit into social culture as well as smaller groups the child learns which natural expressions are acceptable and which are not. This helps to develop the child's basic understanding of life and creates the reality maps that guide behavior throughout life.

A mother's devotion

At the start of life an infant is completely dependent on its primary caregiver and there is a corresponding natural increase in biological activation of caregiving qualities in the caregiver. This is part of a mutual developmental process aimed at creating a perfect environment for the child. The caregiver's state of caring devotion to the newborn child is so special that it has been described as "a state of temporary, constructive madness" (Winnicott, 1965). This increased activation of caring is a preprogrammed biological process designed to make the caregiver a medium for the child's positive development. It makes the caregiver extra sensitive to the needs and general welfare of the child and it contributes to the caregiver's ability to meet and satisfy the child's needs with nearly perfect timing. An increase in practical sensitivity is supplemented by the caregiver's growing openness and affection for the child. For a caregiver, this increased sense of caring makes the child's needs and life more important than the caregiver's own needs and life.

135

The caregiver's increased nurturing behavior comes from a powerful neuro-chemical process in the caregiver. Loving interaction with a child releases oxytocin, endogenic opioids and other chemicals in the caregiver (Panskepp & Biven, 2012), a neurochemical activation that calms, relieves pain and increases empathic ability. This activation of the organism's reward system creates a sense of well-being when caring for a child. The reward system's activity is at maximum from birth through the first period of the child's life. After a while this positive biochemical activation decreases but caring behavior has by then become imprinted into the caregiver's personality.

As the child grows and becomes more independent, the biochemical reward system's heightened activation level decreases and the caregiver returns to being themselves, so to speak. Focus shifts slowly back to the caregiver's own needs and comfort and what Winnicott calls a state of madness turns to more balanced care for the child. In this way the caregiver's biologically supported nurturing follows the child's development toward greater independence and formation of an individual identity. The child's process of separation is supported by the caregiver's natural biological process.

Emotional wounds

If a caregiver is unable to be in emotionally attuned resonance with the child and therefore cannot regulate the child's experiences and expressions, the child must withdraw from its experience. The caregiver's function as a safe haven for the child when it cannot deal with its experience becomes instead a source of anxiety. The child is forced to dissociate, which means that the child stops expression of unmet activated affects or emotions and distances itself from feeling its withheld expression (Schore, 2012). If this occurs repeatedly, a relational pattern is established that causes emotional activation and its expression to be experienced as threatening. A relational trauma occurs, a break in the relational connection between child and caregiver with negative consequences for the child's development, self-organization and future relational behavior. A natural expression of affect or emotion now becomes a threat to the relational wholeness between the child and its caregiver. In order to avoid expression and contact with the emotion, defense mechanisms and fear activate every time the threatening emotion is activated.

A little girl expresses anger naturally if she does not get what she wants. If her mother does not meet the girl's anger but instead withdraws from contact with her and/or becomes cold or angry, the girl is alone with her response. She experiences that her anger is not accepted and she receives no help in regulating it. A break in relational connection occurs between the girl and her mother. If this becomes a pattern in their relationship it creates a relational trauma in the form of painful memories of relational separation. When anger is activated later in similar situations, it will be connected to these painful memories and the girl's expression of anger will automatically be held back.

Rejection of a child's needs and response processes is experienced as a separation from the caregiver and an injury to the child's relational body, which is the internalization of a child's important relations. Since a child is dependent on its caregiver this injury is considered life-threatening and unacceptable to the human organism. When the emotional process is activated later on, the child will hold back emotional expression and dissociate itself from the experience in order to survive and protect itself from this life-threatening experience. The child's experience of relational injury feels exactly the same as physical pain and the child cannot deal with it. The organism protects itself by contracting and defense mechanisms steer the child's awareness away from what is happening. Later on, the child will keep the focus of its awareness away from this pain and protect itself from whatever might provoke the pain again.

Relational trauma is an *emotional wound* (in Greek, *trauma* means wound or injury). The psychiatrist Stanislav Grof (2012) describes emotional wounds as "condensed experiences" that cause psychological disturbances later in life. Most of the problems and difficulties we experience later in life are essentially due to intense experiences of relational separation. The same type of emotional wound can occur when a child or adult is unable to express and regulate high-intensity affective activation. This is what happens in so-called *shock trauma*. In shock trauma a person is suddenly confronted with life's vulnerability. The person experiences the ultimate relational separation of death without a chance to express and complete the natural response to it. The response and its action potential remain in the organism and cause emotional, social and cognitive disturbances from that point on.

A caregiver's attuned interaction with a child does not have to be perfect for the child to avoid an experience of separation. A delayed, attuned interaction in which regulation comes a bit too late or a so-called repairing interaction in which a caregiver returns to attunement with the child after having fallen out of attunement are actually positive for a child's development. Psychoanalyst Donald W. Winnicott (1965) called this behavior and dynamic "good enough mothering".

According to Winnicott a good caregiver does not always need to be in perfect regulatory attunement with their child. Breaks in the connection between a child and its caregiver are natural and children are not always met in perfectly attuned resonance. However when a caregiver notices that the connection is broken, it is important to return to the child in attuned resonance in order to repair the connection.

A relational pattern in which a caregiver breaks their connection and then quickly returns to attuned caring that repairs the break is a natural and healthy part of child development. It gives the child a necessary challenge to develop and it supports the child's ability to relate to and regulate uncomfortable feelings on its own. In this process the child learns to deal with fluctuations in the level of emotional activation even when it goes beyond what the child is used to and able to regulate. The message for the child to learn in this delayed response regulation is: "I can lose my foothold and regain it. Losing my foothold is OK." This is a natural and fitting developmental dynamic. In learning to allow and tolerate unpleasant feelings the child is supported in the process of separation from its caregiver.

The consequences of relational trauma

Relational trauma and emotional wounds result in an unconscious defense dynamic that holds back expression of three separate but connected response processes. These are: the primary need response, its subsequent emotional response activation and the so-called life-promoting positive response processes. These are called *unregulated response processes*.

The primary need response involves a basic need such as the child's need to feel safe and receive the loving contact they need and support to stand on their own. If a primary need response is not met with attuned interaction from the caregiver, an emotional response such as sorrow or anger naturally activates. If this response is not met and regulated either, the child experiences relational separation. Later, expressions of the child's primary need response and the subsequent emotional response will be experienced as threatening. When this emotional need response or its subsequent emotional response are activated in similar situations, personality will automatically defend itself to avoid losing safety and stability.

The development of positive response processes such as happiness and love is part of the organism's natural response development. Relational trauma stalls this development and it is only when the unregulated, emotional response activation and need response is regulated that development can continue. Happiness and particularly love can then be allowed to develop and their regulation and integration can begin.

Chapter 10

Defenses

When unregulated emotions and needs are activated, personality defends itself against their expression. *Defenses* are our personality's survival strategies to prevent expression of unregulated emotions. They remove awareness of contact with these emotions and thereby keep us from conscious contact with the emotional wound that threatens our inner stability. Our defense is a strategy to avoid emotions that we have learned we cannot tolerate (Schore, 2012).

The dynamic of our defense can be separated into two subprocesses. Expression of an activated emotional process is first stopped, fear is activated and conscious focus shifts away in disassociation. Following this comes what is usually referred to as the defense mechanism itself, an avoidance behavior that keeps us from feeling our fear and the halted emotional process.

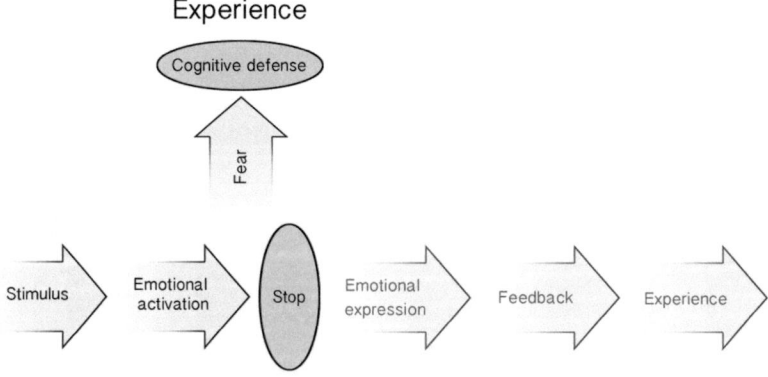

Figure 12: Emotion – fear – cognitive defense
Fear moves conscious focus away from a stoped unregulated emotion and then our cognitive defense keeps us from conscious contact with the fear. In this way, defense mechanisms indirectly protect us from unregulated emotions.

The defense mechanism is a cognitive defense which keeps us unaware of the first process. Our cognitive defense moves the focus of our awareness away from contact with our body's response processes to other people, situations, or our own thought processes. Fear in this case is a process of dissociation away from a threatening emotional process. The task of the cognitive defense is to keep us from coming into contact with this fear. If we came into contact with our fear, we would also come into closer contact with the unregulated emotional activation that triggered our fear. In this way, our cognitive defense makes sure we avoid contact with unregulated emotional activation.

Psychoanalytic theory classifies cognitive defense behavior into a number of defense mechanisms such as splitting, projective identification, repression, denial, affect isolation, rejection, reaction formation, identification, regression, projection, rationalization etcetera (Laplanche & Potalis, 1973). Defense mechanisms are the ways we cognitively avoid coming into contact with fear and thereby unregulated emotional processes. Which defense mechanism we use depends on our particular defense system and its dynamic. Our defense system is built during early childhood and its specific dynamic depends on when it was established during the development of personality.

Defense systems

In child development, a series of universal stages follow in succession as new abilities appear. These stages are connected to brain development and each developmental stage consists of an important theme with associated abilities and skills which the child needs to explore and integrate so they can become a part of personality. To achieve positive development and integration of a theme's skills into personality, it is important that the child receive support from its caregiver. If support is not provided during a developmental stage, the part of the child's personality connected to that developmental theme cannot mature and become integrated into personality. As a result personality begins to defend itself against related, unregulated needs and response processes.

The way a child defends itself against unregulated responses depends on its level of development and resources at the time the disturbance took place. Mobilizing its resources, a defense system is built with a specific defense dynamic. The defense mechanisms we use as adults are built on top of this basic defense dynamic. For example our earliest defense system uses the only defense dynamic available to an undeveloped nervous system: splitting or dissociation, in which personality screens itself off from experienced reality and denies its existence. When disturbances occur in later developmental stages, personality is able to make use of the cognitive skills that have become available and use a more mature and advanced defense mechanism such as rationalization (Shore, 2003). If development is disturbed at several stages, the person will often come to use one specific defense system which then can be supplemented with other defense systems as needed. For instance, a person may normally use a mature defense but under specific circumstances use a more immature one.

The structure of personality including its defense systems is fully developed at five to seven years of age (Lowen, 1958; Totton, 1998). Development during the first two years has major consequences for the fundamental stability of personality and continued development up to about seven years of age has a major influence on the specific character of personality. It is during these first seven years of life that the most important developmental stages of personality formation take place, and the general dynamic and character of the defense system depends on when disturbances in this development occur.

The following is a classification of developmental stages during childhood and the defense system that arises when a stage is disturbed. This classification is based on Alexander Lowen's theory of character structure (1958), later development of this theory and on the functional development of the brain and body (see for example Marcher & Finch, 2010). Approximate ages are listed for each stage to give an idea of when they occur. These stages are however processes in an individual's biological development; their beginning, end and duration depend on many individual circumstances. The stages also overlap and skills continue to develop as new ones begin.

In this presentation of the five stages of development, our focus is on the developmental theme for each stage and the basic defense dynamic that results from a disturbance in need satisfaction during that stage.

Stage of development	Approximate age	Defense system
Existence	3 rd trimester to 3 mths	Dissociative
Needs	1 mth to 1.5 years	Dependent
Autonomy	8 mths to 2.5 years	Manipulative
Will	2 to 4 years	Withholding
Achievement	3 to 6 years	Overachieving

The first stage: Existence

An infant's first stage of development begins before birth at the beginning of the third trimester and continues until it is about three months old. This is the time immediately before and after birth and the theme for this period is existence and fulfillment of the infant's basic security. To develop positively, the infant needs to feel welcome and that life and its immediate environment can satisfy its need for physical and emotional security. If this is achieved and development continues normally, the infant experiences a basic feeling of safety and security in life.

At this time the infant is in a developmental stage in which physical processes are organized and coordinated, supported by the infant's relation to its caregiver (Stern, 1985). The basic structure of personality on which adult personality rests develops in this relational interaction. Since infants at this stage of development do not have an individual "I", they are completely dependent on their caregiver to ensure a stable basic structure. To satisfy the infant's need for security, its caregiver must be very responsive to the infant's needs and able to support necessary regulation. During this stage the infant requires that its physical needs be met as well as regulation of its budding emotional processes. This regulation takes place in direct, attuned physical contact in which attunement and mirroring are important elements. This is the stage in which attachment begins and the infant needs to experience that the caregiver is a safe base that it can rely on and that the caregiver participates in creating a safe base in the infant itself.

If an infant's needs are not met during this stage, if it feels rejected or if it experiences that its environment is cold and hostile, the earliest form of defense system will develop: a dissociative defense. Since an infant is completely dependent on and exists in a symbiotic relationship with its caregiver, the infant

143

experiences that its existence is threatened if the caregiver is unable to meet its need for basic safety. The brain's limbic system is far from fully developed and the infant has limited ways to defend itself against this experience. The only defense possible is to shield itself from contact with the experience of a threatening reality by dissociating, shifting the focus of awareness away from the unacceptable experience and denying its existence.

When the infant's need for basic safety and security is not met at this early age, it can result in a personality without a stable structure at its core. Without a safe base in early life, a conviction grows that the world is unsafe and dangerous. The person's personality risks becoming colored by a focus on polarities such as yes/no, good/evil or black/white. Life becomes a question of either/or rather than both. Other people will for example be seen as either good or bad, they cannot be both. In this way, a person shields themself from the threatening feeling of contact which can lead to an experience of inner insecurity. Since contact with physical reality is experienced as threatening, people with this defense system tend to live in a fantasy world to a greater or lesser extent. They often completely avoid physical and emotional contact and tend to focus on mentally abstract views and perspectives on life. People with this defense system often experience a deep feeling of loneliness and isolation due to the early absence of mutually attuned contact with a caregiver.

The dissociative defense system

Dissociation (from Latin *dissociare*, to separate from fellowship) is a defense established against disturbances in the first stage of development: existence. Dissociation involves completely shifting the focus of awareness from one's own feeling of emotion and denying its existence. A dissociative defense system develops with the objective of avoiding emotional feeling. A person with this defense protects themself by always being cut off from feeling emotional contact and denying its existence. In this way, the person shields themself from experiencing deeply felt insecurity and related, unregulated emotions. The attitude is either/or: either I do not feel emotional contact and am safe, or I feel emotional contact and experience the threat of annihilation. When a person with this defense system feels emotional contact, their personality tends to be overwhelmed and the person experiences that they are in the same mortal danger that they had to dissociate from earlier in life.

144

Behavior

People who mainly use a dissociative defense system are often creative and quick thinkers. They have many ideas, thoughts and words and display a high degree of mental flexibility. They are pioneering, perceptive and easily find new angles and paths. However they tend to be relatively indifferent to reality's limitations or if it is possible to actually realize their ideas. They can be very engaged and positive about an idea or project and then suddenly withdraw and become distant both in terms of presence and attitude. If pushed, or just before they experience emotional contact, they can seem to be confused and/or make others around them confused. They often have good intuition and a feel for what is about to happen before it actually takes place, an ability they use to defend themselves from contact with their own emotional feeling. They are hypersensitive to their surroundings, making them apt to identify possible threats.

While able to sense what is happening in their more distant environment, people with this defense do not always notice what is happening in interactions with their immediate physical and relational environment. This can express itself in a certain awkwardness in their relations with other people or objects. A general pattern in the life of people who use this defense may also include difficulty in finding a place for oneself in life both privately and professionally, since "landing" in physical reality and relating to it is experienced as threatening.

Integrative dynamic

A person with a dissociative defense system needs to feel welcome and experience safety and security when feeling emotional contact. This defense system is based on a fundamental distrust and lack of confidence in life and emotional feelings, which makes the person dissociate even more when pressured to feel emotional contact, just as anyone would defend against threatening annihilation. To support a process of integration, a person with this defense system needs to experience that it is not dangerous to feel emotional contact. Trust has to be built slowly; the person should be gently invited into the process of emotional regulation. In this way the person may experience some control over the process.

For this person, existence was once threatened and they meet that old experience again when they feel emotional contact. The dynamic of defense quickly

145

removes the person from emotional contact. Emotional integration requires a slow return to feeling emotional contact.

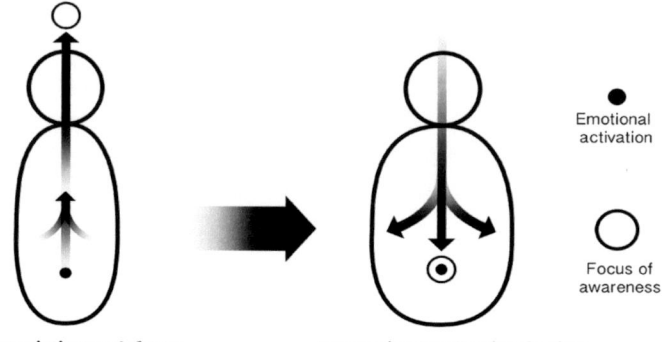

Dissociation as defense   Integration by allowing feeling

Figure 13: The dissociative defense system and its integrative dynamic
Dissociation is the movement of fear away from experienced reality which is later maintained by the dissociative defense system. To discover possible threats, the dissociative defense keeps awareness away from the body in a state of alert attention. Integration is facilitated by inviting the person into contact with their feelings, dissolving fear and returning to physical emotional contact.

The second stage: Needs

This stage of development has the theme *needs* and is concerned with satisfying the basic physical and emotional needs of the child. The child's separation from its caregiver begins during this stage and the child develops from being a part of the caregiver to becoming an independent person. This development coincides with hierarchic development and integration of the limbic system in the brain. It begins as early limbic structures unfold, giving rise to autonomic emotional reflexes and ends with later limbic structures in the neocortex that make it possible for us to inhibit emotional activation (Schore, 2003).

During this stage, children gradually gain greater access to their emotional and relational system and areas of the brain involved with mirror neurons begin a process of maturation (Bentzen, 2015). Since birth, the child has had many experiences within the emotional spectrum and at this stage, the child needs a caregiver who can help it relate to these processes in order to later be able to regulate them on its own. The ability of children to enter into relationships and relate to others increases during this stage of development. Children begin to

146

act as a coherent self in relation to their environment. The primary relational mission during this stage is to develop what developmental psychologist Daniel Stern termed the *core self* (Stern, 1985). In this process, the child develops a clear understanding of itself and its individual personality in relation to others.

To develop naturally during this stage, the child is dependent on a caregiver to satisfy its basic need for physical nourishment and attuned, loving contact. As previously described, children communicate their needs through eye contact, sound and movement. The caregiver satisfies the child's need for attuned contact by regulating its expression and providing loving care. It is important for a caregiver to be attentive to the child and satisfy its needs by showing interest and providing the loving care that the child needs: attention as needed, food when necessary and emotional regulation when called for. A child also needs its caregiver to function as a source of emotional charge during this stage of development. In this way, the child gets new energy and vitality as it explores itself and its surroundings. This happens for example through caring and stimulating eye contact with the caregiver. A balanced satisfaction of the child's needs gives it confidence in life and an experience that life provides for its needs.

If a child's needs are not met, this stage of development cannot be completed and its theme cannot be integrated. The resulting experience is one of being unsatisfied and painfully abandoned (Lowen, 1975). An inner longing to be filled up and satisfied arises and an emotional wound is created. This experience activates natural emotional responses, particularly anger, which the caregiver does not regulate. This makes the child hold back emotional expression and avoid feeling contact with the emotion. To survive, a defense system is established that makes the child extra sensitive and receptive to the needs of the caregiver and others. By paying attention to the needs of its caregiver and satisfying those needs, the child avoids experiencing its own lack of need satisfaction, its own pain and associated, unregulated emotions. By making itself needed in this way, the child holds onto a symbiotic relationship with its caregiver and at the same time loses the possibility of standing on its own two feet.

Adults who did not achieve satisfaction of needs at this stage of development will experience that they are unable to fill the emptiness within themselves. They often experience an uncomfortable, empty hole within themselves that they believe needs to be filled by others. This makes them tend to experience a need for others and they become dependent on others in an attempt to fill themselves out and avoid discomfort. They achieve this for example by entering into various symbiotic relationships similar to their early symbiosis with a caregiver. They can become dependent on other people or develop various forms of addiction such as to food, sex or drugs. Their behavior is driven by a longing for more of whatever they are addicted to, as if they can never get enough.

This behavior covers up and numbs the underlying experience of being unsatisfied. However, regardless of the number of symbiotic relational contacts or other attempts at filling the hole, they are never satisfied because their longing stems from an early lack of attuned contact and need fulfillment. Attempts later in life to compensate for this lack is a way of defending themselves from the emotional pain and unregulated emotions of early childhood. These attempts may provide a moment's relief, but craving and discomfort quickly return since their cause remains unaddressed.

The dependent defense system
The defense system that develops when there is a disturbance in the stage of needs is based on dependence on one's environment. A person with a dependent defense system holds onto others or other things and does not let go. In this way, the person tries to fulfill themselves. As long as the person holds onto their dependency, they avoid experiencing the discomfort that would result from standing on their own. The dependent defense system keeps a person from experiencing the discomfort of independence. Since this person's early need for emotional nourishment was not met, the person does not trust that their needs will be met later in life. The person does not believe that they can stand on their own and get their needs met, so they become dependent on others. Exaggerated, independent behavior is a reactive form of this defense. By resisting their own dependence, pretending to be independent and saying "I do not need anyone at all," this person defends themself against the uncomfortable feeling caused by the absence of early need satisfaction.

Behavior
A positive quality of people who use the dependent defense system is that they can be extremely sensitive and attuned to others. They are good listeners with

148

great sensitivity to others' needs. They are good at taking care of others and are flexible and easy to work with. This is behavior learned during their early relationship with a caregiver to avoid experiencing their lack of need satisfaction and inner deficiency. They are often passive when it comes to their own needs but can be quite stubborn if they have decided on something. They are also good at supporting others but find it difficult to take command over and be responsible for their own life. Despite the fact that they do not feel their own needs, they often expect someone else to come and fulfill them, someone who will give them a roadmap for their life. They often ask what others think and want help in living their life.

Integrative dynamic
To come out of their position of dependency, a person who uses the dependent defense system needs to learn how to stand on their own two feet. They must learn to make decisions and get by on their own, daring to have and express personal opinions.

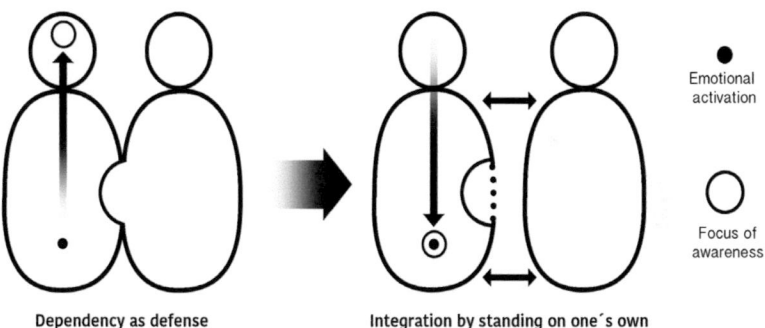

Dependency as defense   Integration by standing on one's own

Emotional activation

Focus of awareness

Figure 14: The dependent defense system and its integrative dynamic
The dependent defense system makes a person dependent on others or other things as a defense against contact with unregulated emotions. The process of integration is facilitated by supporting the person to stand on their own two feet and express their opinions, feelings and needs.

This can be a difficult task since the integration process brings the person into contact with associated, unregulated response processes. Since they did not receive support at this stage of their development, they now need support to stand on their own and fill the emptiness in themselves instead of hoping that someone else will do it for them. They need to stand on their own two feet and to feel and express withheld, unregulated emotional processes. By standing for these response processes, the person regains self-confidence and learns to feel their own needs. This leads to an experience that life will provide for their needs. The person learns to express their needs and relate to the response they get.

The third stage: Autonomy

The next leap in child development occurs at about eight months of age. At this point, a child discovers that it has a mind (i.e., a well-defined, independent consciousness), that other people also have a mind and that inner experiences and intentions can be shared (Stern, 1985). This stage of development has the theme of *autonomy* and is concerned with healthy separation from the caregiver. During this developmental stage, the child's ability to deal with significantly higher levels of pleasure and vital excitement increases, particularly in dyadic interaction with its caregiver.

This development mirrors the development of dopamine circulation from the limbic system to the orbitofrontal cortex (Bentzen, 2015). The orbitofrontal cortex connects our experience of external events with inner states and feelings and makes it possible for a child to distinguish itself from its environment. In earlier developmental stages, the child's basic needs were met. Now the child begins to feel itself more independent from its caregiver, a development that goes from the environment being only a source of mechanical need satisfaction to one in which others become a source of relational interest. For the first time, the child experiences itself as separate from its caregiver and able to communicate subjective experiences that can be understood by others. The child begins to differentiate its own emotional expressions from others' and experiences itself as an autonomous, psychological unit in relation to others.

During this period of separation, the child explores the world and its own feelings. The child needs to be independent yet still needs intimate contact with its caregiver, a process of separation in which the child can be free to leave its caregiver and then return to intimacy. While exploring being itself in relation to others and acting on its own, the child needs to experience that it is accepted, allowed to make its own decisions and that its boundaries are respected. This results in an experience of positively supported autonomy and independence.

If a child does not receive support for the autonomy it needs at this stage and is instead governed by the caregiver's needs and will, the child will feel controlled. It may be that the child's efforts at autonomy are met with ridicule, criticism, indifference or other negative expressions of nonacceptance. In this way, the child's psychological space and intimate sphere are violated by the very people on whom the child is dependent. The child is manipulated to relate to the caregiver's needs and will, under the pretense that they are the child's own needs. In this process, it is not the child's needs that are met but rather the caregiver's, often with the intention of discouraging the child's process of independence and binding the child to its caregiver.

If a child's need for autonomy is not met and supported, the child will experience relational separation from the caregiver. This is a painful and unacceptable situation that creates an emotional wound. Other emotions activate in autonomic response to this and when these are not allowed either, a defense system is created that keeps the child from feeling contact with its pain and autonomously activated, unregulated emotions. To defend itself, the child learns to control and manipulate its environment. The victim of manipulation defends itself by manipulating others.

The manipulative defense system
In order to always stay in control of interpersonal relations and never become a victim again, those whose needs have been disturbed in the stage of autonomy defend themselves by charming and manipulating their environment. In the manipulative defense system, the main theme is about control of the environment and it is necessary to deny feelings that may be connected with closeness and intimacy. Contact with these emotional feelings is experienced as a weakness that risks making the person a victim again. The person is in conflict with their own need for closeness and intimacy, which is associated with the earlier relational separation and unregulated emotional processes. A person with this defense system tends to lift themself up and away from their emotional feelings and to charm others. The person is outgoing, appears powerful and actively manipulates and binds others to themself.

Behavior
People who use the manipulative defense system often appear to be dynamic, powerful and full of initiative. They can be experienced as a dynamic center of

151

power, able to bring others together and motivate them toward a common goal. They are often articulate, argue persuasively and have a well-developed ability to convince others of their own excellence. As a defense they have created a self-image and façade of being extraordinary and omnipotent. Initially those around them believe and accept this but the image cannot be maintained, the façade cracks and a negative, controlling behavior becomes obvious. People with this defense system need followers and sycophants. It is difficult for them to be confronted with their flaws and negative behavior. They come alive by making others need and follow them, although this is a defense against feeling and expressing their own needs and feelings. They are persuasive and specialists at directly or indirectly attracting others to themselves. To stay in control they need to constantly be the center of social attention and find it difficult to be part of a team or group process.

People who mainly use this defense system also tend to be insensitive to the pain of others. If pressed, they may display a lack of empathy for others to a greater or lesser extent. In its extreme form, the behavior of people with this defense system resembles that of people having the much-discussed psychopathic personality disorder, which is characterized by narcissism, impulsiveness, absence of conscience, lying and manipulation (Dutton, 2012).

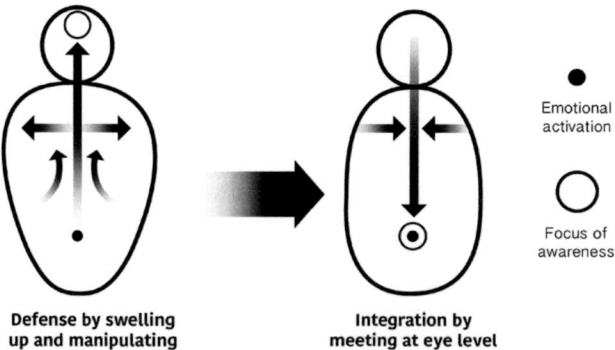

Figure 15: The manipulative defense system and its integrative dynamic
A person with a manipulative defense system defends themself against unregulated emotional responses by lifting themself up and manipulating others. The process of integration is facilitated by supporting the person to come into contact with and express what they feel.

Integrative dynamic

To be able to be in the world without directing and controlling it, a person with a manipulative defense system needs to come into contact with and express unregulated emotional processes connected to closeness and intimacy (Figure 15). To support the process of integration, a person who uses the manipulative defense system needs to meet others as an equal and interact honestly with their feelings and needs. They need to show who they are behind their defenses in relations with others, a process in which they meet their fear of becoming a manipulated victim again. From this position, they can develop natural autonomy and pride as opposed to the inflated, narcissistic self-esteem that they usually display.

The fourth stage: Will

In the developmental stage of will from about two to four years of age, interpersonal regulation between a child and its caregiver shifts towards socialization and the child begins to deal with social and cultural norms. In the previous stage of autonomy, the child made itself independent from the caregiver; now the developmental challenge is to retain this independence in relation to others. This stage of development has the theme of socialization and is concerned with learning to balance one's own needs with others'. The child begins to see itself as an independent individual interacting with others (Stern, 1985). The child must now find a balance between its own freedom, which involves standing up for its own needs, and being an independent part of the relationship with its caregivers. The child needs to learn how to combine its need for freedom and being its own individual self with responsibility and respect for others' needs. These are two considerations that must be balanced and conflicts between them must be resolved.

At this stage, the limbic system in the brain is fully developed and the child can influence its emotional expression. The child begins to express anger towards others more directly and in some situations may react with unprovoked anger. Moderate levels of natural shame help the child to relate to and influence its emotions and relationships. This helps the child to adjust its expression so it does not come into conflict with its environment. To enter into a social context, shame in its natural, balanced form functions as an incentive to self-regulation of expression and behavior (Hart, 2006).

At this stage, children need support in their growing independence and freedom. They need to feel accepted in their exploration and mastery over themselves, their impulses and their will. Children need to experience that they are allowed to be themselves and express themselves. This is why it is important for caregivers to be sensitive when setting boundaries and to pay attention to the effect it has on the child. A child can in this way be supported in the exploration of its power and emotional expression, and can learn to regulate emotions on its own.

One example of this development is the child's exploration of the word "no". "No" is an expression of a new quality of anger directed at others that the child comes into contact with and needs to learn about. By expressing "no" in different situations and ways, the child explores how to achieve more freedom in a relationship. The child experiments to discover when the word can be used, how strongly and how often it can be used and boundaries for its use in different relationships. In this way the child learns to be both free and part of a relationship.

If a caregiver's insensitivity forces a child to choose between its own will and the will of its caregiver, an impossible situation arises. The conflict cannot be resolved and due to the child's dependence on its caregiver, it is forced to obey the caregiver's will. If a caregiver's love is conditional on the child's obedience to the caregiver, the will of the child is broken. In this case if the caregiver does not return later to repair the relationship with love, the child experiences the caregiver's correction as a punishment, which causes the child to feel shame.

To protect itself from the emotional wound and unregulated emotional processes caused by this relational separation, the child begins to act submissively and holds back honest expression. The child learns that it must obey to get love and the dynamic of an otherwise balanced and socializing shame becomes part of the child's defense system. Instead of expressing naturally activated anger toward the caregiver, the defense system directs anger at the child itself in the form of shame. As a result, the child (and later the adult) will experience shame when expressing its own will, needs and emotions. The child learns to hide its natural feelings, particularly anger, since this leads to the child being unaccepted and unloved. The child instead complies and does what others tell it to do in order to show that it is good enough and worth loving. Despite this, the child never experiences that this is the case since its compliance is a defense against an emotional wound and unregulated emotional processes. The child will in the future also avoid relational conflict out of a fear that unregulated emotional processes, particularly anger, might explode into expression.

The withholding defense system

A person whose main disturbance occurred during the stage of will holds themself back and is willing to do what others want them to do. This is a withholding defense system in which the person keeps their honest feelings, needs and will to themself as in a pressure cooker. The person is in conflict with their own honest expression since they have learned that they can only be loved if they do what others want. Strongly self-critical, they redirect anger toward others back on themself in the form of shame. They are wounded internally and have a thick shell around themself to defend against contact with their own expressions of will and response and they do what they believe others want them to do. The person experiences being not good enough, which continues into adulthood. Love has been connected to pain and the person holds onto this pain and suffers. Through a submissive attitude towards others, the person avoids conflict but at the same time finds it difficult to honestly engage and become involved in others' ideas and standpoints. They are never really satisfied and are at the same time afraid that their dissatisfaction will come out.

Behavior

A person with a pronounced withholding defense system often has a high work capacity, is dutiful, readily takes on tasks and sacrifices themself for others. Their efforts are good, stable and reliable. Due to their withholding defense system, this person does not express what they feel, want or need but instead follows the opinions of others or whoever decides. A distinguishing feature for this person is that they keep secrets about themself and their family, secrets that have to do with how things really are or were. This defense system tends to express itself in the form of mild depression that can appear as low energy and heaviness. When taking on tasks, they tend to complain and indirectly air discontent. They rarely or never complain directly, since that might create a conflict and cause them to come into contact with the anger that threatens them. In these indirect expressions of how hard their life is, a victim mentality makes itself known. The person experiences themself as a victim of circumstances and, in their own perspective, without other alternatives or choices.

The person's withheld anger can also be expressed in a passive-aggressive way. Instead of clearly expressing thoughts and feelings, pent-up irritation and dissatisfaction is indirectly expressed in the person's behavior. It may be that the person more or less consciously slows down processes, forgets important details and agreements or undermines the will and needs of others. This is a way of expressing anger without open conflict yet still retaliating. A person with a withholding defense system typically has a lively and infectious humor and in the right environment can display an exuberant joy of life.

Integrative dynamic

To let go of shame and open up, a person who uses a withholding defense system must dare to face their insecurity about expressing honest thoughts, feelings and needs. They need to speak out about how they are doing, what they stand for and what they want, though fearful that they will not be accepted if they do this. It is therefore crucial for the person to experience situations in which this does not happen.

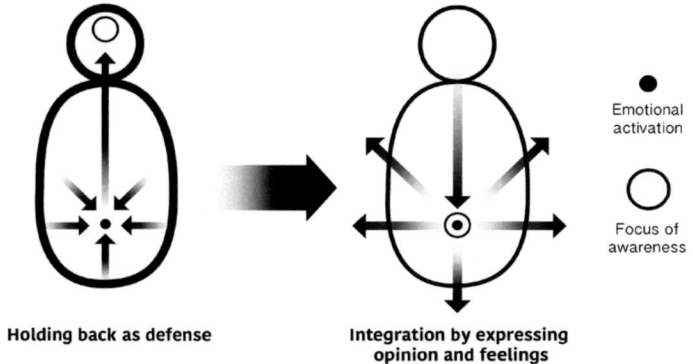

Holding back as defense   **Integration by expressing opinion and feelings**

Emotional activation

Focus of awareness

Figure 16: The withholding defense system and its integrative dynamic
A person with a withholding defense system defends themself against contact with emotional feelings by holding back honest expression. The defense dissolves when the person dares to express their honest opinion and emotional responses without letting the resulting discomfort activate shame.

This is a process in which the person needs to experience that they are free to express their own will and what they stand for without reprisal from others in the form of withheld love and contact. This experience makes it possible for the person to open up and reveal the secrets they carry. This openness also supports a reduced shame response, which is otherwise strong. An increased willingness to express and accept their own anger is another important element in emotional regulation. This is the anger that shame redirects toward themself. If the person succeeds at this, they will move from the experience of being a victim of circumstances to the insight that they are free to express their will and be themself.

The fifth stage: Achievement

After the previous stages, the child has attained a relatively self-sufficient and independent personality. In this stage, from about three to six years of age, the child finds out who they are in the world. This developmental stage is about the child taking its place in society and learning to be a part of a social community that is larger than family and their closest group. A child needs to find its place in this larger community and it is important for the caregiver to support the child's abilities and development during this stage. The child now begins to take social initiatives and compete with others, forming alliances and dealing with group affiliation. Using body and voice to break through social structures and reach others, the child explores the effect it has on its social context.

During this stage, the child also becomes aware of sex and gender. Budding sexuality and love appear as a theme and positive development during this stage requires support from the caregiver for the child's exploration. Regardless of whether the topic is the child's place in the community or its exploration of sexuality, it is important that the caregiver does not place demands on the child that are too high. With each step it takes, large or small, the child needs to feel accepted and loved in its exploration.

A relational separation is created if a child does not feel that it is loved for who they are, regardless of achievement. To defend itself against experiencing this separation and related, unregulated processes, the child is driven to focus on its achievements to gain acceptance. Love becomes connected to high performance. An achievement-driven personality is created, and since the child never experiences that its achievements are good enough, the drive to achieve never stops. If a caregiver does not accept the child's exploration of its budding sexuality, the child will experience that its longing for love has been rejected. To avoid experiencing this emotional wound and related, unregulated processes that the experience of absent love creates, the child defends itself by separating sexuality from love.

When spoken language develops at three to four years of age, children become able to experience guilt (Schore, 1994). Children at this age begin to understand social and cultural norms and the need to follow them. To comply with these norms, the child begins using a natural form of guilt to adjust its behavior. However if the child is exposed to demands that are too great, it will use this socialization process as a defense against feeling the emotional pain arising from relational separation and associated, unregulated emotional processes. By using guilt the child directs activated, unregulated anger at itself, punishing itself for not being good enough and at the same time pushing itself to ever greater achievement.

The overachieving defense system
The defense system of a person who did not get support during this stage is characterized by a dynamic and relatively inflexible attitude focused on achievement. This is an overachieving defense system that does not let the person relax and come into contact with how they feel. A person who uses this defense system tends to press themself as well as others to achieve ever better results. They defend against unregulated emotional feelings by being practically oriented and focusing energy on work, projects and tasks.

This person tends to shut down emotional feelings since they disturb their highly structured life and are associated with vulnerability. This is why others may experience them as tense and inflexible. The lack of support that the person experienced when exploring their budding sexuality resulted in sexuality and love being confused. Love is separated out and replaced by a tendency toward high levels of sexual activity focused on potency. In this way the person avoids experiencing their inner longing for love and related, unregulated emotional processes. The experience of love makes the person vulnerable and is therefore viewed as a threat. As a defense against inner vulnerability, the person avoids feeling by focusing on outer, physical reality.

Behavior

A person who uses an overachieving defense system often has a competitive mentality and wants to show how competent they are. This person has a concrete and realistic view of life, is focused, takes the initiative and possesses the strength to follow through with different tasks. The person is driven to achieve their goals but once those goals are achieved, they do not pause to appreciate the results. The person has a large capacity for work and long, hard effort does not bother them much. They are however rather inflexible and if they have a point of view, it can be difficult for them to change it and admit that someone else is right. The person is a doer who finds inactivity and idleness difficult. As compensation for the early absence of love and thereby self-love, the person enjoys showing their worth through the challenge and struggle of competition. This is why this person often gives the impression of being strong, proud and independent. They often strongly identify with their sexuality and potency. This is displayed in a tendency to both sexualize contact and quickly move toward sexual intimacy.

Integrative dynamic

For a person with an overachieving defense system to open up to unregulated emotional feelings and the process of integration, they must come into contact with the vulnerability that lies under their inflexible, hard surface.

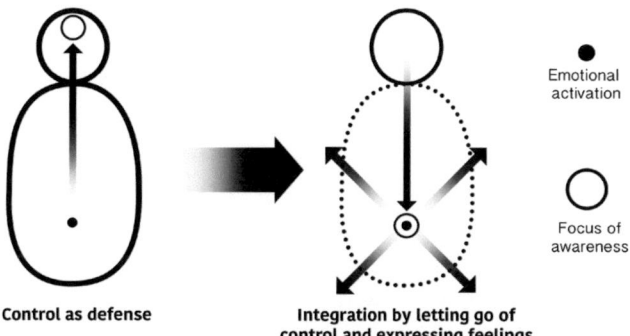

Control as defense

Integration by letting go of
control and expressing feelings

Emotional
activation

Focus of
awareness

Figure 17: The overachieving defense system and its integrative dynamic
The overachieving defense system defends against contact with unregulated emotions through self-control and a focus on achievement. The process of integration is facilitated by letting go of their hard attitude, with a focus on physical reality and opening up to vulnerability and self-acceptance.

159

This person needs to learn that they can experience the love they long for without being hard om themself and pushing themself and others. They need to let go of their inflexible attitude about what is right and wrong and accept that they do not need to be perfect. The person needs to allow themself to experience and express soft, subtle feelings, care and love. They need to live in the here-and-now instead of always thinking a few steps ahead and focusing on their next project and goal. When this person stops to feel their own vulnerability, they discover that they do not need to achieve anything to feel good. The person also needs to understand how they have confused love with sexuality and that their focus on sexual activity does not provide them with the love they need but instead strengthens the defense against love.

They need to give love a chance in their relations with others and in this way find self-love. To give in to this, a person with an overachieiving defense system needs to come into contact with and express unregulated emotions, in particular the relational pain and sadness caused by the experience of absent love.

The defense system is integrated into personality

When a child's needs are not met by its caregiver during a developmental stage, a specific defense system is automatically created in personality. Since the process of development takes place in stages, a disturbance in one stage influences the development of later stages. A person can experience different degrees of disturbance at different developmental stages and personality can contain defense dynamics from several types of defense systems in a general defense system. For instance, a personality with a mainly overachieving defense system can contain elements and behavioral dynamics from the dependent or dissociative defense systems. Also, our temperament predisposes us toward a specific defense dynamic. Fusion takes place as the defense is organized and as outer circumstances interact with our inherent temperament (see Chapter 11), an individual quality of defense behavior is formed.

Usually a person makes use of a primary defense system and its related dynamics, but in the face of special challenges or at certain times, they may use another defense system. In practice a person has one to three defense systems: one defense system is clearly dominant and one or two underlying systems appear in specific situations. Over time or through a process of development and integration, the dominant defense system may shift to one of the underlying defense systems. A person who begins emotional integration with a withholding defense system may after a while display a primarily dissociative defense.

The defense system is always active and its activity increases when our personality is threatened by unregulated emotional activation. The defense system becomes integrated into personality and our personality reflects the defense system in its normal interactions with our environment. The person we define ourselves to be with our skills and qualities is therefore in part used to serve our defense system. This means that skills and qualities which normally have a positive personal, social or cultural value do not promote our life process if they are used as part of a defense system. For instance caring for others is something everyone sees as a positive quality but if caring is used to avoid standing on one's own feet, as in the dependent defense system, it does not promote emotional integration or the integration process. This so-called positive behavior keeps the person from a threatening emotional process and provides a form of positive recognition or at least less negative attention. This kind of recognition or attention is the next best thing for a child when it is unable to experience emotional support and love. However, when we continue this behavior into adulthood without reflection, we repeat the child's defensive dynamic and in so doing actively oppose integration of natural parts of ourselves.

Chapter 11

Adult personality

Our personality is formed by our experience of relational reality in early life, first and foremost in relations with primary caregivers but also in relations with other important persons and social groups. The caregiver's selective attunement teaches the child which expressions are accepted and which are not. In this way, a child learns the basic behavior of approach and avoidance. The child learns which part of itself that is accepted and which is to be avoided. This inner dynamic is mirrored in our interactions with people and situations. We approach safe situations and avoid situations that could activate unregulated emotional processes. This behavior of approach/avoidance becomes part of our behavioral template, which we use to determine safe patterns of behavior in relation to inner and outer reality.

Developmental psychologist Daniel Stern (1985) described how children learn to use schemas or working models in interactions with their caregivers as a means of relating to and organizing existence. These models are based on our cognitive reality maps (see Chapter 7), which become the implicit, unconscious memories we use to relate to inner and outer reality (Cozolino, 2014). These memories become biological structures in the form of neural networks that influence development of the young child's brain. In this way safe behavior that sustains life is integrated into the biological organism. A child's early relational reality together with learned behavioral patterns develop into an understanding of reality that lays the groundwork for its cognitive processes, that is, the way we perceive and interpret the world.

Over the years that follow, our personality and basic understanding of life become more solidified every time we repeat learned behavioral patterns. This may change or shift somewhat during our earliest years if we experience a substantial change in external circumstances, but otherwise it remains the same. Since personality forms in layers with our earliest experiences at the center, relational disturbances and inadequate satisfaction of the need for loving care during childhood will influence later development of physical, emotional and social competencies. This is why emotional disturbances in early life often cause later disturbances in personality development.

Those parts of ourselves that have not been accepted can be regulated and integrated later in life through close, loving and stable relationships such as those found in adult partnership, close friendships and therapeutic relations. Neuroplasticity, which continues as long as we live, makes it possible for regulation later in life to eventually change neural structures of personality formed in the brain at an early age. However it is not certain that neural structures and behavior can be changed if the early disturbances were massive. Several studies of children in institutions indicate how destructive it can be to grow up without emotional support. These studies show how a lack of emotional support negatively influences physical, emotional and cognitive development. It is possible to reactivate this development later but it is often impossible to achieve normal levels of development and function (Fisher et al., 1997; Spitz, 1946).

It seems that personality does not change in any essential way after the age of six (Nave et al., 2013). As a result our basic understanding of life as adults is the same understanding we developed much earlier, when we were dependent on caregivers. We do not question this basic understanding since it is the foundation for our conscious understanding of who we are and the world around us. You might say that there is no place on our (reality) map for an alternative understanding of reality. As a result, as adults we relate to ourselves and the world around us just as we did when we were much younger even though our reality is quite different. If we learned when we were a child that life is a risky, insecure place to be in, we will continue to live according to this deep and unconscious conviction which automatically steers our behavior. As an adult we use the same basic behaviors of approach and avoidance learned early in life but now solidly rooted and supplemented by an inflexible cognitive defense that validates our behavior.

To put it bluntly, adults travel through the same landscape they traveled through as children. We may have learned sophisticated ways to hide those parts of ourselves that we find difficult and we may have found positive ways to use the abilities we have access to but our fundamental personality structure, understanding of reality and relational behavior remain basically the same.

Adult personality consists of a suitable self-organization for the organism in relation to its environment together with a defense system. The self-organized part of our personality is the part in which needs and developmental themes were regulated and naturally integrated into personality, supported by a caregiver. This part provides us with increased behavioral flexibility and the ability to meet life responsibly and in a way that is consistent with who we are. The defense system on the other hand prevents integration of unregulated emotional processes and healing of emotional wounds. It continually holds back natural processes from contact and expression. As a result, we experience inner conflicts, conflicts with others and a recurrent feeling that we are not ourselves, if we allow ourselves to feel at all.

Personality creates its world

Early relationships create our understanding of reality and this understanding becomes the way we perceive and experience reality later in life. We interpret and frame perceived reality using our learned understanding and by doing so we shape reality to conform to our preconceived understanding. This dynamic can also be found in psychoanalytic theory regarding transference and countertransference. According to this theory, as adults we recreate early relational patterns with important people and social structures (Grant & Crowley, 2002).

In the enormous amount of information our senses receive every moment, the organism's primary concern is to discover threats. This includes situations that are threatening, situations that remind us of threatening situations and situations that might develop into threatening situations. Neuroception automatically and continually scans our inner and outer environment and compares this information with previous situations experienced as threatening. Since information regarding our safety has the highest priority, it appears in the foreground and is what we mainly register and deal with. Parallel with this process of threat assessment, we notice information that is familiar to us and which confirms our understanding of life as we already know it. The organism uses its ability to recognize patterns to create predictability; we interpret our experiences on the basis of templates created early in life.

If we experienced life as threatening in early life, we will selectively perceive information that confirms this. On the other hand, if we became convinced at an early age that life is filled with possibilities, then that is the information we perceive and deal with. We shape our world to conform to a world we already know.

The dynamic of our original family and particularly our relationships with caregivers is often recreated in adult life. This occurs in important relationships, especially in love relationships but also in social groups, friendships and at work. In love relationships we tend to be attracted to people who have qualities that remind us of our early caregivers. As most of us have discovered, relations between adult couples may for example have a dynamic that is reminiscent of the relationship between mother and son or father and daughter, with conflicts similar to old, unresolved conflicts with our parents.

Steven is socially active but finds it difficult to make and keep close friends. Every time he wants to deepen a friendship, he experiences that his new friend does not share this wish. Even if the chemistry is good, he often experiences that friendships slowly evaporate if he does not actively maintain contact. It is extremely discomforting and frustrating for Steven to experience being unacknowledged and feeling unimportant. During therapy, Steven relives a situation from his first years at school when he felt lonely and isolated. In his mind's eye, he sees himself sitting alone in a room like a glass bubble. Becoming aware of this image, he feels pain and sadness well up and he experiences being closed off from friends and especially from his mother. Steven's unsatisfactory adult relationships awaken the old pain of his relationship with his mother and the feeling of being unimportant and unloved. Friends turn away from him in the same way he experienced his mother turned her back on him when he was a child.

We often choose to enter into a long-term relationship with someone who gives us a feeling of deep recognition and therefore makes us feel safe. The kinship and community felt in our original family constellation is recreated with the other person. Recognizing elements of our early family dynamic gives us a basic feeling of security even if the original family dynamic was insecure and filled with conflict. In adult relationships, the personality we have developed will often fit with our partner's personality like two pieces of a jigsaw puzzle. We are formed by our caregivers and family and this dynamic creates our behavior. When we later in life meet someone who fits into this pattern, we experience a natural and strong attraction. We feel at home with them.

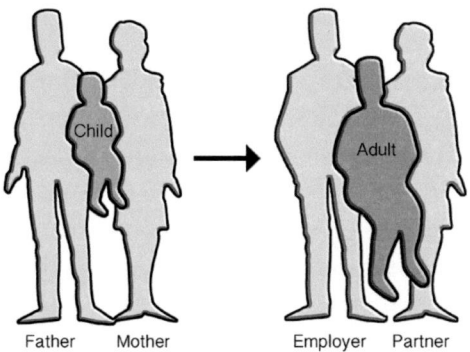

Father   Mother   Employer   Partner

Figure 18: Our personality seeks a known relational context
Personality is formed to fit our early relational contexts and we tend to create or find ourselves in similar relational contexts later in life. Like a piece in a puzzle, we find a context into which we fit.

The security and attraction we feel for something we recognize can be so strong that in extreme cases a person may choose to remain in a physically or psychologically destructive relationship for a long time although recognizing the danger.

Since adult relationships are permeated with a dynamic established much earlier, they also activate unregulated emotions, defenses and conflicts from that time. An early and partially conflicted dynamic is reenacted together with a longing for the love and acceptance that we did not get from our caregiver. Since we automatically defend ourselves against activated, unregulated emotions, we tend to repeat conflicts and difficulties from our original family in close adult relationships. For instance we may feel anger and sadness because we experience that we are not acknowledged. At the same time, recreation of an old, unresolved relational dynamic opens up the possibility of regulation and personal development. Becoming aware of dysfunctional relational patterns in ourselves, we have an opportunity to integrate previously unregulated emotional processes. In this way adult relationships give us the opportunity to resolve inner conflicts and heal emotional wounds. This is why close adult relationships offer the most potent paths of development and are an opportunity to become familiar with and accept more of who we are.

The basic themes of personality

If we zoom out and look at the big picture of our life, we see that conflicts and problems encountered in life tend to resemble each other. We often see two or three general themes showing up in various situations with a common dynamic and complex of problems. As an example, let us look at the case of Pamela:

Pamela began a therapeutic process because she experienced relational problems at work and with her husband. She experienced that her manager did not listen to her or take her seriously at work and felt that her husband did not support her at home. She could see that not being listened to was a theme that constantly popped up in her conflicts. She had also begun to have physical problems. Pamela was tired, slept poorly and she often felt like boiling over in frustration without knowing what to do about it.

After a few therapy sessions, Pamela came to realize that she had always felt lonely as a child and that the related pain and anger were unbearable. She had been unable to express these emotions in her relationship with her mother because that would have led to her being even more lonely. Pamela had not been acknowledged and her natural, activated emotions had not been regulated. To avoid the pain of her early broken relationship with her mother, she was forced to keep anger away and defend herself against it. She had learned to use submissive behavior as her defense against anger and to avoid coming in contact with her anger. Not wanting to seem too forceful and thereby push people away, she began to generally avoid expressing what she felt, in particular when she experienced that she was not respected. She was able to maintain this unconscious behavior for a time but it had begun to wear her down and resulted in bursts of frustration.

Over the course of the therapeutic process, Pamela discovered that these two areas of conflict had a common theme: she refrained from raising objections because

167

she was afraid of pushing others away and instead appeared to others as sweet and accommodating. Because of this attitude, she was not respected. Using submissive behavior learned in early life, Pamela had unconsciously created the conflicts she was experiencing in her adult relationships both at work and at home.

A few basic emotional wounds are the source of many conflicts and problems we experience in life. They later lead to dissociation in which we stop natural emotional activation and defend ourselves against emotional activation in new situations. This creates new wounds that confirm our earlier experience. For example if we learned early in life that acting on our anger when our boundaries are violated makes a situation worse, we later hold back anger when it activates. By holding back anger we make it possible for our boundaries to be violated again, creating new traumas and new emotional wounds. Later emotional wounds are in this way the result of basic emotional wounds and connected to them.

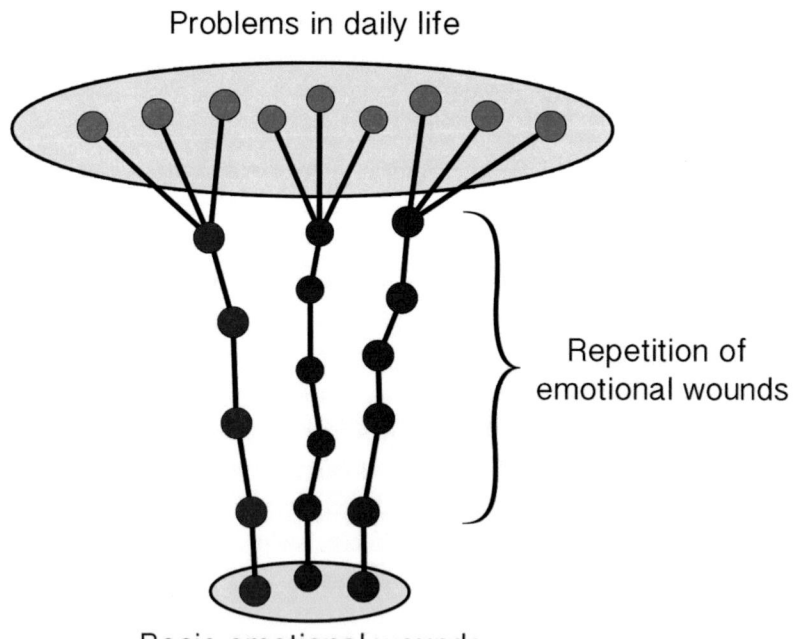

Figure 19: Basic emotional wounds and their symptoms in daily life

Figure 19 shows how problems and challenges in everyday life are connected to basic emotional wounds. One example of a basic wound is when an infant experiences separation from an emotionally unavailable caregiver after birth. This is a life-threatening experience that the infant cannot deal with and the infant emotionally dissociates from the situation. After this, a second wound comes when the caregiver is unable to emotionally embrace the infant's bubbling joy of life and instead closes down. The infant learns to avoid spontaneous expressions of natural happiness and frustration. As a pupil in school, the child has learned to be generally withdrawn and therefore finds it difficult to develop social relationships. This causes a frustrating loneliness, new emotional wounds and the process continues. A series of similar wounds follow one after the other and as an adult, the person finds it difficult to establish and maintain close relationships and experiences isolation. These relational problems are symptoms of our basic emotional wounds and withheld emotional processes in everyday life.

Early in life, we learn to deal with similar situations and avoid unregulated emotions using our defense system. We repeat the process and create new wounds. In this way basic emotional wounds resulting in withheld emotional responses express themselves as relational conflicts in daily life.

The core self: the source of personality

Personality is a functionally organized, relatively stable ensemble of behavioral patterns that expresses the human life process. To put it another way, early relational interactions between the life process and its environment organize and shape the life process into the personality that we identify as ourselves. This individual life process and energy come from the source of personality: the *core self.* The organism's core self consists of relatively stable, constantly repeated and developing biological and neurological processes (Damasio, 2006) that express themselves through vitality affects and emotions. If these natural expressions are stopped, disturbances arise in the human organism and its natural development. To a great extent a balanced, healthy personality functions in resonance with processes in the core self.

Temperament
The core self's unique quality is called *temperament*, which is the inherent, individual quality on which personality is built. We are not born as a tabula

169

rasa; we are born with different preconditions. Our development is based on these basic preconditions and this is the main reason why children with the same upbringing, such as siblings, can have quite different personalities. We cannot change our temperament; all we can do is relate to it and support its integration into personality (Siegel, 2010).

Biologically, temperament is connected to our DNA and properties of our nervous system which together are the functional starting point for the biological system. As such they are the basis of our relational system, for example the amount of sensory stimulation we need before a response activates as well as the quality of that response.

Temperament also creates individual personality traits such as inclinations and interests. Children react differently to the same stimuli due to individual differences in temperament and they therefore have different needs in order to achieve optimal development. Just as there is no single best way for adults to live a balanced life, there is no single best way to raise a child; different children need to be treated differently. Some children need clear boundaries; others need soft boundaries; still others need to find their own way. Some children are active and need a lot of physical activity while others are less active and need peace and quiet. Favorable child development is the result of a positive interplay between the child's temperament and its environment.

Expressions of the core self

The organism's primary driving force is its needs, which cause the organism to release energy and focus its activity. Needs motivate the organism and point out the direction for development. Each level of need, from developmental needs (both physical and relational) to higher, more complex human needs (Maslow, 1946) is expressed through homeostatic response processes. The human organism is in continuous development toward higher systemic complexity and efficiency, from basic needs to more refined expressions of need. When one level of needs is satisfied, the next level appears naturally: from the basic need for physical survival, to social needs such as community and family all the way up to the need for self-realization through creativity, spontaneity and altruism. The development and integration of needs are natural expressions of our life process. It is a lively, continuous process of ever greater complexity. If we become sick this process may be interrupted while focus shifts to recovery but the development of needs can also continue through a period of illness when we discover and integrate new sides of ourselves. A human organism's potential is in this way the result of interactions between our life process and our environment, and our potential expresses itself in the development of increasingly complex needs.

This description of human developmental processes may be compared to the process of evolutionary change known as *phylogenesis* (Laszlo, 1996). Phylogenesis is a natural system's self-creative process caused by interaction with its environment. Living in a changing environment naturally results in life finding new paths. In a similar way our *core self* expresses itself in a self-creative way through personality as it interacts with our changing environment.

Our core self is the dynamic source that forms personality through needs. The extent to which we experience being in contact with ourselves depends on how open we are to connection with this living process. The intensity of this experience is related to our ability to follow our needs and integrate the core self's life processes into personality.

Expressions of the core self in the form of needs, affects and emotions enter consciousness and are understood through feeling. Feeling makes it possible for us to navigate and decide if a behavior expresses who we are, that is, if it is an expression of our core self and needs or if it is an expression of our defense system, which is in conflict with the core self. Natural expression in resonance with our core self is uncomplicated, without inner conflict and promotes life. It is interesting to note that Carl Jung maintained that the goal of life is to fully express who we are without conflict between our life process and our personality. The integration process described in this book is a process of learning to express, regulate and trust this autonomic, self-regulating process through experience. Our core self points the way through needs and responses and we, that is our cognitive self-awareness, experience more flow and balance in life when we listen to this process, learn from it and become its vessel.

Model over the human organism

We can summarize the human organism in a model of its main processes and internal dynamic. This model is a simplification of a complex living system; as with the brain, the human organism functions as a unit and not through interactions among clearly separated functional levels.

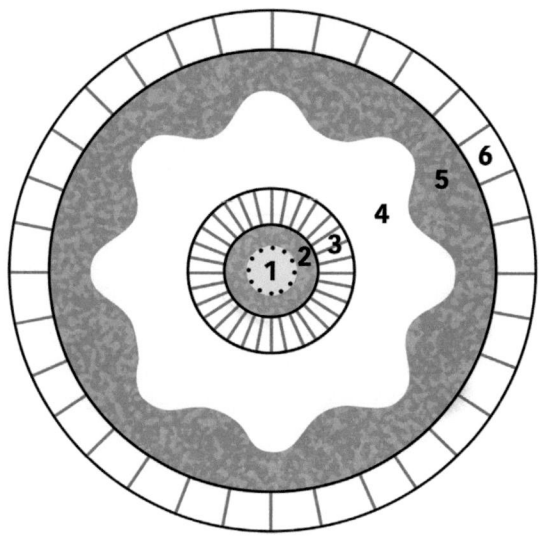

Figure 20: A human being is a living organism
This model consists of two main parts: the core self and personality.
The core self consists of the life process (1) and individual temperament (2).
Personality consists of basic personality structure (3), integrated personality (4), a defense system (5) and cognitive self-awareness (6).

The core self (1, 2) is at our center. This is partially or entirely the biological center of human beings out of which life processes emanate. Life processes (1) express themselves as affective responses moving through our body and personality. The structure of the core self is its temperament (2), a pre-programmed template which points out direction. It directs the organization of personality, and determines how the life process will be expressed as well as its precise quality of expression. Temperament is the individual quality of a human being that gives each individual its unique expression in the world.

After this we come to the structure of personality (layers 3, 4, 5 & 6), which manifests the core self's processes and determines how they are expressed in relational reality. If a child receives the support it needs in its first years of life, personality self-organizes. Personality's first layer is the basic structure of personality (3) and the rest of personality is built on and around this. Personality's basic structure is the first organized layer of personality, created immediately before and after birth during the developmental stage of existence. If this organization is disturbed, varying degrees of deficiency in basic stability will arise. Depending on the amount of disturbance, the result may be a vulnerable personality or if disturbances are more serious, a tendency for mental illness.

Influenced by basic personality structure, the next layers of personality are organized by two processes: natural integration (4) and the defense system (5). Personality's behavioral patterns are organized in relation to the organism's emotional response processes. These emotional response processes are either naturally integrated in resonance with the core self's expressions and processes (4) or they are stopped and defended against by our defense system (5). Our defense system shields our personality from unregulated emotional processes. The processes and behaviors of layers (4) and (5) are intertwined in personality. Since the organism always prioritizes survival, a major part of our personality's behavior is influenced by our defense system. This means that the defense system's organization and dynamic may be clearly seen in normal behavior and that the defense system often determines the way we act. Since the affective and emotional processes that create personality are physical response processes, personality also manifests itself in a somatic, physical dimension. Our defense against unregulated and withheld responses shapes our body and we may experience the muscular consequences of unregulated emotions (see Chapter 12).

The outer layer of personality consists of cognitive self-awareness (6), which includes our cognitive focus and behaviors and is a direct consequence of personality's organization in layers (3), (4) and (5). This layer consists of our cognitive attitude toward ourselves and our environment, that is, how we cognitively relate to incoming stimuli and where we focus awareness. We are able to abstract from the core self's processes, which are the basis of self-awareness and use this ability to defend against unregulated needs, emotions and other affects. By moving conscious focus away from inner conflicts in deeper layers of personality, the cognitive defense enables us to shield ourselves from emotional contact with those conflicts. We make ourselves totally unaware of any conflict or emotional activation at all. All our attention turns to our thoughts and outward to our environment as our cognitive defense keeps us unaware that we are defending ourselves against our own responses.

Since this process can be consciously influenced, we are able to direct cognitive focus back on layers of personality that are somatically manifested (layers 3, 4 & 5). If we do this, we experience discomfort from inner conflicts and it becomes possible to feel our unregulated emotions. This is the first step in an organism's process of self-integration.

PART IV

WHOLENESS DISTURBED

Chapter 12

Emotional trauma

To enhance the ability to live in resonance with ourselves as an organism we must learn to support the integration of unregulated emotional processes. In learning to do this, the first step is to acquire a deep understanding of the dynamics of the organism's emotional disturbances and how emotional traumas influence us.

The function of all emotional activation is to initiate and support a pre-programmed physical response and expression focused on survival, either physical or relational in a social setting. Emotional activation can take the form of a relational approach, as when we feel happy to see an old friend again, or in the form of relational distancing, as when anger activates in order to protect us, set boundaries and physically survive. An emotion's physical activation subsides when emotional expression achieves its desired result, for instance when a boundary is established or when we discover that emotional activation is no longer necessary. When this happens the emotion's effect on the organism disappears, processes of the parasympathetic nervous system are activated and enter the foreground, and body and mind become calm. However when an emotional activation is connected to an emotional wound from an early relational separation, this natural process is disturbed and our defense system shuts down all expression. The activated emotion is halted without being completed.

The dynamic of trauma from emotional wounds caused by relational separation is basically the same as the dynamic of shock trauma. Shock trauma occurs in extreme situations when, at any age and without warning, we are confronted with the fragility of life and the reality of death. It occurs in sudden situations of high emotional intensity such as war, accidents or abuse. It can also occur when we are confronted with the misfortune or death of others. In these extreme situations, emotional intensity is so high that personality cannot take it in, which is to say we cannot regulate it. By taking a closer look at the dynamics of shock trauma, we can learn about the process of relational trauma and early emotional wounds.

Peter Levine, a pioneer in trauma research, has described how the human organism's biological and physical survival systems are violently activated in life-threatening situations (Levine, 2010). An example: if you are brutally mugged one evening, your automatic response might be to resist or run away. If this survival response does not help against the threat and you experience that you are unable to escape, emotional activation cannot be completed. The activated emotional process is halted before it can be expressed and completed. This results in a physically tense stiffness or a motionless collapse. Phrases such as "terror-stricken" and "paralyzed by fear" describe the physical experience of this intense fear. Cognitive dissociation takes place simultaneously with these physical reactions and attention shifts away from what is happening and the feeling of threatening emotional charge. In this way we automatically close down awareness of our incomplete survival activation. The initiated emotional expression's charge is thereafter trapped in the body through an automatic survival strategy that the organism activates and carries out without conscious involvement.

One of the reasons a situation results in shock trauma is that the response activation lacks a build-up phase. In shock trauma, we are unable to relate to the situation and prepare for what is about to happen. Response activation is instantaneous and intense and at almost the same time its expression is shut down more or less totally. The body and nervous system are in a situation similar to what would happen if you pressed down on a car's accelerator and brake pedals at the same time: the motor races at full speed but the car does not go anywhere.

Shock trauma results in both physical and cognitive disturbances. The body may feel stiff, alien and insensitive. As long as emotional charge is not allowed to naturally express itself, the body remains in a condition of stress and relaxation is impossible. In a situation such as this, it is often difficult to focus and collect our thoughts and our thoughts often have a negative charge strongly influenced by fear. We distance ourselves cognitively from present reality and our contact with feelings, particularly from the feeling of threatening emotional activation. Cognition's anchor in physical reality is thereby lost. Simple, everyday routines may suddenly seem difficult or impossible to perform.

The human organism's three defense strategies

According to Stephen Porges' polyvagal theory (Porges, 2011), a human organism has three possible automatic response strategies when faced with a threat: social engagement, mobilization and immobilization. These correspond to the three developmental levels of the brain and nervous system described in Chapter 2. They use the sympathetic and parasympathetic nervous systems as well as the tenth cranial nerve, also known as the vagus nerve.

The first response strategy: Social engagement
Social engagement is the latest response strategy developed in the nervous system and it is transmitted via the vagus nerve. Using the ventral branch of the vagus nerve (the myelinated vagus which runs down the front of the body), we can adjust sympathetic emotional activation, enabling us to consciously act in a threatening situation (Rothschild, 2017). This branch of the vagus nerve assists in lowering heartrate and stimulates facial musculature to greater focus and involvement in relational interactions (Fredrickson, 2013). The response strategy helps us make contact with whoever or whatever threatens us and create a relationship. This ability to connect the brain's self-aware areas in the cortex with older areas makes it possible for us to self-regulate emotional activation without affective action. This strategy supports calm social behavior in which we can regain our composure and remain open and receptive to our surroundings. It is the only strategy that supports the organism's growth and development, which explains why it is the strategy used in affect regulation. With this response strategy we can meet the challenges of life and grow with them.

The second response strategy: Mobilization
This is the fight-or-flight response that activates the sympathetic nervous system and the HPA (Hypothalamic-Pituitary-Adrenal) axis, which releases stress hormones. It is the survival activation of mammals which autonomously mobilizes the organism to immediate, intense muscular action that can continue for a long time. To survive, we can either fight or flee. This response strategy

prepares and activates the body by allocating resources to the striated skeletal muscles used in the situation.

The third response strategy: Immobilization

In evolutionary terms, immobilization is the oldest response strategy and we share this strategy with reptiles. The dorsal branch of the vagus nerve which runs down the back of the body activates as a defense when a threatening situation cannot be resolved through activation of the sympathetic nervous system (Ogden et al., 2006). Using this response, heart rate and respiration in humans and other mammals slow down, muscle tone relaxes and we appear to "play dead". When an organism is brought to a stop in the face of a threat that it can neither fight nor flee, the immobilization reaction is a response strategy that lowers the organism's metabolism and focuses the organism solely on staying alive. This activation is for example seen in different kinds of abuse when a victim cannot escape and therefore stops resisting. An important effect of this response is that it raises the pain threshold and reduces the experience of pain in the situation. Many victims of physical abuse have even reported that they felt no pain at all during the abuse (van der Kolk et al., 1996). In the animal world, the immobilization response is connected to other functions of survival as well. Some predators can only identify prey that moves and others lose interest in lifeless prey because it signals that the flesh has gone bad.

The principle governing when these three strategies are activated is the same as that governing all neural structures. Generally, later structures inhibit or control earlier structures. When a structure developed later cannot ward off a threat, an earlier structure takes over (Jackson, 1958). In a similar way, the first response strategy to be activated in a threatening situation is social engagement. We initiate proactive social engagement and consciously communicate with whoever or whatever threatens us. In this interaction, emotional activation is self-regulated and we remain open and receptive in the situation. If social engagement does not resolve the threatening situation, mobilization and the sympathetic nervous system activate and automatically take over. This is the emotionally intense response strategy that activates muscles and fixed action patterns. If this strategy does not resolve the threatening situation, immobilization occurs. Immobilization is a low-intensity strategy that reduces affective charge to a minimum. The organism plays dead in a final attempt to survive.

In general, these strategies activate one after the other in order. When social engagement fails, it is replaced by mobilization; when that fails, immobilization activates. However when other strategies are autonomously assessed as being insufficient in an extreme situation, the strategy of immobilization may activate at once. It might also be that previous experiences have taught the organism that mobilization does not resolve threatening situations, making immobilization the second activated strategy when social engagement fails. Correspondingly, autonomous mobilization or immobilization may be activated before social engagement is activated and tested.

The window of tolerance

The strategy of social engagement is a basic condition for optimal biological, emotional and cognitive growth and development. When an organism is able to use this strategy, the organism is within its *window of tolerance*. Our window of tolerance is our capacity for arousal, that is, the amount of emotional charge we can regulate, allow and relate to without activating the other two autonomous response strategies (Siegel, 1999; Ogden et al., 2006). Our window of tolerance widens through expression and regulation of emotional charge. This means that the more we express emotion within our window of tolerance, the more we increase our capacity for emotional arousal without autonomous activation of the other two strategies.

The window of tolerance can be compared to a muscle. If you train a muscle to its limit, it becomes larger and stronger. In a similar way, emotions expressed at the limit of our window of tolerance stretch our capacity for arousal and increase our ability to handle higher levels of intensity.

A well-functioning and stable personality normally uses the strategy of social engagement, which inhibits the other two autonomous response strategies. We meet the challenges of life and allow emotional activation without triggering the other two autonomous response strategies. A person who has experienced shock trauma or relational trauma will have a narrower window of tolerance for a specific emotional activation and the two autonomous response strategies will more easily activate in the face of a threat. This is why people suffering from shock trauma can usually only tolerate low emotional charge before the other strategies automatically activate. This reduces their ability to regulate and relate to even low levels of emotional activation in daily life, which in turn inhibits cognitive ability and the ability to participate in social relations.

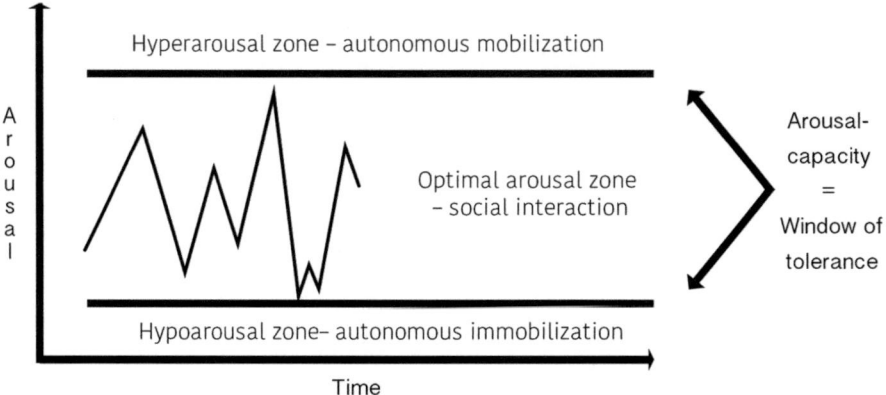

Figure 21: The window of tolerance (Ogden et al., 2006)
Our arousal capacity is the intensity of emotion that personality can regulate without having to defend against it. An unregulated emotion can be regulated when its intensity is more or less within our window of tolerance. If arousal is too great, a strategy of mobilization or immobilization will autonomously activate.

The same dynamics appear in relational trauma. If a specific emotion is not allowed, the organism learns to activate the other two autonomous defense strategies at the first sign of the emotion's activation. The organism has a narrow window of tolerance for this emotion and as a result our ability to relate to this specific emotional activation is limited. As a consequence, our emotional free-dom of action is restricted and we begin to arrange our life to avoid situations that might activate the threatening emotion.

Emotional wounds cause three types of somatic chronic immobility

When activation of the two autonomous response strategies (mobilization and immobilization) cannot be completed as in the cases of shock trauma and relational trauma, it has consequences for the physical organism. A physical, emotional response that has been activated but not completed remains incomplete and does not dissolve. Instead the autonomous response strategy stays active in the body in the same way as in shock trauma. A chronic disturbance in the organism is created and this dynamic causes disturbances in normal physical and emotional regulation.

The physical consequences of an incomplete emotional process may be clearly seen in the striated skeletal muscles that we use to perform the emotion's fixed action pattern. When mobilization's physically tense, sympathetic activation is not expressed and brought to completion or when an immobilized collapse is not completed, the response strategy's action pattern freezes. Muscles in the organism continue to display the activated response strategy even after the threat is over.

This leads to chronic muscular immobility which intensifies when threatening, unregulated emotions are activated. This *chronic immobility* takes the form of either *chronic mobilization,* that is, chronic muscular tension (muscular hypertonicity) or *chronic immobilization,* that is, chronic muscular collapse (muscular hypotonicity). Intensification of chronic immobility can be felt in the body. For example if we do not speak out to defend ourselves when someone violates our boundaries, anger naturally activates in the situation but its expression is held back by autonomously intensified chronic mobilization (increased muscular tension). Later that same day we still feel strong tension in our neck.

Incomplete automatic response strategies continue because the organism continues to perceive a threat. In the case of shock trauma, the threat is no longer external but a consequence of what has happened. A withheld emotional response risks overwhelming personality and is therefore held back by chronic immobility. In the case of relational trauma, chronic immobility is a defense against unregulated emotions, but there is also another reason for chronic immobility. Repeated experience of a caregiver who does not regulate specific emotions causes the organism to improve the efficiency of its defense by not letting the defense completely disappear when it is no longer needed (Ogden, 2015). The defense is continually activated as the most efficient way to keep unregulated emotions from expression. The logic behind this is: the best defense is a defense that never ceases.

Incomplete response strategies appear in three possible forms of chronic immobility: chronic mobilization, chronic immobilization and chronic shock. These are all chronic states in which a response strategy is held in a fixed position after the immediate threat is over.

Chronic mobilization

Chronic mobilization is a form of chronic immobility that occurs when a response strategy of mobilization does not complete and dissolve. It is discernable as a fixed, tense, sympathetically activated physical state. The quality of this state is similar to the muscle tension that precedes action at the start of the fight-or-flight response. Awareness is in a hyper-ready state of orientation and increased charge, a prelude to activation of the fight-or-flight response. This heightened preparedness is used to identify and evaluate any threat before a response is triggered (Ogden et al., 2006). If a threat is perceived as persistent, the organism remains in a state of sympathetically activated immobility. The body is kept in a state of fixed tension in which the nervous system and muscles are prepared to carry out fixed action patterns. Tension in the muscles of the upper body and jaws can be felt in particular.

Chronic mobilization causes a feeling of muscular stiffness and a slightly irritated attitude. It is like a pressure cooker that occasionally lets pressure escape in reactive outbursts of irritation and frustration. These outbursts provide only temporary relief however, since they do not remove the cause of excess pressure. By maintaining sympathetic activation and muscle tension, we gain indirect control over the cause of the pressure and at the same time keep the focus of awareness away from contact with the underlying emotional activation. This type of chronic immobility is often seen in people with mild cases of personality disturbance, often referred to as "being neurotic".

Chronic immobilization

Chronic immobilization is a form of chronic immobility that occurs when a response strategy of immobilization does not complete and disappear so that muscles remain in an immobilized, collapsed state. This is the continuation of a parasympathetically activated collapse which keeps unregulated emotional charge from entering into striated skeletal muscles. In chronic immobilization, striated muscles lack tonus and appear limp, kinetic potential is nearly non-existent. This protects us from emotional activation by numbing us. Normally, emotional charge manifests itself in skeletal muscles and is expressed in action; here, there is collapse. Emotional charge cannot be detected and in this way it is kept away from our awareness. Striated skeletal muscles appear lifeless, as if dead, which may also be the way the person feels (Levine, 1997). Chronic immobilization is often seen in people with more severe personality disturbances.

Chronic shock

A shock trauma can lead to a form of chronic immobility called chronic shock. This is a fixed state of highly intense collapse. Chronic shock is caused by a response intensity so overwhelming that it causes the nervous system to shut down, resulting in an inner collapse (Rothschild, 2017). This is a parasympathetic shock reaction to an unbearable level of sympathetic response intensity. In this form of chronic immobility, both the sympathetic and parasympathetic nervous systems are activated at the same time. This causes muscle contraction and an experience of paralysis (Siegel, 1999). A person in contact with the threatening emotion behind chronic shock feels terrified and immobile. The experience is one of being stuck in a terrible situation without being able to escape.

These three types of chronic immobility are the organism's autonomic defense against contact with a threatening emotional charge. The defense against unregulated emotion is therefore not simply cognitive but also highly physical. An unregulated emotional process is first automatically stopped through increased chronic immobility. Afterward, our cognitive defense shifts the focus of our attention away from the withheld, interrupted emotion.

To a greater or lesser extent, every human being suffers from both chronic mobilization and chronic immobilization. When faced with a threatening, unregulated emotional activation, the type of chronic immobility that increases for a given individual depends on that individual's previous experiences.

The memory of trauma

Trauma and emotional disturbances continue to influence our life because the organism remembers them. Human memory can be divided into explicit memory and implicit memory. We can recall explicit memories and bring them into our awareness in daily life, while implicit memories cannot be recalled.

Explicit memory consists of memories that may be sensory, semantic, episodic, narrative or autobiographical. We use explicit memory to remember people, places, cultural norms, language and other learned facts. Explicit memory is the narrative base for our personality and self-understanding. It is constructed as a conscious story of our life and everything we have learned. Explicit memory makes us aware of how the physical world fits together as a whole. We are also able to recall these memories to process and expand on our knowledge.

Implicit memory consists of memories that are sensory, emotional and procedural (for instance, how to ride a bicycle). Implicit memory contains everything else we have learned about life, a background understanding to both our self-perception and the way we interpret reality. Implicit memories create a basic structure for both personality and explicit memory in the form of reality maps created early in life (see Chapter 7). We view the contents of implicit memory as given facts of life, a basic understanding of the world that is not questioned. Relational and emotional memories (that is, the way we understand and interpret emotional and relational reality) are primarily stored in implicit memory and constitute the basis of our behavior.

Since we are unable to remember much from before the age of two to four, we have few explicit memories about how our understanding of reality was formed during those first years of life. Children have what is called infantile amnesia, which means that they learn things without registering them in explicit memory (Cozolino, 2014). The absence of explicit memories from our earliest years is due to the fact that the brain's conscious memory center develops later in the hippocampus and other areas of the brain. Experiences and learning during our first years are instead registered in more primitive areas of the brain and stored as a basic understanding of life in order to promote safety and survival. This is where for instance our basic approach/avoidance behavior is established.

Early emotional wounds are also stored in implicit memory and become part of our background understanding of life.

Infantile amnesia explains why we may find it difficult to understand where our (sometimes problematic) relational behavior comes from and why we feel the way we do about life and our environment. Our self-aware and cognitively focused personality would like to understand why we are the way we are and why we experience what we experience. Personality wants a story that provides predictability and security in life, but the closest we can come to our earliest, conscious memories is in vague recollections of sensory impressions and moods without direct connection to a comprehensible narrative.

Emotional memory

Emotionally intense experiences are stored in implicit memory for safety reasons, as described previously (see "The memory of fear" in Chapter 5). The organism learns to activate fear in the face of real danger and in potentially dangerous situations. Once we have learned that a particular situation is a threat to our safety, situations that resemble it will also activate fear.

This dynamic applies to all emotional processes. We autonomously and unconsciously learn to connect certain relational situations with specific emotional activations. For instance, some people become angry if they are not listened to while others become sad and still others do not care. The same situation triggers different emotional responses in different people due to their personal emotional memories. Antonio Damasio called these learned emotional responses secondary emotions as opposed to primary emotions, which innately activate in a similar way for everyone (Damasio, 1994).

Emotional memories and learned response activations are connected to emotional wounds. The organism activates an emotional secondary response due to an earlier emotional wound. We learn to activate a specific secondary emotion in a certain situation. The situation itself does not trigger emotional activation; it triggers an emotional memory which in turn activates the emotion. The secondary emotion is activated solely because the situation resembles an earlier situation and relational context, not because of the actual situation we are in. This dynamic applies to most emotional response activation that we experience in life.

It can be difficult to free ourselves from implicit memories and their associated emotional responses. As explained in Chapter 5, memories of fear have a dynamic that is fundamental to survival and these memories are difficult to erase. The human organism prefers to activate fear a thousand times for no reason than forgetting to activate fear the one time danger is real. Learning is quick; unlearning is a long, slow process.

Unlearning an emotional secondary response involves expressing and regulating the emotion in a safe environment (see Chapter 13). In this way, previously withheld expression of an unaccepted emotional process can be completed without negative consequences. The emotional wound heals in this process and its associated implicit memory is erased (Schore, 2012). This is a process that slowly and gradually regulates more and more of an unregulated emotion. However, a basic emotional wound and its emotional memory may never completely disappear; a learned secondary emotion may continue to activate for the rest of our lives. This shows that it is important to not simply free ourself from threatening emotional activation but also to learn self-regulation, that is, learn to accept and deal with activated emotional responses to minimize their negative effects.

Trauma shuts down memory

In the case of emotional trauma, an interesting dynamic takes place between narrative, explicit memory and emotional, implicit memory. After a shock trauma the victim often has no clear idea or understanding of the traumatic situation. A victim of shock trauma experiences only fragments of the traumatic event. Research into trauma has shown that when shock trauma is reactivated in a laboratory setting, the brain's frontal lobe, which includes areas of the brain used to put feelings into words, shuts down (van der Kolk, 2014).

In shock trauma our explicit, conscious, verbal memory and implicit, emotional memory lose contact with each other. Explicit and implicit memory normally cooperate, which helps us understand what we are feeling and provides greater behavioral flexibility. However when there is massive activation of the emotional system as in shock trauma, the emotional system takes over. Conscious contact with areas of the brain such as the hippocampus and thalamus, responsible for integration of memory data, is broken off. This is why trauma is not stored in verbal memory as a continuous, logical narrative. We remember only fragments of sensory impressions, images, sounds and physical and emotional experience. In the midst of trauma, the organism shuts down our ability to understand what is happening. Our memory of trauma is broken into pieces that neither fit together nor make sense. This dynamic is a defense against reactivation of withheld, unregulated emotions from the trauma. When we cannot remember what happened, we are kept from reactivating unregulated emotions that have become a threat to the stability of personality.

As a result of this dynamic, victims of shock trauma often experience flashbacks. A flashback occurs when a specific sensory impression in the present triggers a fragment of emotional experience and cognitive memory from the traumatic event. The person relives a part of the traumatic experience, sometimes so intensely that they believe that they have completely or partially returned to the chaotic, traumatic situation. Flashbacks can occur both shortly after a traumatic event or much later. A person may even experience flashbacks many years after a traumatic event without being able to connect them with the event or even understand what is causing them.

Sensory impressions or thoughts associated with a traumatic event such as a sound, a situation, an image or a scent can be stimuli that trigger an emotional memory and cause a flashback. The sensory impression functions as a key that unlocks memory and opens up a floodgate of incomplete emotional processes otherwise held back and hidden from consciousness. The released memory takes over consciousness and is experienced as real. In this way a flashback takes over a person's perception of reality. The person is overwhelmed by unpleasant feelings and inner images from the traumatic event when emotional pressure escapes and floods consciousness.

To dissolve, regulate and integrate shock trauma, a procedure in trauma therapy involves careful focus on physical experiences and emotions that are successively triggered. In this process, scattered memory fragments are slowly permitted to organically come together and cognitive understanding is built bit by bit. Emotional integration gradually takes place and the halted, unregulated emotional response can eventually be expressed without overwhelming consciousness. Emotional expression and regulation lead to memory integration, which in turn brings successively greater understanding of the traumatic event.

This is a reciprocal process in which emotional expression generates cognitive understanding, which leads to stability and enables stronger emotional expression. The reciprocal process between expression and understanding continues until unregulated emotions from the trauma have been regulated and integrated into personality. Cognitive fragments of memory fall into place like puzzle pieces joining to form a complete picture that enables us to understand what happened. In other words, a person does not have to try to comprehend what happened; a narrative understanding of a trauma comes about as a natural consequence of successive emotional regulation.

To a great extent the process of dissolving relational trauma is the same as the process involved in shock trauma. Situations, physical experiences and thoughts activate emotional memories from a relational trauma just as in shock trauma. The emotional activation of relational trauma does not however intensify as rapidly or as much as in flashbacks from shock trauma. Our defense system stops a great deal of the emotional activation from relational trauma but does not keep it from influencing cognition and distorting our understanding of reality. It still influences us, expressing itself in a behavior of avoidance (LeDoux, 2015). If we for example become angry when someone does not respect us, we implicitly believe that the other person wants to hurt us. Our anger is not allowed to express itself and we withdraw from the other person despite the fact that they may not have meant to hurt us. Another example is when sadness activates because someone forgot to show up for a meeting and we believe the person does not like us. In both examples, emotional activation comes from an earlier relational trauma that left an emotional wound in memory. Something in the present resembles an earlier situation and activates its associated unregulated emotion. The unregulated emotion's activation causes us to interpret the situation in the same context as earlier. We automatically assume that present reality is the same as past reality.

Body memory: the somatic consequences of emotional wounds
A body expresses its history and as such our body is part of our implicit emotional memory. Our body is to a certain extent shaped by the two types of chronic

immobility caused by emotional wounds. The following example shows how an emotional wound from absent need satisfaction and its associated unregulated emotion physically manifests itself in the form of chronic muscular immobility caused by the interruption of fixed action patterns:

> A sad child reaches up and out with its arms and eyes, seeking closeness and comfort from its caregiver. If this reaching out is not acknowledged or if it is rejected, anger or sadness will naturally activate. If rejection continues and is repeated many times, it may result in an emotional wound: an experience of painful, chronic, inner relational separation. The emotional wound causes the child to defend against expression of its needs and emotions in similar situations. As a result, chronic immobilization occurs in muscles that naturally express needs and emotions, for example arm and chest muscles used to reach up and out and eye muscles that express the need for contact. A muscular collapse takes place in order to avoid contact with relational pain. At the same time, withheld anger keeps muscles tense in the jaws, upper arms and back. As a result, the upper body is collapsed in the front and overly tense in the back. Muscle defense and body memory fixates the child in a position that avoids pain and unregulated, activated emotions. With the objective of quickly defending the child and later the adult in similar situations, this body position becomes chronic.

When a person repeatedly holds back emotional expression, it affects the body's muscles, posture and movement patterns. Function precedes form in our biological body and the body is shaped by repeated patterns of movement (Todd, 1959). The body's physical form is shaped in direct relation to the physical consequences of emotional disturbances in the form of chronically tense or collapsed striated muscles. In this process, our body becomes part of our defense against emotional contact. The body's physiology, posture and movement adapt automatically to our defense in order to secure predictability and stability for survival.

The body of a child is influenced during early development by interactions with caregivers. The way a child's expressions are received has physical consequences and over time the child's patterns of movement and its posture become a living map of its history. We learn what we are allowed to express and what we are not. We learn what we can approach with openness and what we must avoid and defend against. Our body automatically relates to these experiences and is formed by them. If we for example have learned that we must constantly achieve to be loved, it may lead us to always be attentive and goal oriented. Our striated muscles will become generally hypertonic and ready for action and this muscle tension will at the same time keep us from feeling the sadness of not having been accepted and loved for who we are.

A specific defense system is established due to a disturbance in a specific stage of child development and each defense system has its own physical organization. Each defense system results in a specific pattern of hypertonic (tense) and hypotonic (collapsed) muscles that affect posture and movement. We can therefore see the defense system a person uses in their posture and movement, thereby gaining an understanding of the person's underlying emotional disturbances and complex of problems (Totton, 2001; Lowen, 2003; Marcher, 2010). Personality is literally made flesh. Formed by emotional processes, our body mirrors our personality. With this understanding of how emotional disturbances manifest themselves in the body, involving the body in personal development, therapy and the process of emotional integration becomes meaningful.

PART V

THE INTEGRATION PROCESS

Emotional integration

To be able to dissolve emotional disturbances and heal emotional wounds, we need to express and regulate unregulated emotional responses. By doing this we integrate our emotional responses into personality and increase response flexibility. As a result we become freer in our relations with others. We need to regulate both the primary need response that was not met in early development as well as the emotional responses that are the consequence of insufficient need satisfaction. These two types of response are connected and we will refer to both as *emotional responses*.

Regulating an unregulated emotional response involves allowing ourselves to express it to another person without it being stopped by our defense system, and then experiencing that it is OK to do so. The intensity of expression should not be too high; it should be within or only slightly outside our window of tolerance. Following this expression, we must be able to accept the other person's response to it. Emotional wounds are created in relation to others and can only heal in relation to others. If expression takes place outside of a relational framework, that is, if there is no one there to receive the expression, the emotion remains unregulated. It is not enough to rage in solitude or cry alone; to regulate an emotional response, it must be expressed in a relational context.

Regulation of an unregulated emotional response is a gradual process and our trust in the emotional process and its expression grows organically over time. Regulation of emotional expression leads to greater arousal capacity and a wider window of tolerance for a specific emotion, which makes stronger and more extensive emotional expression possible. As long as we neither hold back nor force expression, the process of integration automatically adjusts the intensity of emotional expression and we avoid increased activation of our defense system. It is a process in which we gradually lower our defenses. This ensures manageable consequences from the process and the organism experiences the situation as safe and predictable.

The first time we express an unregulated emotion, our window of tolerance is relatively narrow. Only a low level of emotional intensity is possible without interruption from our defense. By repeatedly allowing emotional intensity to reach the limit of our window of tolerance, it gradually widens until it is possible to express the entire emotional charge. This development takes place at the limit of our window of tolerance and follows the body's natural rhythm of contraction and expansion. It corresponds to the process Peter Levine calls *pendulation* (Levine, 2010) in which the process of regulation in an organism autonomously swings between an experience of security and a slow, gradual increase in emotional intensity (insecurity). By remaining in conscious contact with our body's natural rhythm we support the process, allowing natural healing and integration of the emotional response.

Defense escalation

Optimal intensity of emotional expression is achieved when we retain some conscious control over the emotional response's charge and can stop it if necessary. Emotional intensity must therefore only be allowed to slightly exceed the limits of the window of tolerance in order to avoid automatic escalation of the defense. If intensity becomes too high, defense activation escalates and the chronic immobility connected to that particular emotion will intensify. In this way emotional expression is stopped in our body.

For instance if the form of chronic immobility we use to defend ourselves against our anger is chronic mobilization, it will increase if the intensity of anger exceeds the limits of our window of tolerance. In the same way, if we have developed chronic immobilization as a defense against unregulated sadness, this will increase if the intensity of sadness becomes too great. Fear activates after the onset of chronic immobility and after this our cognitive defense activates to keep awareness away from both the emotional response and the fact that its expression has been interrupted by chronic immobility. The focus of our awareness shifts from bodily processes to our thoughts and surroundings. In this way our defense system makes us unaware of a withheld emotional response.

The intelligence of life: integration finds its way

The basic principle of life is to strive for ever greater systemic complexity and efficiency. In this process, disturbances and challenges are stimuli that trigger autonomous (survival) responses which are then expressed and naturally integrated, leading to learning and growth. As far as we know, humans are the only organisms that actively interrupt this process, preventing a natural return to balance after an emergency survival response. Unlike the natural behavior of other living organisms, human personality does not always allow the organism to rectify disturbances in its physical, homeostatic balance. A bird may for example crash into a window and be shocked. The bird will fall to the ground and appear to be dead, but after a few minutes it will get up, shake off the shock and fly away. Humans also become shocked and in different ways may appear dead, but our defenses do not always permit us to return to our inherent balance, that is, to let go of the shock and complete the activated response processes.

The road back to balance and flow is obvious from this perspective. To achieve regulation and integration of an emotional disturbance, we must become aware of the defense and re-establish contact with the organism's own striving for greater levels of systemic complexity and efficiency, our inherent ability to self-heal. A defense that autonomously holds back the organism's natural process of integration requires energy to sustain itself. At the moment of trauma, personality provides this energy to secure its stability. We become however used to doing this and continue to allocate energy without noticing it. In this way being more or less constantly on the defense against ourselves and our natural emotional responses becomes standard behavior.

With this in mind, there are two tasks involved in facilitating an integration process: first, becoming aware of the way we actively defend against the integration process, and second, interrupting our defensive behavior. In the absence of an active defense, the process of regulation and integration begins automatically.

The somatic defense disturbs homeostatic balance

The somatic defense's chronic immobility disturbs the body's natural homeostatic balance and flow. This disturbance becomes part of the body's affective background activity that we perceive as background feeling. In a healthy and balanced living system, processes that sustain the organism mostly take place in the background of awareness. If a disturbance in a process creates an imbalance in the system, a feeling of imbalance naturally makes itself known when it enters the foreground of awareness. This feeling of imbalance makes the organism aware that something needs to be remedied in the same way that the experience of pain from an injury leads us to do something about it. However when our defense's chronic immobility interrupts emotional expression and creates a physical imbalance, our cognitive defense keeps us unaware of what is happening. We must therefore consciously oppose our cognitive defense and come into contact with our background feeling. This makes it possible for the feeling of imbalance to enter our focus of awareness.

Each emotional activation has a specific fixed action pattern. The specific form of chronic immobility that interrupts an emotion in a given situation will therefore be connected to the specific emotional process that is activated. While the defense holds back the emotional process, the emotional response's action potential begins to exert pressure on the nervous system (see Chapter 12). If the defense is not in a state of high alert, we can use interoception to relatively easily come into contact with and feel the interrupted and withheld unregulated emotion as well as its action potential. However if the emotional threat is assessed as high, the intensity of the defense increases instead. We then lose emotional contact as our focus of awareness shifts away from feeling the emotion. We again become unaware of both the emotion and the defense against it.

The integrative dynamic of feeling

When we become aware of our background feeling during an integration process, chronic immobility enters the foreground of awareness. We feel how our body holds the emotion back. If we are willing and cognitively open, this contact leads us to the unregulated emotion and is experienced as an emotional feeling. The emotional feeling's charge will then naturally intensify and become clearer and clearer until the charge reaches a point at which the emotion is expressed (see Chapter 8, Figure 10). After this, the emotional charge decreases and the emotional feeling in the foreground of awareness dissolves. We experience once again only a general background feeling coming from the body's homeostatic processes as they maintain life in an organism in flow.

This describes the human organism's natural and autonomous process of integration in which previously withheld emotional responses are allowed to express themselves and become integrated as part of the organism's autonomous striving for homeostatic balance. It is a process of development that consists of several subprocesses or cycles of emotional regulation, similar to the dynamics of pendulation described earlier in this chapter. Each cycle widens our window of tolerance and contributes to complete regulation of the emotion.

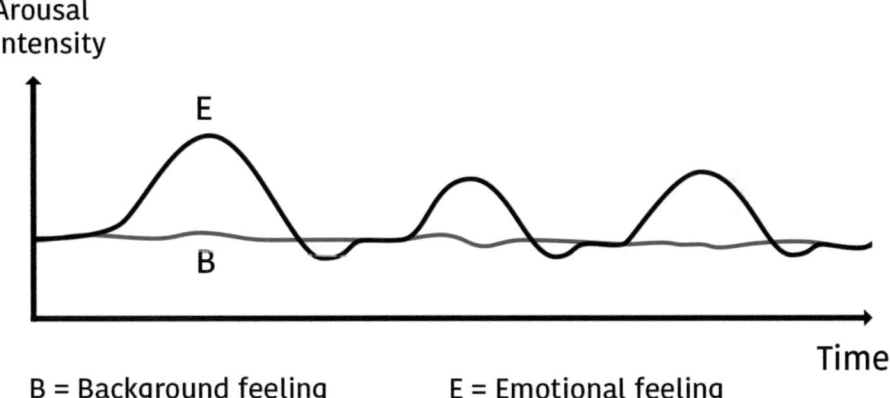

B = Background feeling   E = Emotional feeling

Figure 22: Feeling as a medium for our natural integration process
While in contact with background feeling, a change occurs as an intensified chronic immobility causes a disturbance in our homeostatic balance and enters the foreground of awareness. The emotional feeling connected to this chronic immobility also enters our awareness and intensifies if it is kept in focus until the emotion is naturally expressed. After this, the intensified chronic immobility dissolves and we return to being in contact with background feeling. This process is repeated after a while and a new cycle of intensified chronic immobility and unregulated emotion emerges. This is an autonomous process in which the organism naturally integrates previously unregulated emotions.

The following is an example of how contact with a background feeling leads to contact with an emotional feeling and an unregulated emotion connected to a lack of joy in life.

Alex had not felt joy or motivation in life for some time. He experienced life as meaningless or in his words, "just a one-way trip to the graveyard." His upper body appeared somewhat collapsed with sunken chest and lifeless arms, a body posture expressing chronic immobilization. Alex was asked to focus on and feel his body, move his upper body a little and experience how his breathing affected it. At first Alex did not feel anything, but as he continued, he became slowly aware of stiffness in his shoulders which intensified and became more uncomfortable the more he brought this feeling into focus. While maintaining contact with the feeling, his focus gradually shifted to include the entire front of his upper body. He experienced an emptiness in his chest which quickly developed into an uncomfortable feeling that spread from his chest to his entire body. While in contact with this uncomfortable feeling, his relationship with a woman that had ended a few months earlier came to mind. Alex's discomfort now developed into an experience of emotional pain. Tears welled up and began to run down his cheeks. Alex felt the sorrow of separation from the woman, something he had kept himself from feeling until now. After sobbing for a few minutes, he stopped crying and became still. The emotional activation subsided and Alex experienced a softness in his upper body. He felt his heart beating and his entire body felt warm. He felt liberated and more alive.

The affective cycle

Upon activation, every affective process naturally follows the same dynamic pattern. If an unregulated emotional activation is supported and allowed to follow this dynamic pattern, it is expressed and integrated. Deviation from this dynamic pattern indicates a disturbance and defense against the process of expression and integration.

Biological affects all share a common dynamic form (Clynes & Nettheim, 1982). They rise and fall in a wave movement, each with their own individual intensity and speed. There are a number of theories regarding this dynamic, but common to all of them is the biological affect's movement with increasing intensity of charge up to a maximum, followed by decreasing intensity until the charge completely disappears (Southwell, 1990; Sabetti, 1993; Geuter & Schrauth, 2001). The same dynamic is seen when an emotional feeling intensifies until it reaches emotional expression and then dissolves.

To thoroughly describe the dynamic process of an emotion we use a model called the *affective cycle*. This model presents the different phases of the process and is useful in understanding and diagnosing emotional processes and defense dynamics. With the help of this model we can identify the point at which a person dissociates from an emotional process and needs support and assistance in regulating an emotion. An emotional response that is allowed to naturally follow its entire cycle will take place within the window of tolerance and be regulated and integrated into personality.

This classification of different phases of the affective cycle builds on the *Change Wave* formulated by psychologist Stèphano Sabetti (Sabetti, 1993), a model of the general dynamics of development and change in life. The following description of phases in the affective cycle are presented as phases in a process of emotional regulation, as opposed to an emotion that naturally activates and expresses itself in real time. The various phases of an emotion's natural development follow seamlessly one after another.

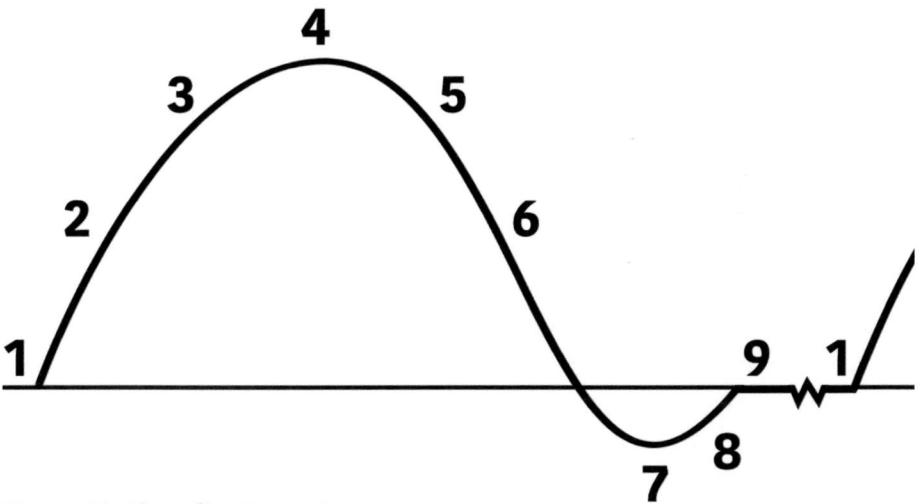

Figure 23: The affective cycle
The phases of the affective cycle are: 1. Perception; 2. Activation; 3. Intensification; 4. Boundary point; 5. Expression; 6. Dissolution; 7. Insight; 8. Behavioral integration; 9. Transition.

The first phase: Perception

An integration process requires contact with the body's natural feedback mechanism, that is, contact with background feeling and openness to the emotional level of feeling in interoception. The person is awake and relaxed, breathing is from the belly and contact with background feeling is clear. Using open interoception, awareness stays focused on the shifting feelings while in contact with the body. When the body is included in the focus of awareness, it provides a somatic indicator of the window of tolerance and in this state it is possible to detect chronic immobility and withheld action potential connected to an unregulated emotion.

Open perception and stable contact with feelings are the themes of this phase. These themes remain necessary in the following phases in order to maintain contact with the natural affective cycle. An emotion's natural process can be interrupted in any phase by dissociating from this open and stable contact with feeling.

The second phase: Activation

Once stable contact with background feeling is achieved, chronic immobility enters into the foreground of awareness followed by the feeling of its associated unregulated emotional response. The experience of low-intensity background feeling shifts at this point to one or more specific body parts which now enter into the foreground of awareness. The person may feel tension, unease, heaviness, coldness etcetera in various parts of their body, often accompanied by discomfort with whatever has entered the foreground of awareness. This discomfort is a negative hedonic tone that the organism has learned in order to avoid conscious contact with unregulated emotions. If the person is able to remain open and in contact with whatever is in the foreground of awareness, the feeling of the emotion will begin to take shape. The unregulated emotion at the root of the problem seamlessly begins to appear; its intensity is usually experienced as low during this phase. Anger may for example be experienced as nervousness, sadness as physical heaviness and happiness as lightness. As long as contact with this low-intensity physical feeling continues, its intensity increases and after a short time the emotion clearly appears both in the body and in awareness.

Personality can defend itself against the emotion during this phase by avoiding feeling or by slowing down and stopping the build-up of intensity. We cannot avoid emotional activation but our defense can interrupt it and keep it from our awareness. This is done by intensifying chronic immobility and shifting our focus of awareness to our thoughts and surroundings.

During the activation phase and in subsequent phases, contact with an unregulated emotion can trigger activation of a fear response. Instead of following the dissociative dynamic of fear when this happens (which would lead away from contact), it is possible to dissolve the fear by maintaining conscious emotional contact with the discomfort of fear. It is important to become aware of any activation of a fear response in order to quickly end it, since fear disconnects awareness from the unregulated emotion and interrupts the affective cycle. In this way we remain in stable contact with the unregulated emotional process that activated the fear.

The third phase: Intensification

When we give space to a feeling of emotional activation in the foreground of awareness, the feeling naturally grows stronger. During the intensification phase, the experience of emotional activation expands from a feeling in a specific area of the body to a whole-body experience. When emotional feeling grows in our awareness during this phase, it may activate fear of being unable to control it. It is necessary to allow emotional intensity to grow during this phase without intervening and allow the emotional process to fill both our body and our cognition.

One defense against intensification is to activate a reactive emotion which discharges the emotional charge and reduces uncomfortable intensity. For example, by becoming irritated with others when sadness intensifies, we give ourselves breathing space. The defense can also keep emotional intensity at a minimum or completely break off contact with the emotion. We suddenly feel nothing, our focus of awareness shifts to our thoughts and we begin to talk about other things.

The fourth phase: Boundary point

When emotional feeling completely fills us and intensity peaks at the end of the intensification phase, the emotional response seeks natural expression. This is the boundary point, after which the process moves from an inner feeling and experience to outer expression in the form of tears, laughter, screaming etcetera.

At this point we go from experiencing, thinking about and talking about the emotional response to being one with the response through expression.

Emotional expression is not a "doing". It is a natural consequence of continuous contact with an intensifying emotional feeling. A certain level of emotional intensity is required to express the emotion. When emotional charge reaches that level, expression occurs naturally. At or just before the boundary point, we frequently experience that we are able to choose between expressing the emotion and holding it back. This is the moment when we become aware of the control we actually have over the defense. If we keep emotional activation inside the body as emotional feeling, we retain a certain control over it; control is lost when we let the emotion naturally express itself. If we remain in contact with the emotional process during this phase without intervening, it overflows into natural expression like an overfilled glass of water.

There is a tendency for the defense to react with powerful resistance at the boundary point since this is the point at which there is a shift from conscious control over an inner experience of emotional feeling to loss of control in expression. Resistance can take many forms: we may harden ourselves and hold back the response; we may collapse and lose all energy; we may dramatically "freak out" in overreactive expression; we may focus awareness on mental activity; we may entirely lose focus; etcetera. This is why it is important to have support during this phase of the affective cycle in order to help us remain in stable contact with the emotional process. In this way we can consciously let resistance dissolve and allow the emotion to reach natural expression.

The fifth phase: Expression
The boundary point is followed by expression of the emotional response. Expression begins slightly before emotional response intensity peaks, continues through peak intensity and then decreases in intensity. Natural expression of an emotional response occurs organically and automatically; we do not need to do anything to make it happen. The organism autonomously expresses its natural fear, sadness, happiness, anger or love. The emotional response's accumulated action potential is released in body movement (its fixed action pattern) and a clear, emotional quality is apparent in facial expression, voice and eyes. We become one with a stable and focused emotional expression.

Expression of an unregulated emotional response may lead to insecurity about how others will respond to it. As previously explained, it was not so much our expression of an emotional response that taught us to hold back the response but rather how the expression was received. Fear of negative consequences can lead us to manipulate response expression in this phase. We may for example influence expression by forcing it and overdramatizing, end expression before the natural response process has completed, or keep expressive intensity low. In this way we manipulate the expression of our emotional response to retain control over it and our relational reality as well as to avoid the risk that we have learned comes with natural expression of the unregulated emotional response.

The sixth phase: Dissolution

Following natural expression, emotional response activation slowly dies out. Expression ends when the reason for activating the emotional response is no longer present and its mission is accomplished. The nervous system calms down and physical components of the emotional response process such as hormones are cleared from the body. As high physical intensity slowly gives way to low-intensity relaxation, body and mind become still. Dynamic activity is followed by relaxation, particularly in striated muscles. Sympathetic activation of the nervous system present during expression of the emotional response gives way to parasympathetic activation. The emotional response completely dissolves and is no longer felt.

This phase can be experienced as threatening since the body relaxes without its usual chronic defense activation. At the same time, expression of an emotional response results in increased trust in the organism's autonomous processes, which helps us dare to remain in a state of dissolution with all its vulnerabilities. By consciously allowing natural relaxation in this phase, we let go of activity and the defense's preparedness. However if we do not follow this natural process, the defense will reactivate. Defense reactivation appears as physical restlessness and/or heightened mental activity. Fear may be activated and an experience of shame and guilt may arise.

The seventh phase: Insight

If we follow the affective cycle all the way through the phase of dissolution and let the emotional response process completely dissolve, body and mind become calm. In this phase an emotional response has been expressed, regulated and dissolved and affective intensity has reached its lowest point. This is the phase in which memory integration occurs and a narrative understanding arises about the origins of our unregulated emotional response. An insight autonomously appears in awareness that makes it possible for us to understand how a withheld emotional response caused the problem that was the focus of our integration process. Insight is a "eureka" experience in which we understand how the challenges that we meet in daily life are connected to situations and relations in early life. This narrative understanding is the result of emotional response expression and regulation and is not formulated consciously. With insight comes clarity about the natural behavioral change that needs to take place to meet the challenges we face. We realize how we should act and take responsibility for ourselves.

To come to this insight, we should avoid quickly activating self-conscious, willful thought processes after the dissolution phase. Insight appears in awareness when we stay in the emptiness that comes after natural dissolution of an emotional response. The process needs time to settle and all the pieces need to fall into place. We need to be open and receptive to insight rather than mentally construct it.

As a defense against losing control and letting insight become apparent to us, we may deny ourselves this necessary time for stillness. We may begin to think about what happened and what we need to do next. These thoughts are accompanied by physical restlessness, an experience of mild discomfort and an inner stress to move on.

The eighth phase: Behavioral integration

Natural, practical, behavioral integration takes place in this phase of the affective cycle. During this phase, inner understanding from the phase of insight becomes manifest in daily life. For example if we have realized that we need to draw a line in a relationship, we draw the line. Behavioral change is an extension of the emotional response process we have been through and the insights it brought us. Change has been made possible by the increased behavioral flexibility we acquired in this process. The new behavior is experienced as natural and responsible even though we may feel some resistance or fear when manifesting our insights in our relationships.

Changes in everyday relational behavior are at times the most difficult part of the affective cycle. To achieve the stability needed to face our relational reality, we must trust both ourselves and the emotional response process. In practice it is often necessary to repeat earlier phases of the affective cycle several times before we are ready to implement behavioral integration. It is important not to rush behavioral integration; great insecurity may be a sign that there are other emotional responses that need to be regulated before behavioral integration can take place. Each time we successfully repeat earlier phases of the affective cycle, we gain more clarity about the process and trust in ourselves. When there has been enough regulation and trust is strong, there is little or no resistance to complete behavioral integration.

Once we have attained sufficient regulation of an emotional response, it is important to transform our insights about behavioral change into real changes in behavior as soon as possible. The quicker this happens, the greater the motivation to do it. As a consequence of emotional expression and the insights it brings, old and entrenched behavioral structures open up. Actual change becomes easier at this point because the organization of personality is highly receptive to behavioral change. This openness and motivation begin to disappear however when the time between insight and behavioral change lengthens. Resistance to change grows if behavioral change does not come quickly.

This means that we can avoid complete integration of an unregulated emotional response by not changing behavior and not allowing practical integration to take place in our relational reality. Procrastination, delays and more or less intentional inactivity cause the motivation for behavioral change to disappear and old behaviors become dominant once again.

The ninth phase: Transition
The affective cycle ends when an emotional response process is completely regulated and behavioral changes have been implemented. This completion opens up possibilities for new emotional response cycles. The organism's first priority is to rectify imbalances. Its next priority is to develop its potential. If the affective cycle of an emotional response is not permitted to naturally complete and therefore remains in focus, room for new possibilities and associated response development is limited. The openness created by a completed affective

cycle liberates our life process and enables emotional response development and transformative personal development. It now becomes possible to develop positive emotions of happiness and love.

The integration process

The integration process takes place in a natural interaction between background feeling and emotional feeling in the foreground of awareness. Through this process, we grow and mature in an interplay with our environment. The integration process is a self-generative developmental process that finds its own way and is influenced by shifting inner and outer circumstances. Every emotional response and integration caused by stimuli from the environment creates a new starting point for the next response and direction. The actual course of development depends on influences from our particular environment. By interacting with our environment, personality develops naturally and continually.

An established defense means that we have learned not to trust the organism's ability to heal disturbances in its emotional system. A main principle in the process of regulation and integration is that the more we allow contact with an emotional response and allow it to reach expression, the more we trust our emotional system. This is why regulation of emotional responses stemming from basic emotional wounds takes place in stages of increasing intensity. Personality needs to gradually experience that the increasing intensity of emotional expression is safe. Partial regulation develops gradually into complete regulation; as long as the problem complex continues to surface in our life, further regulation is needed (see Figure 24). Incomplete regulation is the reason why the same type of problems and conflicts tend to appear over and over again in our life.

Feeling as the medium of integration

From a functional perspective, feeling is a cognitive ability and conscious contact with the organism's emotional responses. From a different perspective, feeling may be viewed as the medium for the integration process. Natural integration of conflicts takes place when we are in contact with feeling, both in relation to ourselves and others (Siegel, 2010). One might say that feeling generates a resonant field of integration in which everything that is fragmented and not whole gathers together again. This is why feeling is an essential part of the developmental process in several meditative practices. For example according to Zen tradition, focus on the natural movement of feeling in the present opens the way to positive, transcendental experiences and wholeness. Here we see how feeling itself is the medium for a developmental process (Kapleau, 1989). In this tradition as well as many others, feeling and the integrative process of feeling is used not simply to regulate disturbances in emotional responses but also to open up to more satisfying dimensions of ourselves and to develop the positive emotions of happiness and love.

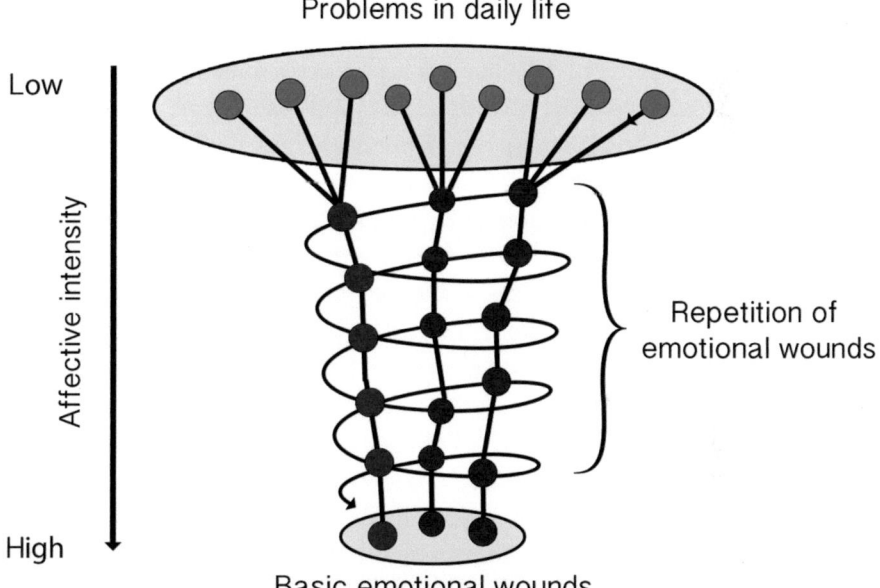

Figure 24: The integration process and basic emotional wounds
The process of integration involves gradual regulation of basic emotional wounds. Basic themes are met repeatedly with increasing intensity until the underlying basic emotional wound is reached. Over time we become able to regulate the emotional response process with increasing intensity until complete regulation is achieved.

Resistance to the integration process

When our defense and its chronic immobility is confronted in an integration process, there may be resistance. Resistance is an automatic emergency survival activation that is triggered when the defense comes under too much stress and expression of an unregulated emotional response is imminent. Early psychoanalytic literature described this resistance as an enemy to be conquered. Freud used expressions such as "the struggle against resistance" and Wilhelm Reich wrote that resistance must be attacked (Reich, 1950; Freud, 1959). For these writers, resistance was seen as something negative that had to be removed or destroyed to promote a person's well-being. Today we know that resistance activates when the defense is put under too much stress and that increasing the stress does not dissolve the defense but rather causes activation to increase in the long run, although it may look like it is actually dissolving at first.

Natural resistance to the regulation and integration of emotional responses and for that matter to all personal development is part of personality's security system, a system tasked with ensuring stability and predictability in life. Resistance may be described as the activation of personality's fight-or-flight response. The process begins when a stimulus such as criticism or a therapeutic intervention brings us into contact with an activated, unregulated emotional response. Our defense interrupts expression of the activated response and then fear triggers the cognitive defense to shift our focus of awareness away from it. This is followed by the resistance impulse, a fight-or-flight response expressed in relation to the source of the stimulus which caused us to come into contact with an unregulated emotional response. In a therapeutic situation, this may be seen when a client suddenly begins to forcefully argue or changes the subject entirely. After this, defense mechanisms activate and the client's focus of awareness shifts to the environment. The process of therapeutic regulation is perceived as a threat to the stability of personality and if pressure on the defense becomes too great, forceful resistance is automatically triggered.

Resistance is a natural survival activation from a system that experiences itself as threatened. The most appropriate way of dealing with resistance is to facilitate dissolution of its sympathetic activation. Contact with the underlying, unregulated emotional response can only be established after this is achieved. Dissolution of sympathetic activation requires steady, sensitive empathy that brings the resistance into our focus of awareness, thereby making it possible to reestablish contact with the integration process.

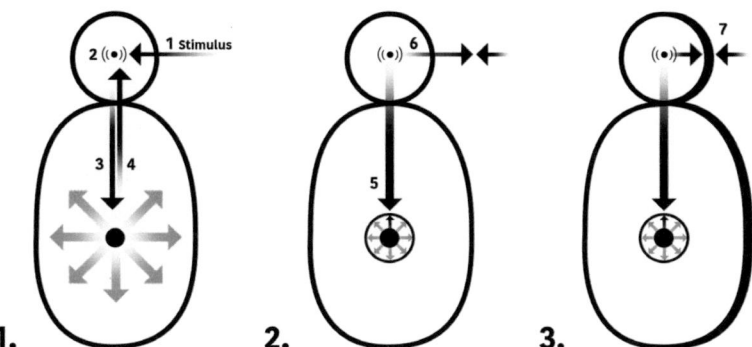

Figure 25: The dynamics of resistance
1: A stimulus (1) brings us into contact with an emotional wound (2). This activates an unregulated emotional response (3) and feedback from this reaches interoception (4). 2: The defense interrupts expression of the emotional response (5) and resistance is expressed (6). 3: The defense system becomes more intense, illustrated here as a thick shell that keeps the threatening stimulus out (7).

Physical, biological resistance

In addition to the resistance of personality there is also a natural physical, biological resistance to the integration process. The embodiment of personality makes behavioral change resulting from emotional response regulation the object of natural physical resistance. Cognitive insight regarding change occurs rapidly, but our body needs more time to adjust and change. One well-known example of this is when we know that we need to reduce stress but find it difficult to do so since our sympathetic nervous system stays activated, our body remains tense and we are stuck in hyperactive behavior.

As we have seen, physical structures and processes are the basis for our thoughts and how we relate to the world. The fact that changes in these biological processes require considerable time may negatively impact on the change process. As a result behavioral change may slow down to the point that old behaviors return, even though our emotional response has been regulated and we have cognitive insight into what we need to do. Our built-in physical resistance can be seen as a default setting that slows change processes for our own safety.

We see an example of this dynamic in the neural networks that govern behavioral patterns. A new behavior requires more energy and focus and therefore ends up with lower priority since it does not have the same neural efficiency as behavior that has been repeated often. To change neural networks so that the new behavior becomes the primary behavior, a combination of activated neurons must change and existing networks must be modified (Cozolino, 2014). A new network needs to be synchronized into the new pattern of activation, a process that requires more energy than the old pattern. While this process requires extra energy, the old neural network continues to be effective and only gradually dissolves after a period of inactivity. If we do not remain aware of this and actively support a new behavior, the old behavior will have a tendency to be automatically used long after all the other phases of the integration process has ended.

Our body and posture also influence our feelings and the way we look at life. As described earlier, life shapes our posture but posture in turn influences our attitude toward life and steers us toward experiencing specific feelings and emotions (Bull, 1945). An alert, dynamic posture full of energy or a dejected posture absent of energy will amplify and facilitate equivalent life experiences. Research has shown that individuals with a collapsed posture find it more difficult to recall positive feelings and thoughts than individuals with an upright posture (Peper & Lin, 2012). This resistance built into our body makes it necessary to repeat a new behavior quite often before it is established as the most efficient and natural. Research also shows that we can support a change process by being aware of body and posture.

Primary and secondary regulation

The most essential parts of the integration process are to express the emotional response and then to experience that our expression is OK and accepted. This regulates the unregulated emotional response. Cognitive understanding, restructuring and behavioral change follow from this. When expression of our emotional response is accepted, the emotional disturbance is regulated and dissolved. While cognitive understanding of a disturbance may create a safe structure for integration of an emotional response, it may also be part of the defense against it. Trying to heal an emotional wound without emotional contact, expression and acceptance of the expression would be like asking the defense to dissolve itself. This would completely contradict the nature and function of the defense.

The inertia of behavioral patterns can make it difficult to change them if we do not consciously support new behavior. We may at times have to use our self-awareness and will to abstain from behavior that we know is bad for us and instead support behavior that we know is good for us and which promotes the integration process.

Regulation and integration can be completed at both a primary and secondary level. The primary level is completed when we no longer experience symptoms from the emotional disturbance. We may for instance no longer crave food when we feel lonely or we may no longer feel nervous and begin to sweat just before we present a project to our colleagues. At the primary level of regulation and integration, we no longer experience an inner conflict in situations that previously were experienced as difficult. The unregulated emotional response has been completely regulated and the entire organism has adjusted to it.

A secondary level of regulation and integration occurs when we have gone through some regulation and gained some insight into the dynamics of our emotional response but there are still symptoms of the unregulated emotional response. Regulation is incomplete but we are aware of and can control our unhealthy behavior. In this case we can support the integration process by consciously supporting new, positive behavior and abstaining from behavior that is unhealthy for us.

An example of these two levels of regulation may be seen in the case of a woman who tends to be attracted to men who are not good for her. When regulation is at the secondary level, the woman is still attracted to these men but understands that they are not good for her. She can resist giving in to her attraction and in this way supports the process of regulation and integration. When regulation is at the primary level, the woman is no longer attracted to men who behave in this way. Underlying, unregulated emotional responses have been completely regulated and integrated into the woman's personality. In other words, it is not enough to understand and partially regulate a disturbance in an emotional response. This may be the first step in an integration process but regulation of an emotional response is only complete when the emotional disturbance dissolves and its symptoms have disappeared.

Chapter **14**

Development of the integration process over time

Emotional and affective responses that are positive and life-promoting

Our defense against unregulated emotional responses not only creates conflicts and problems but also reduces vitality and impedes the development of positive response processes that promote the development of life.

One consequence of early emotional wounds is that the natural, human process of emotional maturation stops. When early relational needs are not met, the defense that is created to protect us becomes a hindrance to realizing our inherent human potential. The defense impedes the development of positive response processes such as happiness and love. Although theories of psychological developmental often do not consider this part of emotional response regulation, positive response processes are important. They complement regulation of unregulated response processes that stem from the lack of need satisfaction and have great significance in regulating them. These unregulated response processes are often referred to as our "negative" response processes: anger, fear and sadness. Activation, expression and regulation of positive emotional responses are a natural part of human development and the integration process. Expression of positive emotional responses strengthens our emotional resilience and stabilizes the regulation of emotional wounds.

In psychological literature, there are two opposing perspectives on psychological disturbances and human development. One focuses on illness and pathology and the other focuses on positive life experiences.

The pathological perspective focuses on personality dysfunctions, personality disorders, their symptoms and explains how they can be alleviated. This perspective is found in psychoanalytic theory and cognitive psychology and has formed the way we in the Western world normally view the dynamics of the psyche. Generally speaking, this perspective lacks a theory of positive human development.

Positive psychology developed in the 1990's as an alternative to psychological research focusing solely on pathology and disturbances. Positive psychology focuses on the positive characteristics of personality, our resources, positive relations and positive feelings. By evoking and nourishing these naturally occurring human qualities and responses a person can achieve increased well-being and enhanced psychological resilience in the face of personal crises and illness (Seligman, 2002). This develops our resources to cope with stress.

It may seem that the two perspectives, pathological and positive psychology, are in conflict with each other, but in reality they complement each other and may be considered two connected elements in a single process. This becomes evident in the dynamic of the process of emotional integration. In this process, emotional wounds and their associated unregulated emotional responses become regulated in connection with the expression and development of positive emotional responses.

Although we strive to experience positive emotions, we often experience life-promoting, positive, emotional responses as more threatening to personality than responses that we normally consider to have a negative hedonic tone. If early experiences of positive emotional responses have not been acknowledged by caregivers, we learn to hold back expression of these positive responses. As a consequence, activation of these emotional responses is experienced as threatening to personality. This occurs partially because expressions of positive emotions are connected to painful emotional wounds and partially because this kind of response requires an open organism without an active defense system.

Of all the positive responses, love is the central process in the development of positive emotional responses. The experience and expression of love towards others as well as self-love are part of the lifelong process of human indivi-

220

duation. We reduce our dependency on others by expressing, regulating and integrating love. Our defense on the other hand keeps us dependent on others. The defense is constructed to avoid feeling relational separation and to make us dependent on attention, acknowledgement and the misconception that we still need care from others. This dependence disappears when we experience and integrate self-love. Integration of self-love into personality causes a shift from dependency on others to self-sufficiency and the experience of joy in our relations with others.

Life-promoting, positive emotional responses are often activated after a hedonically negative, unregulated emotional response has been expressed and dissolved in a regulation process. Following this regulation, the experience of negative hedonic tone shifts to positive hedonic tone accompanied by an experience of openness, warmth and flow in the organism. If this new process of integration is allowed to continue, the hedonically positive background feeling can develop into a clear, positive emotional response. When we become aware of contact with activated, positive emotions and support the growth of these feelings, our window of tolerance widens. As a result, positive emotional responses will play a larger role in our response repertoire and activate more often. Increased awareness of positive emotional responses also supports the regulation of emotional wounds. It increases trust in the organism's ability to lead the way in the regulation process, which decreases defense activation. As long as the process of integration continues, expressions of positive response processes grow in intensity and frequency.

Positive, life-promoting emotional responses stabilize the regulation process, increase happiness in life and strengthen psychological resiliency. It is therefore important to pay careful attention to these emotional responses when they are activated because of the risk that our defense system will not allow the activation to increase in intensity and will stop it before we become aware of it. At the beginning of a regulation process we often experience positive response activations as flow, warmth, liveliness and being deeply touched. By maintaining focus on these feelings, they grow over time and become clear, affective cycles of happiness and love, and we sense being part of a greater whole. These cycles cannot be created at will, but for them to develop we must be aware of them when they automatically activate. It is not however enough to simply become aware of a positive emotional response. To develop a positive emotional response, integrate it into personality and give it more room in our life, it is necessary to express and regulate it in a relational setting, that is, in relation to another person.

Phases of the regulation and integration process

The process of regulation and integration supports natural development of the emotional system. Over time it is possible to distinguish three phases in the regulation and integration process, each with its own specific dynamic. These phases can also be seen as levels of emotional maturity. The phases mirror the developments and changes that our emotional system and personality go through as well as our increased acceptance of and access to the emotional system.

A regulation process is often begun in the midst of a crisis. Life may seem difficult and stressed, conflicts arise, we are depressed, feel anxiety or cannot feel anything at all. It may be caused by our general life situation or there may have been a specific incident that triggered a personal crisis. We may experience that life has come to a halt and that we are trapped in old patterns that feel impossible to change.

The first phase
A characteristic of the first phase of the regulation and integration process is the defense system's strong resistance. At the beginning of the regulation process, the person often experiences negative emotional, physical and relational symptoms stemming from the underlying emotional disturbance. Contact with the emotional response is weak and the person will often display depressive or reactive behavior toward response activation and the environment in this phase. Due to the strength of the defense, it is often necessary to receive help from a therapist or coach, an outside person who can also provide support during the other phases as needed. The first important task in this phase is to support a shift from the person's focus on mental processes to a focus on feeling and to establish initial trust in the emotional regulation process. Trust is established by carefully approaching an unregulated emotional process, at first allowing only short glimpses of the unregulated emotion and later experiencing it for longer periods. Focus during this phase is on coming into contact with the emotion, giving space to it and developing trust in the emotional response system.

The first phase is facilitated by verbal reflection on emotional processes, the defense and how these are connected to the person's present life and behavior. These reflections help the person develop an understanding of negative behavioral patterns and how they constitute a defense against unregulated emotions. It is important to identify processes of shame and guilt in this phase. If not identified and understood, shame and guilt can disturb or completely disrupt a process of regulation and integration. If the person experiences a lot of fear, it is important to strengthen the person's understanding of fear and its regulation by learning about the general function of fear and how it can be physically regulated. Theoretical understanding of fear provides predictability and increased trust in the regulation and integration process.

The second phase

As trust in the emotional system begins to grow, the regulation and integration process enters its second phase. Focus during this phase is on the process of emotional regulation. The emotional response system is now experienced as a relatively natural part of the person. As a result, the defense is not mobilized against the regulation process to the same extent as previously. When it does mobilize, it is easier to become aware of it, dissolve it and return focus to unregulated processes. During the second phase, acceptance of all emotional processes begins. Some of these emotional processes might however be experienced as easier to accept than others. Ability to follow the complete affective cycle of an emotional process increases, and emphasis is placed on emotional expression and regulation. Fear activation is quickly identified and regulated.

In the second phase, emotional regulation regularly results in cognitive understanding which supports trust in the emotional response system. As the process of emotional regulation continues and deepens, the pain of emotional wounds and the person's lack of early need satisfaction begin to appear. After some time, it becomes possible for the person to allow direct contact with the emotional pain of relational trauma and the needs that were never met and regulated. The regulation process does not at this time only deal with secondary emotional responses from emotional wounds. It also begins to regulate primary need responses. The previously strongly negative hedonic tone of unregulated emotions shifts to a more neutral hedonic tone and emotions become easier to express. Positive experiences of emotional expression make expression less uncomfortable.

During the second phase, the development of positive, life-promoting emotional responses begins. There are brief glimpses of happiness, pleasure and a growing self-love. Behavioral changes in the person's life are typically seen in this phase, often with life-changing consequences. These behavioral changes are a natural extension of the regulation process and our increased access to both ourselves and our response system. When this phase is complete, the person has a clear sense of being able to take responsibility for themselves and their expressions. The person has a greater ability to self-regulate emotional response activations and the challenges of life are met with motivation and confidence.

The third phase
During the third phase, a person's inner longing to become liberated from whatever is holding the person back from living a full life serves as a motivating factor to continue the integration process. There is an inner clarity that more regulation is needed to experience the freedom, connection and self-love that is within grasp. Basic emotional wounds continue to trigger the defense to activate but at this point the person is often aware of them and can to a great extent self-regulate them. There is however a sense that even greater regulation is possible. Motivated by an inner wish to live a more authentic life, the process continues with positive motivation and openness.

This third phase is characterized by curiosity about unregulated emotions and emotional wounds. Trust in the response system is high, which keeps the defense and resistance at a low level. Resistance is quickly dissolved if it activates and an emotion's affective cycle is allowed to progress relatively naturally. During this phase there is greater focus on regulation of primary need responses and their associated emotional pain. This process quickly opens up self-acceptance and self-love, which make it possible for basic emotional wounds to heal. Strong contact with the core self is often experienced and there is a natural thankfulness, at times expressed in a tearful, liberating process.

Since the influence of the defense system is dramatically weakened during this third phase, personality goes through a major reorganization. Basic trust in life grows and dependency on acceptance from others weakens. An increase in self-love awakens natural interest in the well-being of others and there is increased focus on living and acting within the context of one's life. Egocentric needs and ideas are less important than they were before.

The integration process does not end here. It continues in the direction taken during this third phase. Basic emotional wounds and the defense system never completely disappear and it is necessary to remain aware of them and the need for further emotional regulation. The response system continues to develop and future difficulties or personal crises may reveal new sides of who we are. We may need outside support once again. As long as there is life there are challenges and developments. From this point on, however, the ability to self-regulate is strong and the person's focus is on developing positive response processes.

15

Facilitating the integration process

This chapter takes a closer look at how to facilitate the integration process in ourselves and others and presents an overview of the basic principles behind facilitation of a regulation process. This will enable the reader to use the theories presented in this book on themselves and others. We will look at three states or qualities of mind that promote the integration process as well as various intervention techniques used to clarify and follow the process. We will also take a look at how the body can be involved in this process.

Three integrative qualities of mind

To support ourselves and others in an emotional integration process, our attitude is of great importance. *Curiosity*, *empathy* and *being present* are natural qualities of mind that support feeling contact and promote emotional regulation. These qualities also support a positive experience of life and authentic contact with ourselves. Curiosity, empathy and being present help us understand and form the process of feeling as well as the flow of information in ourselves and our relationships. These qualities support a natural interest in the integration process and strengthen our ability to discover disturbances, make room for them and confront them. At the same time curiosity, empathy and being present express that we are taking responsibility for ourselves and our own processes since these qualities keep us in contact with our feeling and support the natural, ongoing integration process. When facilitating another person's integration process, the facilitator must display these three qualities. In addition to supporting the process, they influence the other person to develop and display the same attitudes and qualities toward themselves.

Curiosity

Curiosity is a fundamental motivating factor for humans. When we are curious we learn more easily and quickly and the process is as satisfying as the goal. Curiosity is part of what Jaak Panksepp and Lucy Biven (2012) call *The Seeking System*, one of the fundamental motivational systems in human organisms. The Seeking System is a network of basic survival instincts that activate us in relation to our environment. This network activates natural, motivational impulses that support engagement with the world around us as part of our survival. When we actively interact with our environment and learn about it and our responses, we enhance our chances of survival. This network of survival instincts gives us a natural impulse to examine, explore and test, which are all basic characteristics of curiosity. In this way the dynamics of curiosity are the same as the dynamics of the basic human life process which strives for increased systemic complexity and evolutionary development at a biological level.

Curiosity contributes to the development of humans and human society at many levels. Curious people create new things, break norms and change the world and our way of life. Curiosity is a fundamental force of life that motivates us to transcend the boundaries of the known.

Curiosity counteracts avoidant behavior which is a feature of fear and the defense system. Curiosity reveals new information to us because we approach and explore a situation instead of running away from it or defending ourselves against it. This approach to difficult relational situations is also the most appropriate and solution-oriented in situations that are not physically dangerous. The defense is static and based on the premise that life will remain as it has been. Curiosity allows for the mutability of life and explores life situations. Curiosity is a proactive approach to our environment as opposed to the defense's avoidant behavior based on past situations. Fear and curiosity are in other words opposites. A person who is afraid is not curious and will not examine the object of fear. By reminding ourselves of our natural curiosity and supporting this attitude, we return the proactive focus of our awareness to whatever we have avoided due to fear.

Many of us have learned to hold back curiosity. We have learned to accept existing norms and avoid challenging accepted truths early in life. We have stopped asking, "Why?" the way children naturally do before they learn to keep quiet. It often takes a personal crisis to crack open this polished, safe surface and once again question our life and the way we are living. Only then do we begin to ask ourselves why we experience what we experience, what it means and why we act the way we do. Curiosity is given another chance.

By approaching ourselves and our relationships with curiosity we open up to learning about who we are, not because we must but because it is an expression of a natural inner process. Curiosity is a fundamental expression of the integration process and when we support an integration process in another person it is important to show natural curiosity about that person and their process. The other person feels seen and accepted by our interested openness which builds trust. The same principle applies to our own life and processes: when we are curious and show genuine interest in ourselves, we support acceptance of our experiences and ourselves.

Empathy

From an evolutionary perspective empathy is first and foremost a social survival mechanism that makes use of our ability to feel what others feel. Empathy efficiently connects people and helps us predict others' behavior. It motivates us to help others as if they were ourselves. When we for example experience another person's pain as our own, we are motivated to relieve their pain. By automatically supporting those closest to us in this way, we strengthen our social group and safeguard our own survival. The fact that empathy is strongest in relation to those closest to us also explains why we feel more motivated to help family members and neighbors than people suffering on a distant continent.

Having empathy for others involves feeling what they feel together with loving care for the feeling mirrored in ourselves. We relate to others' feelings by experiencing them ourselves and lovingly regulating our mirrored feelings. Empathy requires the ability to self-regulate the affective and emotional processes activated in us when we mirror others' feelings. To be able to be empathic with another person's emotional process we must be emotionally mature enough to experience, accept and regulate the process in ourselves.

If we are unable to contain and regulate the emotional state of others in our-selves, we can only be friendly and sympathetic but not empathic. When we display sympathy toward another person, we understand their difficulty either cognitively or because we have experienced it ourselves, but cannot regulate the feeling. If the other person's emotional process activates our own fear and defense, our behavior will become driven by the desire to remove the other person's suffering in order to avoid experiencing it ourselves. Instead of supporting acceptance and regulation, sympathy supports the other person's conviction that their experience is a threat and ends up supporting the emotional dysfunction. An example of sympathy is when we say, "Don't be sad" when a person is sad and needs to be sad. Another example is when a friend is angry and we say to them, "You shouldn't spend so much time on this, it isn't worth getting angry over!". In these situations, mirroring the other person's emotion causes us to experience discomfort and we try to reduce or stop it.

Empathy requires emotional maturity and the ability to self-regulate in order to be able to allow the affects and emotions of others to touch us and become regulated with loving care. With empathy we understand that the other person's emotion is mirrored in our own emotional system and do not lose ourselves in this mirrored emotional activation. Instead we give it the care needed to regulate it. Empathy is an attuned, caring touch that supports another person to regulate what they are feeling, the same caring touch we received from a caregiver as a child. It makes room for the other person's activated inner processes so they can be safely expressed. Empathy sends the message: "It is OK, you do not have to fight, you can let the process unfold," and this creates a safe space for the other person, for example by expressing the sadness that has been held back.

We feel empathy not only for others but can also feel empathy for ourselves when we accept what we experience with loving care. This self-empathy is decisive for our ability to self-regulate. Through self-empathy we consciously and proactively make room for and accept unregulated emotional activation. For example we allow ourselves to feel pain when a friend has died or anger when we are betrayed. This self-acceptance allows us to feel our own emotional activation and give it space. It is also only with a well-developed self-empathy that we can deeply regulate our personality's basic emotional wounds.

Being present

Being present means focusing awareness on our present experience without an abstract, narrative understanding of what is happening. Being present opens us up to the human organism's autonomic responses so they can be expressed and regulated. Also, only by being present can we express and develop natural curiosity and empathy.

The closest we can come to conscious contact with the present moment is by being aware of the organism's responses to the present moment. What we sense and feel is not actually the present moment but rather an interpretation based on the organism's affective responses (Damasio, 1994). The present moment influences our senses and this activates the organism's autonomous affects, vitality affects and emotions. Our feeling of these responses is our experience of the present moment. In other words, the present moment we experience is in fact a delayed interpretation of the actual present moment. This delayed experience of the present moment is the closest we can come to actually being in the present. This is what we mean by being present.

When we begin to think about what is happening or try to establish a narrative understanding of what has happened, we leave the present moment even further and begin to relate to our experience of the present moment. Our thoughts about what is happening is never direct contact with the present. Thought is an abstraction from the present moment and always comes after our experience of the present moment. Our cognitive defense often dwells in these abstract thought processes.

Our experience of the present moment as feeling is the organism's interpretation of reality. It takes time to turn emotions and other affects into feeling. Humans can register a sequence of separate events that last between 20 and 150 milliseconds. However to make sense of these events, personality needs to group them in functional and conceptual units of at least three to four seconds each (Stern, 2004). These functional units are not conscious thoughts but unconscious interpretations of what is happening that guide our behavior in relation to our inner reality maps (see Chapter 7). Certain meditative disciplines train awareness to liberate itself from this connection to unconscious interpretation of the present moment and thereby personality. This involves perceiving affective responses without interpreting them as conceptual units. In the natural process of integration on the other hand we use information from feelings, that is, the implicit interpretations of our experience of the present moment. Emotional regulation results in an adjustment of our implicit interpretation so that something which was previously interpreted as uncomfortable and threatening becomes interpreted as neutral or positive. In this way the regulation process can change our reality maps, the basic understanding of life formed in our earliest years of life.

In the integration process, being present involves contact with our experience without breaking the flow. We feel activated vitality affects and emotions in their natural processes as they respond to perception, that is, as they activate and reach completion. We can only maintain contact with the present moment by letting our responses be. If we interrupt a response process or break off contact with it, we lose our experience of the present moment. It is not possible to experience the present moment if our focus of awareness is on anything other than what we are experiencing. Abstract thought and understanding in the form of a narrative is only possible if we create distance to the present. This means that our cognitive defense cannot function while we are fully in the present moment since it is a reaction to responses activated by present reality. When we stay in the present we support our activated emotions to reach completion.

Our capacity for being present is directly related to our ability to self-regulate the organism's autonomous responses as they unfold in the present moment. Being present requires allowing affective responses to flow through us and is necessary for emotional regulation and integration. It is not possible to integrate unregulated emotions by talking about them. We need to experience the emotional process in order to achieve integration, and by being present we are always in contact with emotional processes that need regulation.

Affective Inquiry

Affective Inquiry is a communication method that facilitates emotional regulation and personal growth. It is a further development of psychologist Stèphano Sabetti's communication technique *Process Inquiry* (Sabetti, 1991). Affective Inquiry builds on knowledge of affective and emotional processes to facilitate problem solving and emotional regulation. It emphasizes emotional processes, draws attention to defense activation and supports emotional expression.

Affective Inquiry is an active communication method that poses questions which clarify and lead us deeper into what we experience, express and think. The facilitator is interested in the causes of a person's problems, the kind of defense used and the underlying emotional facts. Affective Inquiry uses the organism's affective expressions to come into contact with the integration process. Becoming aware of the affective process and following it as it unfolds leads to regulation of deep-seated, unregulated emotional processes. In facilitating regulation, Affective Inquiry disrupts existing defense patterns to uncover a problem's underlying cause. Openness and understanding are not enough to facilitate this process since the defense will hinder it. Problematic and unconscious patterns of thought and behavior must be disrupted and challenged in order to open up. The disruption needs to be strong enough to open up these problematic patterns, but not too strong, since this would intensify the defense.

A behavioral pattern provides us with a safe and predictable structure. The pattern may be physical, mental or emotional. An Affective Inquiry facilitator makes visible the behavioral patterns of the defense and what the person is defending against, that is the feeling of affective or emotional activation. The verbal techniques of Affective Inquiry, called *interventions*, disrupt the defense and bring the person into contact with feeling and the integration process (intervention comes from Latin intervenire, which means "to come between"). Interventions disrupt the defense's behavioral patterns by bringing these patterns and the emotional processes that activate them into the focus of our awareness.

Here is a short example of how Affective Inquiry works:

> **Sam:** Life is heavy right now.
> **Facilitator:** You feel it is heavy? (connection to the feeling in Sam's body is brought into focus)
> **Sam:** (nodding) It feels like everything is a struggle.
> **Facilitator:** A struggle against what? (the defense is clarified and the inquiry directs Sam's focus toward the process that Sam's defense is fighting against)
> **Sam:** That I am so sad about the way my relationship is going (tears).

Sam experienced low-intensity sadness as heaviness. His heavy experience was due to his defense, which kept his sadness from being expressed. Sam's cognitive defense cut off his awareness of feeling sadness as well as his defense against it. Focused inquiry into Sam's heavy feeling disrupted his defense. He shifted from abstract mental concepts to a clear experience of the present moment. As Sam's contact with feeling was allowed to continue and develop, he experienced that he was struggling and became aware of what he was struggling with and defending himself against: sadness. By becoming aware of his defense, Sam was able to dissolve it and the activated emotion (sadness) that triggered the defense could naturally develop toward expression and regulation.

Every problem we have and every challenge we face has the same dynamic. Our cognitive defense, which is a mental behavioral pattern, consistently keeps awareness away from our inner conflict with unregulated emotional activation. Affective Inquiry disrupts this avoidance pattern by focusing awareness on the inner conflict and inquiring into feeling as it is experienced in the present moment. Once contact with feeling is established, our background feeling leads us to the emotional feeling that we are defending against. Here is another short example of this process:

> **Ellen:** I am so tired of listening to my husband!
> **Facilitator:** Do you feel this tiredness right now?
> **Ellen:** Yes… (sighs deeply)
> **Facilitator:** How does that feel?
> **Ellen:** (squirming in her seat) Frustrating.
> **Facilitator:** In what way frustrating?
> **Ellen:** I feel irritated.
> **Facilitator:** Irritated? About what?
> **Ellen:** Ohhh… (becoming red in the face and around the throat) I am
> sick and tired of him and fed up with all his excuses!
> (the session continues, following the affective cycle of anger)

Ellen's cognitive defense caused her to experience anger as tiredness. The initial intervention brought Ellen's focus of awareness to the feeling of tiredness, which made it possible to develop a clear feeling of anger. Ellen's tiredness was caused by withheld anger that required regulation. Regulation involves becoming aware of the inner conflict between an emotional activation that naturally seeks expression and the defense that holds expression back. Ellen's cognitive defense was disrupted by focusing on her feeling of frustration, which clarified her low-intensity anger in the form of irritation. Affective Inquiry effectively tracks Ellen's affective activation, breaks through the defense and reestablishes contact with the regulation and integration process. When this is accomplished, Affective Inquiry provides support by following the organism's natural integration process until the cause of the problem and disturbance in Ellen´s inner balance dissolves.

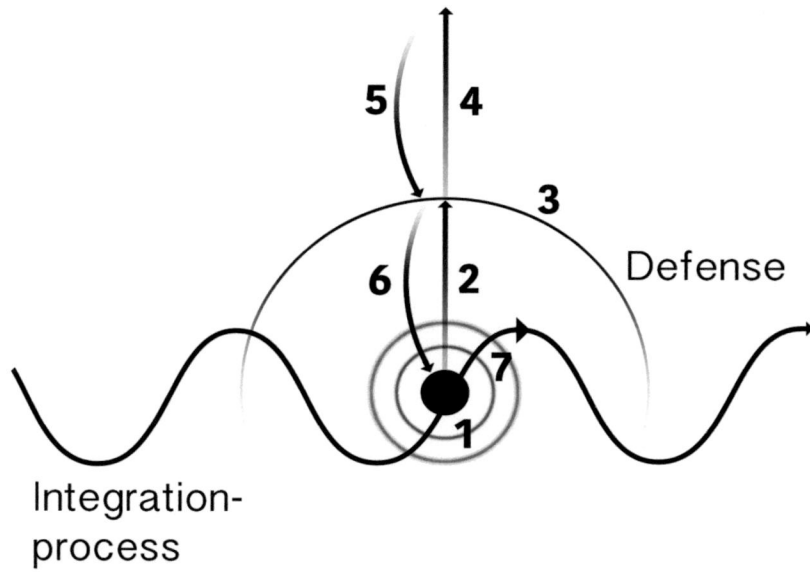

Defense

Integration-
process

Figure 26: The dynamics of Affective Inquiry
A problem or conflict arises when an unregulated emotion activates and is stopped (1). Fear activates and contact with the emotion is removed (2). The intensity of the cognitive defense increases after this (3) and the focus of awareness shifts away from the defense (4). Using Affective Inquiry, awareness returns to the cognitive defense (5) and focuses on the emotional activation that the person is avoiding (6). In conscious contact with unregulated emotional processes, Affective Inquiry facilitates continued contact with the emotion's affective cycle in its development as part of an integration process (7).

Affective Inquiry cuts through the complexity we experience in our problems. This complexity is the product of our cognitive defense that resists the simple solution of expression, acceptance and regulation of unregulated emotions. When in contact with what we feel, the techniques of Affective Inquiry make it possible to focus on the simple solutions hiding behind our complex mental tangle. Affective Inquiry interventions function as signposts that help us follow the natural unfolding of emotional response processes in the integration process. If dissociation from the integration process occurs, interventions are used to bring the dissociation into our focus of awareness and reestablish contact with feeling. Understanding the cause of a problem is the natural result of a completed emotional cycle. We do not need to seek a solution; it comes to us.

To defend ourselves is essentially a denial of personal responsibility. We think someone or something else caused our situation and we turn ourselves into a victim of circumstances. The core focus of Affective Inquiry is to reestablish personal responsibility by acknowledging our reality and what we feel. When a person for example talks about everything but their experience of the actual problem, Affective Inquiry breaks through this avoidant behavior and focuses on supporting the person into taking responsibility for what they experience. An Affective Inquiry facilitator does not interpret what a client says and expresses; the facilitator supports the client in their inquiry until answers appear through regulation and integration.

Affective resonance

In facilitating an integration process, the most important tool in Affective Inquiry is the facilitator's ability to achieve affective resonance. The ability to affectively resonate with another person makes it possible for the facilitator to experience affective charge in the other person's nervous system. Affective resonance together with knowledge of the way affective processes physically express themselves make it possible for the facilitator to follow and influence a person's contact with their affective system and feeling.

One way to effectively facilitate an integration process is by continuously observing and experiencing a person's physical affective processes. Affective resonance is achieved through attuned, affective mirroring that provides immediate information about changes in the client's affective state. We can see and experience when the intensity of contact with a feeling naturally increases and when the defense decreases in intensity. At the same time, affective resonance naturally supports regulation of a person's emotional processes. It is however necessary that the facilitator's emotional system is mature and trained to perform this mutual co-regulation properly. Without this, there is a risk that the facilitator's own defense will activate and negatively influence the client's process.

Affective resonance reveals both a person's affective intensity and the type of defense that is active. Affective intensity ranges from open, parasympathetically activated stillness to intense, sympathetically activated, dynamic activity. In affective resonance, the facilitator can notice when the client's emotional expression becomes mixed with fear activation as affective intensity becomes too great and chronic immobilization begins to take over. Eyes widen, respiration becomes shallower and faster, and emotional expression accelerates. These are signs that the intensity is becoming too great and indicate the need for an intervention to dissolve activated fear. If it is not dissolved, the defense's chronic immobility will intensify, emotional expression will stop and the cognitive defense will take over once again. Affective resonance keeps the focus on shifts in affective intensity, and through interventions, the facilitator helps adjust the client's process so emotional expression stays within the window of tolerance.

Affective tracking

Dissociation and defense activation involve every level of the human organism. When the defense keeps us from our integration process, it influences our natural, parasympathetically activated openness. The defense influences us physically, cognitively and in how we relate to others. Both our affective responses and the defense system appear on all three of these levels. During Affective Inquiry they function as signs that keep us on track toward unregulated emotions.

Affective resonance helps us perceive the affective trail and keeps us focused on signs that an affective response is about to break through the defense. The Affective Inquiry facilitator then supports the client's process back to clear contact with the activated emotion and the integration process. During this process the facilitator supports continuation of the integration process when the facilitator notices intensification of the defense in what the client says, their physical expression and/or in a relational context. The process of sensing and perceiving signs of emotional activation and the defense is called *affective tracking*. There are three forms of affective tracking: verbal, somatic and relational.

Verbal tracking

Verbal tracking involves paying attention to words and how they are used. What we say and particularly descriptive words are often connected to an underlying emotional activation. Something may be described as hard, difficult, fun, sorry or frustrating, or we my say that we love, hate, are confused, conflicted or do not understand etcetera. By focusing on and exploring what the words express, we draw attention to them and make room for them. This enhances contact with the emotional processes behind the words. With training it is possible to use affective resonance to sense when words are directly connected to a heightened affective charge and explore those words. Here are two examples of this dynamic:

> **Kevin:** It was hard to figure out what to do when she said that.
> **Facilitator:** In what way was it hard?
> **Kevin:** I was surprised.
> **Facilitator:** Surprised? Is that all?
> **Kevin:** Yes, surprised and irritated!
>
> ⁓⁓⁓⁓⁓⁓⁓⁓⁓⁓
>
> **Linda:** I feel ambivalent about what he said.
> **Facilitator:** Ambivalent? How so?
> **Linda:** Hmm... cold and confused.
> **Facilitator:** In what way cold?
> **Linda:** Well, (swallows)...so I would not have to feel how much it hurt.

The facilitator's interventions should convey curiosity, empathy and presence. These are necessary for effective inquiry and regulation. These qualities are expressed in the inquirer's presence, contact with feeling and interest, and are conveyed through the quality of the facilitator's voice and body language. In the above examples, the facilitator's focus on particular words made it possible for Kevin and Linda to feel the affective charge behind their words. It made them stop and focus on what they were actually saying. Asking directly about the emotional processes behind the words avoids discussion of what was said, which would tend to strengthen the cognitive defense.

Another example of verbal tracking is to draw attention to ambiguities, avoidance and contradictions in what is said. These verbal dynamics are often symptoms of unregulated emotional processes. By focusing on them, they can be used to directly connect to feeling and the integration process.

Somatic tracking

Since our bodies are the medium of the affective and emotional systems, our bodies automatically and continually provide information about these processes. Affective response activation is naturally expressed in the body and we are able to observe this activation and how a person relates to it when their defense reacts bodily with chronic immobility. This process is most clearly observed in the eyes, physical position, body movement, breath and voice. When Affective Inquiry draws attention to these phenomena, the client becomes aware of them and this enhances the affective process.

When we use somatic tracking, we follow signs of the integration process or the defense in physical expression and then track the physical process of affective charge. The facilitator intervenes for example when they observe autonomic body movements connected to affective activation. The observations may be movements in any part of the body but are most clear when hands and arms suddenly move due to an increase in affective charge. The facilitator can then enhance contact with the affective process by directing the client's attention to this movement and asking them to repeat it a few times to connect the client's movements to their feeling of emotional activation. By supporting the development of movement the client become aware of the muscular defense and it becomes possible to let go of the chronic immobility and allow an emotion to reach expression.

If a person holds their breath or breathes in a controlled, unnatural way, somatic tracking can draw attention to the somatic defense and explore what the person is holding back by breathing in this way. Another approach is to ask the client to breathe in a different way. For instance, if the client's breathing is rapid and shallow, the facilitator might ask what would it be like if the client breathed slowly and deeply. In Affective Inquiry it is also possible to directly ask how the body feels and then follow the development of this feeling. This is an intervention that bypasses the cognitive defense and offers direct contact with an activated, unregulated emotion. Asking directly about feeling in the body effectively focuses awareness on emotional processes and the integration process.

Relational tracking

When the defense system intensifies we are cut off from an activated emotion. When expression of an unregulated emotion is held back in relation to another person, we also defend against an open feeling of relational contact with that person. This can occur in relation to the one who activated the emotion but it can also be in relation to others nearby. Closing off the feeling of open relational contact is a defense against unregulated emotional activation. When facilitating a regulation process this may be observed in a client's lack of contact in their interaction with the facilitator. The client is more or less distant and does not open up in the relationship. The client may for example engage by talking about a problem but does not share how it affects them.

Using relational tracking, the facilitator discovers relational distancing and makes the client aware of it. The facilitator points out that the client is maintaining relational distance in the interaction and in this way defending against unregulated emotional processes. In relational tracking, the facilitator reads the relationship and asks the client about signs of a defense used in the client-facilitator relationship and openings in the defense. The facilitator may for example ask the client what they are trying to avoid by remaining relationally distant and what would happen if they returned to relational contact. The process can then continue with other interventions to keep awareness focused on contact with the affective process.

An important aspect of relational tracking involves making a person aware of the general pattern of interaction that appears in the client-facilitator relationship, for example the role or attitude the client takes in interaction with the facilitator and the role or attitude the client invites the facilitator to take in the interaction. In psychoanalysis this relational dynamic is referred to as transference and countertransference, which deals with how we as adults relate to important people in the same way we learned to relate to early caregivers (Grant & Crawley, 2002). Part of our defense against unregulated emotions involves taking on a specific role or attitude in our relationships, which also encourages the other person to take on a specific role, often one that is similar to that of an early caregiver.

This role or attitude is part of the defense system and contributes to maintaining the client's inner emotional conflicts. If the client for example learned to steer clear of unregulated anger either by letting others explain what needs to be done or by never daring to speak honestly about what is on their mind and what they are feeling, this will become manifest during the inquiry. Often the client does not take responsibility for the process and instead wants the facilitator to provide all the answers to their problems. An inexperienced inquirer may be tempted to provide answers, but with relational tracking, the focus of awareness is directed toward the behavior itself and the facilitator explores what the person is defending against. Dissolving the client's relational defense leads to direct contact with the unregulated emotional process.

Somatic focus in the integration process

An emotional response is a physical process in which emotions become activated to support physical expression and movement. When there is a disturbance in this process, emotional expression is held back by chronic immobility. A somatic focus on the emotional integration process draws attention to this physical defense and directly intervenes with it. In this way muscular chronic immobility dissolves and contact with the unregulated emotion is established. Using this method and without the client needing to think at all, the facilitator can support the completion of the interrupted emotional movement and come into direct contact with the emotional process that is being defended against.

The physical dynamic of an emotional disturbance makes it possible for a specific, conscious, emotional movement to continue expression of a withheld, unregulated emotional process. This is done either by relaxing an activated chronic mobilization or by activating chronic immobilization. In this way, an unregulated emotion can be facilitated to reach expression without cognitive participation or other stimuli. The decisive factor is direct influence on the muscular defense, which helps an incomplete sequence of emotional movements to reach completion. The emotion reawakens when we activate and become aware of an interrupted sequence of emotional movements.

Bypassing the cognitive defense, this method makes it possible to directly complete withheld emotional expression. When body movement is used in the integration process, emotional expression attains its natural focus. This reinforces the client's contact with emotional expression. Involving the body also strengthens awareness of the emotional process, which makes it easier to dissolve the cognitive defense. At the same time, trust is efficiently established in the emotional process and the body's response system. Instead of remaining an anxious and passive spectator of emotional conflicts, a somatic focus helps the client to become a proactive and responsible participant in the process of emotional regulation and integration. By being proactive, the client experiences having some control over the process.

A somatically focused integration process does not require much verbal communication to achieve emotional expression and regulation. In this process, cognitive understanding of the cause of an emotional conflict develops parallel to or after emotional expression and regulation. After completion of a somatic process, it is therefore important to cognitively work through the completed process in client/facilitator reflection and consider what the process has meant for the client.

The benefit of a somatic focus in the integration process lies in the efficiency with which it can break through years of emotional rigidity, inertia and automatic defense activation. A somatic focus can be of great support to the regulation process if the facilitator uses it without pressure as an invitation to actively explore what the client's body tells them.

Somatic signs of the window of tolerance

We are able to remain in emotional contact as long as emotional intensity is within or only slightly outside our window of tolerance. If emotional intensity becomes higher, the defense automatically activates. When a client's body is actively involved in a process of emotional regulation there is a risk that the intensity of emotional charge will rapidly exceed the limits of the person's window of tolerance. This may for example occur when a person who lacks a stable basic personality or a person who suffers from shock trauma makes emotional contact. To avoid this and to keep the defense from interrupting contact with the emotional process, it is necessary to pay attention to somatic signs that indicate when emotional intensity is within the limits of a person's window of tolerance and when the intensity is clearly outside this limit. The facilitator must be able work with this process, known in body psychotherapy as *grounding* (Lowen, 1976).

When the strategy of social engagement is active, our body displays somatic signs of being within the window of tolerance. In this state, expressions of the body's natural, affective responses are allowed and integrated without autonomic intensification of the body's muscular defense. As long as this remains within the limits of the window of tolerance, parasympathetic activation of the nervous system continues. This is indicated for example by good circulation to the extremities and the digestive system and a relatively natural respiration. During a process of emotional regulation, sympathetic activation and chronic immobility does not completely take over and the emotion can be expressed and regulated in conscious contact while the client maintains a form of control over the process. In this process the vagus nerve plays a central role in mediating inhibition of what would otherwise become a comprehensive, emotional, sympathetic activation (Frederickson, 2013).

A facilitator who is in affective resonance will register when the intensity of an emotion begins to move outside the limits of the window of tolerance and fear is activated. The facilitator will counteract this with verbal interventions that support a parasympathetic, physical openness. For instance by focusing attention on changes in respiration and supporting deeper and more relaxed breathing, an escalation toward hyperventilation caused by fear can dissolve. This lowers heartrate and sympathetic muscular contraction, which makes it possible for the client to feel their entire body. Active support of emotional movement in the torso, arms and legs also promotes parasympathetic openness in the body. The facilitator may for example provide feedback regarding a physically withheld emotion and suggest movements that support a balanced emotional expression without activating the defense.

242

Once we have learned to identify somatic signs of the window of tolerance and fear, we can facilitate expansion of the window of tolerance and make regulation of greater emotional intensity possible. By actively involving the body, the client is able to regulate higher intensity than they otherwise could contain.

Fear in the integration process

An important part of the process of emotional integration is the facilitator's ability to read the extent to which an unregulated emotion threatens the stability of the client's personality. The threat level of fear appears in the type of chronic immobility the defense intensifies. Determining the type of chronic immobility helps us understand the level of activated fear. Once we have determined this, it is relatively simple to choose the type of intervention that best fits a given integration process.

The relative intensity of fear can be seen on a scale from low to high. The scale can be divided into four different levels. The lowest level is the strategy of social engagement and the higher levels correspond to the three forms of chronic immobility.

Fear level 1: The strategy of social engagement
The lowest level of fear occurs when the strategy of social engagement is active. This is the natural fear that activates when we meet something new and uncertain. The experience of fear at this level is one of attentive readiness with a hedonic tone that ranges from slightly negative to slightly positive. We may feel butterflies in our stomach or be slightly nervous with an elevated pulse. This low-intensity level of fear may be accompanied by natural curiosity and expectation. This kind of fear activation is however often experienced as slight discomfort and insecurity. This is the feeling we have when we experience a loss of control while being aware that there is no real danger. Examples of this are when we go alone to a party where we do not know anyone, make a speech at a friend's birthday party or begin a rollercoaster ride. Common to all of these situations is that they activate the sympathetic survival system because we are entering uncertain territory. There is a naturally heightened readiness that occurs in situations which may become dangerous although there is no negative behavioral disturbance. This low-intensity fear can also

have positive effects in that it can help us focus and perform better. In a process of emotional regulation, low-intensity fear indicates to the facilitator that it is possible to intervene directly in relation to the unregulated emotion and support its expression. The client's personality is capable of coming into direct contact with the unregulated emotion and beginning the regulation without becoming unstable.

If an unregulated emotion constitutes a greater threat to personality, the emotion's intensity will exceed the limits of the window of tolerance. When this happens, chronic immobility intensifies, fear activates and the cognitive defense shifts the focus of awareness away from what is happening. The type of chronic immobility exhibited provides information about the relative intensity of fear. The types of chronic immobility are chronic mobilization, chronic immobilization and chronic shock.

Fear level 2: Chronic mobilization

Increased tension in striated musculature is a sign that chronic mobilization has intensified as a defense. Muscles tense to interrupt and control emotional expression and to prevent feeling contact with the emotion. The amount of muscular tension corresponds to the level of threat that the unregulated emotion represents to personality. A relatively low threat level appears as light tension and fear activation is low. This may be seen for example in patterns of autonomic muscular contraction and relaxation that display the shifts between the feeling of fear while connected to an unregulated emotion and interruptions in this contact. This is for example seen in physical restlessness when a client cannot sit still, or as movements that resemble tics with small tremors in hands, mouth or other parts of the body (ten Have-de Labije & Neborsky, 2012). If the relative intensity of fear becomes higher, it leads to more extensive chronic mobilization. This chronic mobilization may appear as physical tension with overly tense jaws, neck, back, shoulders, stomach and legs that cause the client to feel stiff and inflexible.

The intensity of fear when chronic mobilization activates is still relatively low. During an integration process the client is still able to relate to the fear and the unregulated emotional process without threatening the stability of personality. The client's personality is able to come into contact with the emotion that is being defended against, express the unregulated emotion and regulate it. The client's fear and withheld emotional processes can be directly confronted without causing defense activation to escalate as in the example of Paul, who experienced that his partner often violated his boundaries.

> **Facilitator:** How are you?
>   **Paul:** I feel tension in my jaws.
> **Facilitator:** How come?
>   **Paul:** (sensing and reflecting as his jaws open and shut) Hmm… it's
>   frustration… and I notice that my neck is tense, too.
> **Facilitator:** How does it feel if you move your neck a bit?
>   **Paul:** (moving his head from side to side) It hurts.
> **Facilitator:** And if you let yourself really feel that pain?
>   **Paul:** Oww… I feel irritated, too!
> **Facilitator:** What does this have to do with your relationship?
>   **Paul:** Hmm… Now I see. I'm angry about the way she acts.
> **Facilitator:** And how does she act?
>   **Paul:** She rejects me and takes over my responsibility just like my mother
>   did and that makes me angry.

The chronic mobilization that made Paul's jaws and neck tense was part of his defense against feeling fear and the underlying unregulated emotion of anger. By gradually becoming aware of stiffness and actively moving his stiff muscles, contact was established with emotional feeling and the emotion that chronic mobilization defended against. When this type of defense is directly confronted, what is noticed most often is not fear but resistance to the contact and discomfort (the hedonic tone of fear), followed by direct contact with the activated emotion.

Fear level 3: Chronic immobilization

When chronic immobilization intensifies, muscle tone in striated muscles collapses. Activation of an unregulated emotion causes the parasympathetic defense strategy of chronic immobilization to intensify and the person dissociates to avoid feeling the threatening emotion and fear. All the person's energy seems to vanish like a discharged battery. The person experiences a general feeling of numbness together with an inner, wordless conviction of being unable to do anything about their situation. The defense may be observed in such things as a slightly bowed torso and a low, monotonous voice. In general the person finds it difficult to experience relational contact and is often only cognitively present with many words, thoughts and fantasies.

When chronic immobilization intensifies, the level of fear is relatively high. The person's defense moves affective charge away from muscles and the person dissociates. The unregulated emotion is experienced as so threatening that it cannot be directly dealt with. In many cases what the client feels cannot be directly linked to an unregulated emotion and the client finds it difficult to explain what they are afraid of. Attempts to force further contact with the emotional activation at this point most often leads to an increased defense and cognitive dissociation.

When the intensity of fear is relatively high, the client needs to increase their capacity to experience fear. This is achieved by carefully and gradually exposing the client to fear activation. When the experience of fear is more or less accepted and stable it becomes possible to facilitate feeling contact with the unregulated emotion. It is often necessary to build up emotional capacity, a time-consuming process in which attempts to force emotional contact risk increasing activation of fear and the defense. Neutral physical contact can be used to support stability in contact with emotional feelings, for instance by encouraging the person to touch their hands, arms and legs and to focus on physical contact. Attention to feeling one's body anchors awareness in present physical experience, which fear moves us away from. This attention supports stable contact with the unregulated emotion and expression within the window of tolerance.

If contact with an emotional process is forced and develops too quickly, chronic immobilization will intensify and abruptly interrupt the client's contact with feeling. A client in the midst of this defense can in extreme cases experience cognitive disturbances such as difficulty with rational thought, blanking out or overwhelming confusion. Losing contact with physical reality in this way is a very unpleasant experience. Attempts to force contact with an unregulated emotion in this situation may lead to an uncontrolled escalation of fear, a process reminiscent of the state of chronic shock.

Fear level 4: Chronic shock

Chronic shock is a state of tense collapse, a seemingly contradictory state described earlier in Chapter 12. When this chronic immobility intensifies, the client can no longer exert self-control and collapses in the grip of a highly tense, affective charge. When a person experiences fear at this level the most important thing is to discharge this tense affective charge before continuing further with affective regulation.

Continued contact with emotional feeling or fear when chronic shock intensifies risks an increase in the intensity of fear, which can quickly escalate out of control. A self-reinforcing spiral of fear occurs. The more fear is experienced, the greater its intensity, a dynamic of fear which seems to take on a life of its own. The relative intensity of fear becomes higher than the client can deal with or defend against and fear takes over. Attempts at emotional regulation or just contact with feeling increases the fear. Physical signs of chronic shock include visibly tight throat muscles like taut wires, shallow breathing and wide-open eyes.

An effective way of deescalating fear is to shift the client's focus to their physical environment such as objects in the room. At this level of escalating fear it is most important to break contact with the fear and other emotions so the person can return to neutral, here-and-now experience in order to stabilize personality. The client will need help to make this shift from an almost exclusively inner to an outer focus, from the experience of being trapped to outer, neutral reality (Rothschild, 2017). This is achieved by focusing on objects in the room and asking the client to describe their form, color, structure etcetera. Slowly repeating this process for a few minutes, the client's focus of awareness shifts to the environment and fear is dissolved. It is a powerful intervention that is necessary when fear escalates in a self-reinforcing spiral and the client's contact with fear must be broken.

When focus has shifted, fear has decreased and its physical effects are gone, the client needs to reflect on the process together with the facilitator. Reflection on what happened helps to create a cognitive structure for understanding the process of fear, when it activates, its initial signs and what triggers it. This provides perspective, predictability and safety and makes it possible for the client to avoid a tense escalation of affective charge in the future. Increased awareness of the fear process and its causes can eventually lead to regulation of the emotional process that caused it.

Learning about the process of fear, the defense and the integration process is also in general valuable for a client in a regulation process. The following example demonstrates facilitation of a regulation process in the case of chronic shock.

> Betty found it difficult to market herself as a consultant even though she was good at expressing herself in writing. Every time she sat down at her computer to write marketing text, she experienced that her thoughts stopped and that she could not continue. In this session, Betty declared a strong wish to present herself, her skills and what her business could provide.

> Focusing on this theme of standing for her own worth and using Affective Inquiry, Betty experienced a slight increase in emotional intensity followed by a sudden blank. Inquiry into the cause of this blank experience, however, took a quick turn. Betty's affective intensity increased rapidly in a visibly distinct upward body movement. Her throat stiffened, her breath became shallow and her eyes glazed over and were empty. This was an escalating spiral of fear and continued conscious contact with the event only led to a further escalation of fear. It became clear that Betty was trapped in a process of intensified chronic shock. Therefore, the intervention shifted focus away from contact with the session's theme and the experience of fear. Betty was distinctly told to look at a colorful picture hanging on the wall and was asked to describe its colors, forms and frame with questions such as, "What colors are used on the person to the right in the picture?" or, "How would you describe the frame?". This was followed by shifting focus to flowers on the windowsill with similar questions and then shifting focus again to the rug on the floor. After three or four minutes of this, Betty's focus of awareness completely shifted to the room and her fear dissolved.

> When Betty was calm again and seemed stable, the session continued by reflecting on what had happened. Betty reflected on how the fear had developed quickly at a certain point and realized that it actually had activated earlier. By shielding herself from the early low-intensity activation of fear, its later activation erupted

with explosive force. Betty understood that this was an important insight. She had ignored low-intensity fear that only led to swift escalation later. According to her, she could see that she had been too "quick in her mind", that she was pushing herself, and a key phrase for her was to "Go slow". With this insight, the session continued. Consciously and slowly returning to the theme, Betty now becomes aware of a low level of fear activation. When this occurred her hands began a grasping movement and she was asked to grab a pillow. This tactile support helped her to remain stable while she felt the emotional process begin as she paid attention to the feeling of fear, which was followed by a feeling of sadness. This feeling of sadness is what had activated the fear. Betty's sadness was expressed in tears and afterward she became still. She felt relieved and deeply understood that it was important for her to go slow so she could stay in touch with what she was doing. In this way she could self-regulate so fear would not take over. This was especially important in relation to standing for her own self-worth, which was the theme of the session and which she had learned earlier in life had negative consequences.

Facilitating a process in which chronic shock intensifies requires clarity and patience. The explosive quality of fear is counteracted by going slowly with a clear focus on external physical reality. At the first sign of dissociation, contact with the emotional process must be broken and focus must shift to the here -and-now to allow fear to subside. After this it is important to cognitively digest what has happened. It often takes several sessions of dealing with fear before work with an unregulated emotion can begin. The session presented here with Betty took place after building trust over eight sessions.

PART VI

THE CONSEQUENCES OF INSUFFICIENT INTEGRATION

Chapter 16

Problems and conflicts

There are many times in life when we think circumstances are against us and we say to ourselves, "If things were different, my life would be better and easier" or "If only I were different, everything would be fine". These thoughts or unconscious convictions can take up a good deal of our awareness and have a negative impact on the quality of our lives. We convince ourselves that something, someone or we ourselves must be different for our problems to go away. These problems can range from minor daily frictions with those we live together with to major conflicts, and from small irritations that are quickly forgotten to deeper existential problems and crises that affect how we function in our daily life.

This is a human dynamic caused by emotional wounds. To avoid experiencing these wounds, our cognitive defense convinces us that something in our environment or our own behavior is causing the problem or difficulty. In reality we are actually defending ourselves from ourselves and our own unregulated emotions. By blaming ourselves or others for our discomfort, we protect ourselves from unregulated emotions and distance ourselves from these emotions in a process of avoidance.

As they all share the same dynamic, we use the term "problems" for our challenges, conflicts and the difficulties we encounter in life. A problem is the circumstance or person that seems to be the cause of a disturbance in our inner calm and balance. When we have a problem, we feel discomfort in a particular situation and experience that we are limited and frustrated. We experience being trapped by a problem because we are unable to avoid or solve it. A problem can be practical or personal and can disturb us to a greater or lesser degree. We often view a problem as an opponent and we struggle with it, try to ignore it or collapse in defeat when we see no solution for it. Regardless of how serious the problem is, our ways of looking at it and relating to it are parts of a learned defense. The defense does not however improve the situation, in fact it does just the opposite.

The term "problem" comes from the Greek word probàllein (pro=forward and bàllein=to throw), a term which illustrates the dynamic in every problem. In this dynamic we shift cognitive focus from our feelings to the world around us. When we have a problem, we are influenced by something that causes an experience of discomfort and therefore shift our focus of awareness away from the experience of discomfort to what we believe is the cause of our discomfort. In this way we avoid having to look at what actually caused the discomfort in us. Discomfort is low-intensity fear activation with a negative hedonic tone that comes as a response to a withheld, unregulated emotion. Our defense against expression of the withheld emotion shifts our focus of awareness away from the emotion to the person or circumstance that activated the emotion. We end up viewing the person or circumstance as the cause of our discomforting problem, rather than the unregulated emotion.

The dynamic of this defense automatically shifts responsibility for our experience onto someone or something else, and we believe the deception. As a consequence, there is a big difference between how we describe an experienced problem if we take responsibility for the situation, as opposed to how we describe it if we do not take personal responsibility for it. Here are a couple of examples of this:

> **Taking responsibility:** "It pains me that I get so mad when I experience him as difficult."
> **No responsibility:** "If he were not so damned difficult, I would not have to fight him so much."

> **Taking responsibility:** "I become frustrated and saddened that I cannot meet my own demands on myself when he is this slow."
> **No responsibility:** "If he could just be a bit quicker, I would not be so irritated."

The dynamic of problems moves our focus away from experienced discomfort. Discomfort is low-intensity fear activation, often an undefined feeling with negative hedonic tone stemming from an inner conflict between on the one hand an activated, unregulated emotion and on the other hand the defense that interrupts the emotion's process and holds it back. Our cognitive defense assists the defense by turning off contact with the feeling, thereby avoiding the discomfort of fear. We experience instead reactive feelings such as irritation, frustration, suffering or hopelessness in relation to whatever or whomever we see as the cause of our emotional activation.

Inner conflicts

In the dynamics of problems we do not accept our reality, that is, the activation of an unregulated emotion. If we accepted our reality, we would naturally come into contact with the emotion and express it. Instead we struggle with our inner truth and find ourselves in a conflict both within ourselves and with our surroundings. Here are some examples of this:

> "I do not accept that we are no longer together because then I would come into contact with the sadness I feel about not being loved."
> "I cannot accept that you are angry because then I would feel how angry I am."
> "I cannot accept that you are happy because then I would feel the pain of my own lack of happiness in life."

When we have an inner conflict, an emotional wound is touched and its associated, unregulated processes are activated. The situation itself does not cause this activation but something in the situation is reminiscent of what happened when the emotional wound was created. Neuroception picks up information that appears to be similar to that early situation and activates the same unregulated emotion as then. After this, the defense activates to keep the unregulated emotion from being expressed. It is this similarity to a previous situation that activates and holds back the unregulated emotion, not the person or circumstance at hand.

The negative consequences of defense activation are that it cuts us off from important personal resources and it limits our available expressions in daily life. Our behavioral flexibility decreases and our relational resources shrink. If we for example learned not to show anger, it becomes difficult to set limits in relation to other people in general. A life without the ability to set natural limits has many negative aspects including the fact that others will overstep our boundaries and not respect us in various ways, as in this example:

> Audrey thinks her manager does not listen to her. She feels overlooked compared to another colleague who gets all the interesting tasks and more positive feedback from their manager. Audrey's manager does not see it this way and thinks Audrey is making a mountain out of a molehill. At times Audrey feels frustrated, as if she is boiling inside but finds it difficult to say anything constructive about it to her manager. Instead she withdraws, which makes her even less visible to her manager.

> During a session, Audrey becomes aware that a boiling anger she finds difficult to deal with is hiding behind her discomfort. She expresses the anger she feels towards the fact that her manager does not take her seriously and in her eyes oversteps her boundaries. Audrey has at this point an insight and recognizes a pattern in all that has happened to her which goes back her to her relationship with her father when she was young. Her sister got all her father's attention and if Audrey became angry about this she got even less attention from her father. By feeling, expressing and taking responsibility for her anger during the session, Audrey came to understand the source of the problem with her manager. The situation at work reminded her of the situation with her father when her anger was not accepted. Audrey also realized that she only noticed this after her manager had ignored her and overstepped her boundaries several times. Accepting her anger and insights, Audrey felt motivated to take responsibility for herself and her boundaries and to begin a constructive dialogue with her manager about her tasks at work.

Audrey thought her manager's behavior had caused her discomfort. Audrey's discomfort was however in reality caused by the inner conflict between her activated anger and the defense that held her anger back. Her anger was activated because the situation at work was similar to the situation with her father where she learned to hold back her anger and avoid demanding her share of attention. As a consequence of this dynamic Audrey found it generally difficult to stand up for herself and set boundaries, which resulted in limited behavioral flexibility and the experience of her boundaries often being overstepped by others.

By withdrawing, Audrey's boundaries became less noticeable to others, they could not sense her boundaries and it became even easier for them to overstep her boundaries. When Audrey began to regulate and accept her anger, she experienced that the anger was not as threatening as before. This increased her behavioral flexibility and it was easier for her to stand up for herself and her boundaries.

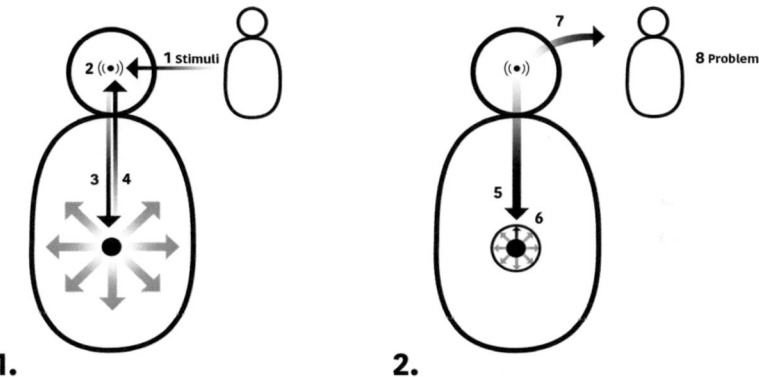

1.   **2.**

Figure 27: Our inner conflict creates the problem
Stimuli (1) are registered in neuroception due to an emotional wound (2) and activate an emotional response (3). The defense detects feedback (4) from the activation and holds back emotional expression by intensifying chronic immobility (5). This causes an inner conflict (6). To avoid feeling the discomfort coming from the inner conflict (the fear), the cognitive defense shifts the focus of awareness (7) away from the conflict and toward what is experienced as the cause of the discomfort. A person or circumstance becomes the problem (8) instead of the unregulated emotion.

While the cause of our problems with someone or something lies in ourselves, it is important to clarify that this does not mean that the circumstances or what another person does is acceptable and right. That is an entirely different question and it has nothing to do with our inner conflict. It is for example a quite natural human response to be upset, angry or saddened when another person treats an animal or another human being badly. However if we feel emotional discomfort for a long time or find it difficult to deal with this emotionally, it means an unregulated emotion has been activated, the defense is holding the emotion back and an inner conflict is ongoing.

Problem-free life?

A human organism is in constant development and as part of a living process we will always be challenged by life. To follow this natural development we must recognize the challenges, conflicts and problems we meet. Many people do not recognize that they face challenges and have difficulties. This is most often a form of highly efficient defense that thoroughly keeps inner conflicts away from awareness. These people hold unregulated emotions back and instead meet others and themselves with reactions that are similar to emotions. They are often unaware of their inner states and are convinced that others, circumstances or their own behavior are the cause of their challenges and difficulties. One example of this dynamic may be seen in the case of a therapist in training who went to therapy as part of her training, although she did not think she needed it. After one year of therapy and self-reflection, this student wrote:

"When I began my training, I did not think I had any major problems. After one year in training, I am happy to say that I have a lot of them!"

This student had discovered how she effectively and automatically defended herself against her own emotional feelings. By regaining contact with these feelings her life had become more satisfying and she had a deeper relationship with herself even though she was now aware of her problems. Her insights also brought her into contact with her own needs and her need to prioritize in order to achieve a meaningful life. Another student who also had an opening in his effective defense against emotional contact commented:

"From living in a two-dimensional, black-and-white world, it is as if I have begun to live in three dimensions and in technicolor. It is not only pleasant, but I feel like I am finally alive!"

If a person effectively closes off contact with emotional feelings, it often requires a personal crisis to crack open the defense. A close relative's death, a divorce, miscarriage or other life-changing events can rupture a solid defense. This kind of high-level emotional strain can make it difficult to maintain the defense, the person will experience inner chaos and they may become motivated to begin a process of personal development. In hindsight the crisis appears as a necessary evil that we do not wish undone. When we live through a crisis and regulate its emotional consequences, we open up to our response system and gain deeper emotional contact with ourselves. We now have the chance to find a more responsible and satisfying way of living in relation to others and ourselves.

Interpersonal conflicts

Conflicts with others are symptoms of our inner conflicts. When we do not accept reality, for instance that a person has a differing opinion, it is because of an unregulated emotion activated in ourselves. The other person becomes a problem for us and if the other person cannot accept our opinion either, then we become a problem for the other person as well and a conflict arises. This is the basic dynamic in every interpersonal conflict: two or more people experience the other person or persons as a problem. They cannot accept each other's behavior or opinions because it activates an unregulated emotion in themselves. Each person's unregulated emotional processes make the other person a problem and conflict arises.

Participants in an interpersonal conflict project the reason for their own inner conflict and discomfort onto someone else. Take this conversation between Larry and Lucy for example:

>   **Larry:** I do not want to visit your mother this weekend. We were there two weeks ago and this weekend I want to watch football at home.
>   **Lucy:** That visit two weeks ago was the only time we have visited my mother in the past six months!
>   **Larry:** I don't want to be with your family all the time. We are never with my family!
>   **Lucy:** You are always thinking about yourself and what you want. You are so egotistical. You can stay home on your own, I am leaving without you! (Lucy slams the door as she leaves)

Unregulated emotions were activated in both Larry and Lucy because of the other's behavior. Both of them thought the other was the cause of this unpleasant, escalating conflict. On both sides, their defense against contact with unregulated emotions was so strong that they automatically expressed reactive resistance instead of engaging in meaningful dialogue. Expressions of reactive irritation created a self-amplifying process in which a reaction from one side led to a new reaction from the other which then led to another reaction and the conflict escalated.

The negative, escalating spiral of conflict continues to grow as long as the two continue to react to each other. Their defenses took over and hijacked their awareness. Both Larry and Lucy were unaware that they were defending themselves. Both of them automatically experienced that the other person wanted to hurt them due to the other's defensive behavior of reactive resistance. This naturally activated their own defensive behavior and a reactive resistance. As long as this dynamic continues to direct their behavior, the conflict will remain unresolved.

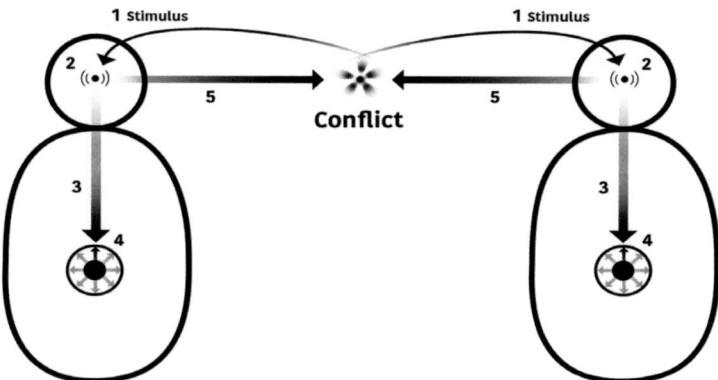

Figure 28: An interpersonal conflict
An interpersonal conflict occurs when two or more people become a problem for each other. On both sides, the behavior and/or opinion of the other functions as a stimulus (1) that activates an unregulated emotion (2). Each person's unregulated emotion is held back by their defense (3), causing an inner conflict (4). Discomfort from this inner conflict causes their focus of awareness to shift away from the inner conflict to what they consider to be the cause of their discomfort, that is, the other person (5). Once the other person is identified as the problem and defensive reactiveness is directed towards them (1), an unregulated emotion is again activated in the other person (2). This is the dynamic of escalating conflict spirals.

To resolve interpersonal conflicts the dynamic of reactive defense must stop. Everyone needs sufficient space to be able to shift focus to getting in contact with their underlying unregulated emotional activations, to express them and to experience that their expression was OK.

This process of conflict solving can be difficult and is often impossible in the midst of escalating conflict. There is a strong tendency for the pattern of reactive resistance and conflict to take over again. External assistance is often needed, a person who can create a safe structure for a process of solution and mediation between the parties. This is not a simple process. It involves helping both parties to confront their own unregulated emotions and later to carefully mediate the dialogue between them.

Afterword

In this book we have seen how affects and emotions are expressions of our human life process. The human organism, body and personality, is an expression of this life process and our quality of life depends on the extent to which we can accept this process and life's unfolding. Life is not a problem to be solved; problems arise when we stop the natural unfolding of life.

Personal development and growth in this context involves turning our gaze inward to discover where and how we stop our life process. Personal development and growth are not goals to be achieved, something to strive for and struggle with or a transformation into someone other than who we are. It is about returning to the present and meeting life as we are, dealing with what we feel and expressing our feelings, needs and intentions. When we take ourselves seriously in this way, we are able to end the dramas created by old, unfinished emotional processes in our life. The complexity of life disappears and is replaced by simplicity when our behavior becomes an extension of who we are.

References

Ainsworth, M. D., Behar, M.-C., Waters, E. & Wall, S. N. (2015). *Patterns of attachment: a study of the strange situation*. New York: Psychology Press.

Armstrong, K. (2010). *Twelve steps to a compassionate life*. Waterville: Thorndike Press.

Averill, J. R. (2011). *Anger and aggression: an essay on emotion*. New York: Springer-Verlag Inc.

Bargh, J. A. (1997). The automaticity of everyday life. In: Wyer Jr., R. S. (ed.), *Advances of social cognition, 10*, 1–62. Hillsdalc, NJ: Erlbaum.

Bargh, J. A., Chaiken, S., Raymond, P. & Hymes, C. (1996). The automatic evaluation effect: unconditionally automatic attitude activation with a pronunciation task. *Journal of Experimental Psychology. 32*, 185–210.

Barrett, L. F. (2017). *How emotions are made: the secret life of the brain*. London: Pan Books.

Bartels, A. & Zeki, S. (2000). The neural basis of romantic love. *Neuroreport. 11*, 3834–3929.

Bentzen, M. (2015). Shapes of experience. In: Marlock, G. & Weiss, H., (eds.), *The handbook of bodypsychotherapy & somatic psychology*. Berkeley: North Atlantic Books.

Bentzen, M. & Hart, S. (2012). Jegets fundament: den neuroaffektive udviklings første vækstbølge og neuroaffektive kompasser. In: Hart, S. (ed.), *Neuroaffektiv psykoterapi med voksne*. Köpenhamn: Hans Reitzels Forlag.

Berceli, D. (2008). *The revolutionary trauma release process*. Vancouver: Namaste Publishing.

Berceli, D. (2015). *Shake it off naturally – reduce stress, anxiety and tension with TRE*. USA: Createspace Independent Publishing Platform.

Bertalanffy, L. (1969). *General system theory*. New York: Georg Braziller Inc.

Bowlby, J. (1969). *Attachment and loss: Vol. 1. Attachment.* New York: Basic Books.

Breiter, H. C., Golllub, R. L., Weiskoff, R. M., Makris, N., Berek, J. D., Goodman, J. M., Kantor, H. L., Gastfriend, D. R., Riorden, J. P., Mathew, R. T., Rosen, B. R. & Hyman, S. E. (1997). Acute effects of cocaine on human brain activity and emotion. *Neuron, 19,* 519-611.

Brown, B. (2012). *Daring greatly.* New York: Gotham books.

Bruner, J. S. (1990). *Acts of meaning.* Cambridge: Harvard University Press.

Buchannan, T. W., Tranel, D. & Adolphs, R. (2006). Memories for emotional auto-biographical events follow unilateral damage of medical temporal lobe. *Brain – A Journal of Neurology,* 115–127.

Bull, N. (1945). Towards a clarification of the concept of emotion. *Psychosomatic Medicine, 7*(4), 210–214.

Bull, N. (1951). *The attitude theory of emotion.* New York: Nervous and Mental Disease Monographs.

Butler, D. & Moseley, L. (2003). *Explain pain.* Adelaide: Noigroup Publications.

Butler, D. & Moseley, L. (2015). *Explain pain handbook.* Adelaide: Noigroup Publications.

Cannon, W. (1927). *Bodily changes in pain, hunger, fear and rage.* New York, London: D. Appleton & Company.

Carroll, R. (2012). På grænsen mellem kaos og orden: hvad psykoterapi og neuroviden-skab har til fælles. In: Hart, S. (ed.), *Neuroaffektiv psykoterapi med voksne.* Köpenhamn: Hans Reitzels Forlag.

Cicchetti, D. & Tucker, D. (1994). Development and self-regulatory structures of the mind. *Development and Psychopathology Journal. 6,* 533-549.

Clynes, M. & Nettheim, N. (1982). The living quality of music: neurobiological patterns of communicating feelings. In: Clynes, M. (ed.), *Music, mind and brain: the neurophysiology of music.* 47–82. New York: Plenum Press.

Coyle, D. (2009). *The talent code.* New York: Arrow Books.

Cozolino, L. (2014). *The neuroscience of human relationships.* New York: Norton.

Damasio, A. (1994). *Descartes error.* New York: G. P. Putnam & Sons.

Damasio, A. (1999). *A feeling of what happens.* London: Vintage.

Damasio, A. (2012). *Self comes to mind.* London: Vintage.

Darwin, C. (1872). *On the expression of the emotions in man and animals.* New York: D. Appleton. (New print: 1965, Chicago: University of Chicago Press.)

Dutton, K. (2012). *The wisdom of psychopaths.* London: Random House.

Eagle, M. & Wolitzky, D. L. (2009). The perspective of attachment theory and psychoanalysis: adult psychotherapy. In: Obegi, J. & Berant, E. (eds.), *Attachment theory and research in clinical work with adults.* New York: Guilford Press.

Ekman, P. (2003). *Emotions revealed.* London: Weidenfeld & Nicolson.

Erikson, E. (1959). *Identity and lifecycle: Vol. 1. Selected papers. Psychological issues.* New York: International University Press.

Fields, D. R. (2009). *The other brain.* New York: Simon & Schuster Inc.

Fisher, L., Ames, E. W., Chisholm, K. & Savoie, L. (1997). Problems reported by parents of Romanian orphans adopted to British Columbia. *International Journal of Behavioural Development. 20,* 67–82.

Fuster, J. M. (1997). *The prefrontal cortex: anatomy, physiology and neuropsychology of the frontal lobe.* Philadelphia: Lippincott-Raven.

Frederickson, J. (2013). *Co-creating change: effective dynamic therapy techniques.* Kansas City: Seven Leaves Press LLC.

Fredrickson, B. (2013). *Love 2.0: creating happiness and health in moments of connection.* New York: Hudson Street Press.

Freud, S. (1959). *Inhibitions, symptoms and anxiety.* New York: W. W. Norton & Co.

Frey, W. H. (1985). *Crying: the mystery of tears.* Minneapolis: Winston Press.

Gallese, V., Fadiga, L., Fogassi, L. & Rizzolatti, G. (1996). Action recognition in the premotor cortex. *Brain, 119*(2), 593–609.

Georgiadis, J. R. & Kortekaas, R. (2010). The sweetest taboo: functional neurobiology of human sexuality in relation to pleasure. In: Kringelbach, M. L. & Berridge, K. C. (eds.), *Pleasures of the brain.* 178–201, Oxford: Oxford University Press.

Germer, C. K. & Siegel, R. D. (2012). *Wisdom and compassion in psychotherapy.* New York: Guilford Press.

Geuter, U. & Schrauth, N. (2001). Emotionen und Emotionsabwehr als Körperprozess. *Psychotherapie Forum. 9*, 4–19.

Gilbert, P. (2009). Introducing compassion based therapy. *Advances in Psychiatric Treatment. 15*, 199–208.

Gilbert, P. & Irons, C. (2005). Therapies for shame and self-attacking, using cognitive, behavioural, emotional imagery and compassionate mind training. In: Gilbert, P. (ed.), *Compassion: conceptualization, research and use in psychotherapy.* 263-325. London: Routledge.

Gould, S. J. (1977). *Ontogeny and phylogeny.* Cambridge: Belknap Press of Harvard University.

Grant, J. & Crawley, J. (2002). *Transference and projection-mirrors to the self.* Berkshire: Open University Press.

Grof, S. (2012). *Healing our deepest wounds.* Newcastle: Stream of Experience Productions.

Haines, S. (2015). *Pain is really strange.* London: Singing Dragon.

Harris, S. (2012). *Free will.* New York: Free Press.

Hart, S. (2011). *The impact of attachment.* New York: W. W. Norton & Company Inc.

Hart, S. & Bentzen, M. (2012). Jegets fundament: den neuroaffektive udviklings første vækstbølge og neuroaffektive kompasser. In: Hart, S. (ed.), *Neuroaffektiv psykoterapi med voksne.* Köpenhamn: Hans Reitzels Forlag.

Hill, D. (2015). *Affect regulation theory.* New York: W. W. Norton & Company Inc.

Hubble, M. A., Duncan, B. L. & Miller, S. D. (eds.) (1999). *The heart and soul of change.* Washington: American Psychological Association.

Iacoboni, M. (2008). *Mirroring people.* New York: Farrar, Strauss & Giroux.

Jack, R. E., Garrod, O. G. B. & Schyns, P. G. (2014). Dynamic facial expressions of emotion transmit an evolving hierarchy of signals over time. *Current Biology, 24* (2), 187–192.

Jackson, J. H. (1958). Evolution and dissolution of the nervous system. In: Taylor, J. (ed.), *Selected writings of John Hughlings Jackson.* London: Staples Press.

James, W. (1884). What is an emotion. *Mind, 9*(34), 188–205. Oxford: Oxford University Press.

Kalat, J. (2001). *Biological psychology.* Belmont CA.: Wadsworth.

Kapleau, P. (1989). *The three pillars of zen.* New York: Anchor Books.

Kohut, H. (1971). *Analysis of the self: a systematic approach to the psychoanalytic treatment of narcissistic personality disorders.* Chicago: University of Chicago Press.

Krishnamurti, J. (1975). *The first and last freedom.* San Francisco: Harper.

Laplanche, J. & Pontalis, J. B. (1973). *The language of psychoanalysis.* London: Hogarth Press Ltd.

Laszlo, E. (1996). *The systems view of the world.* Cresskill: Hampton Press Inc.

LeDoux, J. E. (1996). *The emotional brain.* New York: Simon & Schuster.

LeDoux, J. E. (2015). *Anxious - the modern mind in the age of anxiety.* London: One World Publications.

Levine, P. A. (1997). *Waking the tiger: healing trauma.* Berkeley: North Atlantic Books.

Levine, P. A. (2010). *In an unspoken voice: how the body releases trauma and restores goodness.* Berkeley: North Atlantic Books.

Libet, B. (1983). *Neurophysiology and consciousness.* Boston: Birkhäuser.

Llinás, R. R. (2002). *I of the vortex – from neurons to self.* Westwood: First MIT Press.

Louw, A. (2013). *Why do I hurt?* Minneapolis: Orthopedic Physical Therapy Products.

Lowen, A. (1976). *Bioenergetics.* New York: Penguin Books.

Lowen, A. (2003). *The language of the body – physical dynamics of character structure.* Alachua: Bioenergetics Press.

MacLean, P. D. (1990). *The triune brain in evolution: role in paleocerebral functions.* New York: Plenum.

Mahler, M., Pine, F. & Bergman, A. (1975). *The psychological birth of the human infant.* New York: Basic Books.

Marcher, L. & Fich, S. (2010). *Body encyclopedia – a guide to the psychological functions of the muscular system.* Berkeley: North Atlantic Books.

Marsden, C. D., Rothwell, J. C. & Day, B. L. (1984). The use of peripheral feedback in the control of movement. *Trends in Neuroscience,* 253–257.

Maslow, A. H. (1943). A theory of human motivation. *Psychological Review, 50* (4), 370–396.

Maslow, A. H. (1968). *Toward a psychology of being.* New York: Van Nostrand.

Meltzoff, A. N. & Moore, M. K. (1977). Imitation of facial and manual gestures by human neonate. *Science, 198*, 75–78.

Meston, C. M. & Buss, D. M. (2009). *Why women have sex.* New York: Times Books.

Mitchell, S. A. & Black, M. J. (1995). *Freud and beyond.* New York: Basic Books.

Moseley, G. L . & Butler, D. S. (2015). *The explain pain handbook.* Adelaide: Noigroup Publications.

Nave, C., Sherman, R. A., Funder, D. C., Hampson, S. E. & Goldberg, L. R. (2010). On the contextual independence of personality: teachers assesment predicts directly observed behaviour after four decades. *Social Psychological and Personality Science, 8* (3) 1–9.

Ogden, P., Minton, K. & Pain, C. (2006). *Trauma and the body: a sensorimotor approach to psychotherapy.* New York: W. W. Norton & Company Inc.

Ogden, P. (2015). *Sensorimotor psychotherapy: interventions for trauma and attachment.* New York: W. W. Norton & Company Inc.

Panksepp, J. & Biven, L. (2012). *The archaeology of mind.* New York: W. W. Norton & Company Inc.

Penguin dictionary (1985). *The Penguin dictionary of psychology.* London: Penguin Press Ltd.

Peper, E. & Lin, I. M. (2012). Increase or decrease depression: how body postures influence your energy level. *Biofeedback, 40*(3), 125–130.

Porges, S. W. (2011). *The polyvagal theory.* New York: W. W. Norton & Company Inc.

Presti, D. E. (2016). *Foundational concepts in neuroscience.* New York: W. W. Norton & Co.

Regan, P. C. & Berscheid, E. (1999). *Lust: what we know of human sexual desire.* Thousand Oaks: Sage Publications.

Reich, W. (1942). *The function of the orgasm.* New York: Orgone Institute Press.

Reich, W. (1950). *Character analysis.* London: Vision Press Limited.

Ross, E. D., Homan, R. W. & Buck, R. (1994). Differential hemispheric lateralization of primary and social emotions. *Neuropsychiatry, Neuropsychology and Behavioral Neurology, 7*, 1–19.

Rotschild, B. (2017). *The body remembers, Volume 2. Revolutionizing trauma treatment.* New York: W. W. Norton & Co.

Sabetti, S. (1991). *Process inquiry.* Sherman Oaks: Institute for Life Energy.

Sabetti, S. (1993). *Waves of change: dynamics and practice of personal change.* Sherman Oaks: Life Enery Media.

Schlaepfer, T. E., Strain, E. C., Greenberg, B. D., Preston, K. L., Lancaster, E., Bigelow, G. E., Barta, B. E. & Pearlson, G. D. (1998). Site of opiod activation in human brain: mu and kappa agonists subjective and cerebral blood flow effects. *American Journal of Psychiatry, 155*, 470–473.

Schore, A. (2003). *Affect regulation and repair of the self.* New York: W. W. Norton & Co.

Schore, A. (2012). *The science of the art of psychotherapy.* New York: W. W. Norton & Co.

Schore, A. (2016). *Affect regulation and the origin of the self.* New York: Routledge.

Seligman, M. E. P. (2002). *Authentic happiness.* Boston: Nicholas Brealey Publishing.

Seth, A. (2021). *Being you: a new science of consciousness.* London: Faber & Faber Ltd.

Shapiro, D. (2006). *Your body speaks your mind.* Boulder: Sounds True Inc.

Siegel, D. (1999). *The developing mind.* New York: Guilford Press.

Siegel, D. (2010). *The mindfull therapist.* New York: W. W. Norton & Co.

Siegel, D. (2012). Følelser som integration: et muligt svar på spørgsmålet - hvad er følelser? In: Hart, S. (ed.), *Neuroaffektiv psykoterapi med voksne.* Köpenhamn: Hans Reitzels Forlag.

Siegel, D. (2017). *Mind - a journey to the heart of being human.* New York: W. W. Norton & Company Inc.

Southwell, C. (1990). Biodynamische Psychologie. In: Rowan, J. & Dryden, W. (eds.), *Neue Entwicklungen der Psychotherapie.* 198–221. Oldenburg: Transform.

Spiering, M. & Everaerd, W. (2006). The sexual unconscious. In: Janssen, E. (ed.), *The psychophysiology of sex.* 166–184. Bloomington: Indiana University Press.

Spitz, R. A. & Wolf, K. M. (1946). Analytic depression: an inquiry into the genesis of psychiatric conditions in early childhood. *Psychoanalytic Study of the Child, 2*, 313-343.

Stern, D. N. (1985). *The interpersonal world of the infant.* New York: Basic Books Inc.

Stern, D. N. (1998). *The motherhood constellation.* London: Karnac Books.

Stern, D. N. (2004). *The present moment.* New York: W. W. Norton & Co.

Taylor, J. B. (2008). *My stroke of insight: a brain scientist's personal journey.* London: Hodder & Stoughton Ltd.

Ten Have-de Labije, J. & Neborsky, R. J. (2012). *Mastering intensive short-term dynamic psychotherapy.* London: Karnac Books Ltd.

Toates, F. (2014). *How sexual desire works – the enigmatic urge.* Cambridge: Cambridge University Press.

Todd, M. (1959). *The thinking body.* New York: Dance Horizons.

Totton, N. & Jacobs, M. (2001). *Character and personality types.* Philadelphia: Open University Press.

Tsai, H. Y., Peper, E. & Lin, I. M. (2016). EEG patterns under positive/negative body postures and emotion recall tasks. *NeuroRegulation, 3*(1), 23–27. http://dx.doi.org/10.15540/nr.3.1.23

Van der Kolk, B., MacFarlane, A. C. & Weisaeth, L. (1996). *Traumatic stress: effects of overwhelming experience on mind, body and society.* New York: Guilford Press.

van der Kolk, B. (2014). *The body keeps the score.* New York: Viking Penguin.

Wegner, D. M. (2002). *The illusion of conscious will.* Cambridge: A Bradford Book.

Williams, K. (2001). *Ostracism: the power of silence.* New York: Guilford Press.

Winnicott, D. W. (1965). *The maturation process and the facilitating environment.* New York: International University Press.

Zajonc, R. B. (1980). Feeling and thinking: preferences need no inferences. *American Psychologist, 35*, 151-175.

Ågmo, A. (2007). *Functional and dysfunctional sexual behaviour.* London: Academic Press.

REFERENCES

Webpages:

Ingraham, P. (2014). Your back is not out of alignment. *https://www.painscience.com/articles/structuralism.php*.

Lederman, E. (2010) The fall of the postural–structural–biomechanical model in manual and physical therapies: exemplified by lower back pain. *CPDO Online Journal, March*, 1–14. www.cpdo.net.

www.etymonline.com

Index